DEVELOPING COUNTRIES AND THE MULTILATERAL TRADE REGIME

This book explores the way in which 'development' has functioned within the multilateral trade regime since de-colonisation. In particular, it investigates the shift from early approaches to development under the GATT to current approaches to development under the WTO. It argues that a focus on the creation and transformation of a scientific apparatus that links forms of knowledge about the so-called Third World with forms of power and intervention is crucial for understanding the six decades' long development enterprise of both the GATT and the WTO. The book is both topical and necessary given the emphasis on the current round of negotiations of the WTO. The Doha 'Development' Round has been premised on two assumptions. First, that the international community has undertaken an unprecedented effort to address the imbalances of the multilateral trading regime with respect to the position of its developing country members. Secondly, that its successful conclusion represents a historic imperative and a political necessity for developing countries. Through a sustained analysis of the interaction between development thinking and trade practices, the book questions both assumptions by showing how development has always occupied a central position within the multilateral trading regime. Thus, rather than asking the question of what needs to be done in order to achieve 'development', the book examines the way in which development has operated and still operates to produce important, and often unacknowledged, power relations.

Studies in International Trade Law: Volume 11

Studies in International Trade Law

Titles in this series:

Volume 1 Basic Legal Instruments for the Liberalisation of Trade
Federico Ortino

Volume 2 The Power to Protect: Trade Health, and Uncertainty in the WTO
Catherine Button

Volume 3 *The WTO, the Internet and Trade in Digital Products*
Sascha Wunsch-Vincent

Volume 4 *Good Faith in the Jurisprudence of the WTO: The Protection of Legitimate Expectations, Good Faith Interpretation and Fair Dispute Settlement*
Marion Panizzon

Volume 5 *Globalisation and Labour Rights: The Conflict between Core Labour Rights and International Economic Law*
Christine Kaufmann

Volume 6 *The World Trade Organization and Human Rights*
Fiona Macmillan

Volume 7 *Redefining Sovereignty in International Economic Law*
Edited by Wenhua Shan, Penelope Simons and Dalvinder Singh

Volume 8 *Law and Ethics in International Trade and Environment Debates*
Ilona Cheyne

Volume 9 *Constitutionalism, Multilevel Trade Governance and Social Regulation*
Edited by Christian Joerges and Ernst-Ulrich Petersmann

Volume 10 *The Human Rights Impact of the World Trade Organisation*
James Harrison

Volume 11 *Developing Countries and the Multilateral Trade Regime: The Failure and Promise of the WTO's Development Mission*
Donatella Alessandrini

Developing Countries and the Multilateral Trade Regime

The Failure and Promise of the WTO's Development Mission

Donatella Alessandrini

•HART•
PUBLISHING

OXFORD AND PORTLAND, OREGON
2010

Published in the United Kingdom by Hart Publishing Ltd
16C Worcester Place, Oxford, OX1 2JW
Telephone: +44 (0)1865 517530
Fax: +44 (0)1865 510710
E-mail: mail@hartpub.co.uk
Website: http://www.hartpub.co.uk

Published in North America (US and Canada) by
Hart Publishing
c/o International Specialized Book Services
920 NE 58th Avenue, Suite 300
Portland, OR 97213–3786
USA
Tel: +1 503 287 3093 or toll-free: (1) 800 944 6190
Fax: +1 503 280 8832
E-mail: orders@isbs.com
Website: http://www.isbs.com

British Library Cataloguing in Publication Data

Data Available

ISBN: 978-1-84946-030-9

Typeset by Columns Design Ltd, Reading
Printed and bound in Great Britain by
CPI Antony Rowe Ltd, Chippenham, Wiltshire

A Letizia e Aldo

Acknowledgments

THIS BOOK IS a revised and updated version of the PhD dissertation I wrote at Birkbeck Law School, University of London, between 2002 and 2007. I owe my gratitude to several people who have provided stimulation, inspiration and motivation during the writing of this work. I am most indebted to Fiona Macmillan. I am sincerely grateful for her intellectual rigour and generous guidance: her knowledge, endless patience, perceptiveness and encouragement have been, and still are, truly invaluable. I have been immensely fortunate to have her as a mentor and friend.

I wish to express my warmest thanks to Brenna Bhandar and Stewart Motha with whom I have spent many inspiring moments. I am particularly thankful to Brenna for the intellectual challenges she has brought to my work and for exploring with me the boundaries of professional friendship. I thank the support staff, the academic staff and the post-graduate community at Birkbeck Law School for their encouragement and support, in particular Patricia Tuitt, Peter Fitzpatrick, Michelle Everson, Elena Loizidou, Valerie Kelly, Jose Bellido, Pablo Ghetti, Victoria Hunt, Sundhya Pahuja, Maria Aristodemou, Adam Gearey, and Costas Douzinas. I also wish to gratefully acknowledge the financial support provided by Birkbeck Law School with the Ronnie Warrington studentship.

At Kent, I wish to thank friends and colleagues at the Centre for Law, Gender and Sexuality for providing me with a stimulating and supportive environment: Helen Carr, Joanne Conaghan, Davina Cooper, Anisa De Jong, Stacy Douglas, Maria Drakopoulou, Emily Grabham, Emily Haslam, Didi Herman, Rosemary Hunter, Suhraiya Jivraj, Toni Johnson, Sarah Keenan, Sarah Lamble, Olga Palevich, Sally Sheldon and Simone Wong. I am very grateful to my colleagues and the students on the International Commercial Law LLM programme for the insights and perspectives on many themes explored in this book, and for making the programme an exciting teaching and learning experience: in particular I wish to thank Kate Bedford, Paddy Ireland, Iain Ramsay, Alan Story, and Toni Williams. Kate and Toni have also provided helpful comments on various chapters of the book for which I am very grateful. Thanks to Lynn Risbridger, Dylan Williams, Liz Cable, Sarah Slowe and Eve Dyer for their help in the past five years and to Kent Law School for the generous financial support provided with the Research Support Fund.

I owe an enormous debt to Judy Fudge for reading the entire manuscript and providing very helpful feedback; Suchetana Chattopadhyay and Chirashree Das Gupta for the engaging discussions on several topics of this book; and the anonymous reviewers from Hart Publishing for their comments. I am also very grateful to Rachel Turner, Mel Hamill and Jo Ledger at Hart for their guidance and patience; Melissa Nelson for the thorough proofreading and Jan Titcombe for the meticulous work on the index.

Thanks to Anastasios Gaitanidis, Iosif Tzanopoulos, Solidea Cocciatelli and Francesca Corsini for their friendship and advice; Maria Tsoukala for helping me finish this project and start thinking about new ones; Sandra Lazoi and Lorenzo Corsini for the strength and motivation provided throughout the years, and for knowing exactly when to listen to me; Pia Cuscito and Francesco de Palo for inspiring me in the first place; and Letizia, Aldo and Luigi for their love and support.

Canterbury, August 2010

Contents

Table of Cases

GATT

Canada: Administration of the Foreign Investments Review Act, Report of the Panel (adopted 7 February 1984) GATT BIDS 30S/140

WTO

Canada: Certain Measures Affecting the Automobile Industry, Report of the Panel (adopted 11 February 2000) WT/DS139/R

Canada: Patent Protection of Pharmaceutical Products, Report of the Panel (adopted 17 March 2000) WT/DS114/R

United States: Section 110(5) of US Copyright Act, Report of the Panel (adopted 27 July 2000) WT/DS160/R

United States: Measures Affecting the Cross Border Supply of Gambling and Betting Services, Report of the Appellate Body (adopted 7 April 2005) WT/D285/AB/R

Introduction

The Failure and the Promise of the Multilateral Trading Regime

> This Conference will initiate the next stage in the development of the trading system, whose focus must be the fuller integration of the developing world ... we have a responsibility, as WTO members and as a Secretariat, to help [developing countries] build ... the capacity to participate fully in the work of the WTO and to derive maximum benefits from it.[1]

IN 2001, TRADE MINISTERS launched the fourth Ministerial Conference of the World Trade Organisation (WTO) in Qatar.[2] This event was to be of historic significance for developing countries as the international trading community undertook the first comprehensive effort to address the reasons for their difficulty to 'participate fully in the work of the WTO and to derive maximum benefits from it'.[3] The establishment of the WTO in 1995 signalled a new era of multilateral trade relations. The precursor of the WTO, namely the General Agreement on Tariffs and Trade (GATT), had disciplined trade relations among states for over four decades. Since its outset, the GATT had had to confront the claims of its developing country members that its rules were unfavourable to their trade interests. As a result, several initiatives were undertaken between the 1950s and 1980s to take into account the specific problems developing countries faced within the multilateral trading regime.[4]

However, trade scholars have pointed out that the development-related trade activity of GATT resulted in an asymmetry of trade rules between developed and developing country members that did not address the source

[1] M Moore, Address by the Director-General at the Inaugural Session (9 November 2001) WTO Doc WT/MIN(01)/12.

[2] WTO, Doha Declaration (14 November 2001) WTO Doc WT/MIN(01)/DEC/1.

[3] See above, text to n 1.

[4] The nature of the challenges developing countries brought to the rules of GATT will be analysed in chs 1 and 2.

of the discrimination against the competitive exports of the latter.[5] According to mainstream trade literature, whereas the asymmetry of rules provided the legal basis for such discrimination, its underlying rationale must be traced back to the erroneous economic assumptions about development and the resulting counter-productive legal claims advanced by developing countries.[6] To put it succinctly, by relying on trade protection as opposed to trade liberalisation and insisting on unilateral measures on the developed countries' part, developing countries failed to obtain the elimination of the discrimination against their competitive exports and consequently to develop their economies by means of liberal trade.

Thus, the entry into force of the WTO legal regime was supposed to have signalled the rational choice by developing countries to abandon their failing economic policies and legal strategies and embrace a rules-based multilateral trading system endowed with an effective enforcement mechanism. By adhering to the same set of rules and the economic rationale they embody, namely the unquestionable belief in the universal beneficial role of trade liberalisation, developing countries would finally be able to demand and enforce compliance with WTO rules so as to enjoy the benefits its legal regime is supposed to generate. However, soon after the entry into force of the WTO, it became apparent that the benefits of multilateral trade liberalisation had not materialised as far as developing countries were concerned.[7] The failure of development within the WTO is imputed to the improper implementation of its rationale and, in particular, to the less than full liberalisation achieved with respect to the sectors of interest to developing countries.[8]

Hence, the Doha Round was meant to finally deliver the long-standing development promise of the multilateral trading regime. Its agenda, as Moore's words illustrate, was informed by three premises: the acceptance of the universal beneficial role trade liberalisation plays with respect to the promotion of development; the persistence of the difficulty developing countries face in fully participating in the multilateral trading regime; and the responsibility of the Organisation and its developed country members to assist them in their development enterprise.[9] Yet, in July 2006, and then again in 2008, negotiations were suspended due to the irreconcilable

[5] Hudec, for instance, has extensively scrutinised the limits of non-reciprocity and the so-called Differential and More Favourable Treatment developing countries have obtained within GATT. See R Hudec, *Developing Countries in the GATT Legal System* (London, Trade Policy Research Centre, 1987).

[6] The various arguments advanced in this respect will be discussed in ch 3.

[7] For a recent comprehensive study on the difficulties developing countries face within the WTO, see JE Stiglitz and A Charlton, *Fair Trade For All: How Trade Can Promote Development* (Oxford, Oxford University Press, 2005).

[8] This contention is epitomised by the so-called agricultural issue which was at the centre of the controversy between developing and developed countries during the Doha Round.

[9] See above, text to n 1.

differences between WTO members.[10] The major issue of contention concerned, once again, the liberalisation of the sectors in which developing countries are supposed to be most competitive. As a result, the development promise of the WTO remains to be fulfilled.

This book is an attempt to go beyond the narrow preoccupation with the conclusion of the current Round and to explore the rationales behind the six-decades-long 'failure' of the development enterprise of the multilateral trading regime. This 'failure' can be viewed from two complementary perspectives. One is to take the development rationales of both the GATT and the WTO at their face value, namely without challenging the inherent normative assumptions about development they embody. From this angle, it will be shown that both the GATT's and the WTO's selective trade practice has violated the development principles they have purported to promote. One obvious conclusion from this perspective is that international efforts should continue in order to finally redress the imbalances of the multilateral trading regime. Indeed, this is the premise that underlies the current market access argument, according to which the WTO will deliver its development promise provided that its developed-country members open up their markets to developing countries' competitive exports.[11]

There is, however, another perspective from which to look at the relationship between the multilateral trading regime and development that problematises the former approach. Once the development rationales of the GATT and the WTO are no longer taken for granted and their inherent normative assumptions are called into question, the focus shifts away from attempts at reconciling trade liberalisation theory and practice. In their place, a different set of questions starts to emerge: how was the relationship between trade liberalisation and development made possible in the first place?; what has sustained it in the past six decades?; and how does it continue to hold such an authority today? The hypothesis advanced from this angle is that development has always occupied a central position within the multilateral trading regime. This is a position filled by a 'science of development' that articulates a mutual reinforcing relationship between a 'civilising mission' and the furtherance of the imperial interests of the

[10] See P Lamy, 'Talks Suspended. Today there are only Losers' (WTO News-DDA, 24 July 2006) www.wto.org/english/news_e/news06_e/mod06_summary_24july_e.htm. See also WTO, 'Day 9: Talks collapse despite progress on a list of issues' (WTO News-DDA, 29 July 2008) www.wto.org/english/news_e/news08_e/meet08_summary_29july_e.htm.

[11] See eg P Lamy, 'WTO Doha Development Agenda: Building on the Uruguay Round towards a freer, fairer world trading system' (WTO News-DDA, 22 November 2006) www.wto.org/english/news_e/sppl_e/sppl50_e.htm.

major capitalist powers.[12] Therefore, the appreciation of the modality through which this imperial science has operated since decolonisation is crucial to understanding the rationale behind the six-decade-long 'failure' and 'promise' of development within the post-war multilateral trading regime.

I THE 'SCIENCE OF DEVELOPMENT' AND 'CAPITALIST IMPERIALISM'

The first argument of this book is that the development-related trade activity of both the GATT and the WTO can be best appreciated in light of the development framework established at the end of the colonial era. Taking the cue from Anghie's account of the Mandate System under the League of Nations, it will be shown that development has been constructed as a 'science' functioning on the basis of a universal economic rationality and a linear, consequential reading of history. This framework relies on three normative assumptions, namely: the establishment of an unquestionable dichotomy between advanced and backward societies; the reliance on a supposedly neutral economic rationality through which to bridge this gap; and the invocation of the help and expertise of the so-called advanced members of the international community and the specialised international economic and financial institutions in order to facilitate the development process. Despite the transformation of the means through which to achieve development, these three elements have consistently been deployed to order hierarchically different societal formations and consequently enforce economic, social and political reforms that have resulted in the wholesale transformation of so-called Third World societies.

In the field of international trade law and policy, the GATT and the WTO have contributed to the creation, consolidation and transformation of a development apparatus that links forms of knowledge about the so-called Third World with forms of power and intervention. This is to say that the representation of Third World societies in mainstream development theories has been crucial to both the GATT's and the WTO's development-related trade activity. In the immediate postwar period, development was defined in terms of rapid economic growth and underdevelopment in terms of a 'failure' by developing countries to pursue the adequate level of growth.[13] GATT participated in the formation and

[12] The expression 'science of development' is borrowed from Anghie's work on the imperial legacy of the Mandate System within the current international financial institutions. See A Anghie, 'Time Present and Time Past: Globalisation, International Financial Institutions, and the Third World' (2000) 32 *New York University Journal of International Law & Politics* 243, 281.

[13] The postwar development norm will be discussed in ch 2.

consolidation of this development norm by positing the failure of developing economies to trade as efficiently as the industrialised countries.[14] Consequently, it established the need for the former to follow the rational trade prescriptions of the latter, namely the liberalisation of trade in goods. With the WTO, the permanence of this failure is made to rest on the developing countries' adoption of the wrong economic policies and legal claims during the 1960s and 1970s and the policy prescriptions that follow are based on a market-based approach to development. As a result, developing countries are required to recognise the rationality of the market and subscribe to the WTO's neo-liberal rationale that extends well beyond trade in goods.[15]

Yet, as the history of the Doha Round shows, there is a profound contradiction between the development rhetoric and the actual practice of the major trading powers. The selective free-trade approach the Americans and the Europeans in particular have pursued within both the GATT and the WTO cannot be explained solely in terms of the 'failure' and 'promise' the development framework perpetuates.

Thus, the second interrelated argument concerns the modality through which the 'science of development' has operated since the end of the colonial period. In this respect, the claim is that the positioning of the development framework with its three normative assumptions as unquestionable has been crucial to the transformation of the imperial project that has taken place in the twentieth century. As Meiksins Wood puts it, 'to understand the "new imperialism"—indeed to determine whether it exists at all—requires us to understand the specificities of capitalist power and the nature of the relation between economic and "extra-economic" force in capitalism'.[16] She argues that 'capitalism is unique in its capacity to detach economic from extra-economic power, and that this, among other things, implies that the economic power of capital can reach far beyond the grasp of any existing, or conceivable, political or military power'.[17]

Thus, whereas previous empires had operated through the employment of direct political and military coercion, the separation of political and economic power during decolonisation has allowed 'capitalist imperialism' to rule through the imposition of market imperatives. Yet for capitalism to operate without political and military intervention, its economic laws need to be extended and implanted everywhere, and this requires the 'extra-economic' force supplied by the state. This work complements Meiksins

[14] GATT, Twelfth Session of the Contracting Parties (1957) BISD 6th Supp (1958) 18.

[15] The shift from the GATT focus on barriers to trade in goods, in particular tariffs, to the WTO focus on market integration which extends to services, investment and intellectual property will be analysed in chs 3, 4 and 5.

[16] E Meiksins Wood, *Empire of Capital* (London, Verso, 2005) 5.

[17] *Ibid.*

Wood's insights by arguing that the three-layered development framework has been, and continues to be, a crucial 'extra-economic' force in furthering the project of the major capitalist states since decolonisation. Hence, 'capitalist imperialism' provides another perspective from which to assess the seemingly inexplicable contradiction between the development rhetoric and the actual development-related trade practice of the GATT and the WTO. As Meiksins Wood writes:

> [C]apitalist imperialism has been affected by one of the main contradictions of capitalism: the need to impose its economic 'laws' as universally as possible, and, at the same time, the need to limit the damaging consequences that this universalization has for capital itself. Capitalism is driven by competition, yet capital must always seek to thwart competition. It must constantly expand its markets and constantly seek profit in new places, yet it typically subverts the expansion of markets by blocking the development of potential competitors.[18]

Thus, the selective free-trade approach of both the GATT and the WTO cannot be assessed independently of the political and economic responses of the major capitalist powers to the challenges brought first by decolonisation, and later by the crisis of the 1970s, to their hegemonic position within the international economy. Thus, GATT's selective liberalisation practice has enabled the ex-colonial powers to access the raw materials and primary commodities necessary for expanding production at home while constraining the liberalisation of goods in which the newly-independent countries had a comparative advantage. Similarly, the extension of the WTO's mandate beyond trade in goods to include services, intellectual property and investment on the one hand, and the less than full liberalisation achieved with respect to the competitive exports of developing countries on the other, cannot be viewed in isolation from the imperial powers' attempt to reorganise the international division of labour between developing and developed countries after the crisis of the 1970s.[19] Yet, it is argued, this has been possible thanks to the operation of the 'science of development' whose three normative assumptions provide the 'extra-economic means' through which the reach of the capitalist interests of the imperial states has been extended 'beyond the limits of [direct] political and military domination'.[20]

[18] *Ibid* 22.

[19] As it will be argued in ch 3, the international economy was restructured along the lines of a trade-service-investment driven market integration which was congenial to the interests of the major capitalist powers.

[20] Meiksins Wood (n 16) 20.

II DEVELOPMENT AS A 'DISCOURSE' AND DEVELOPMENT AS A 'TRAP'

I therefore borrow the insights offered by Anghie's analysis of the 'science of development' and Meiksins Wood's study on 'capitalist imperialism' to explore the endless failure and promise of development within the GATT and the WTO. I need to make two clarifications at this stage. The first concerns the conceptualisation of development as a 'discursive practice'. Drawing from Foucault's work on the dynamics of discourse and power that helps in 'unveiling the mechanisms by which a certain order of discourse produces permissible modes of being and thinking while disqualifying others and even making others impossible',[21] Escobar, for instance, sees development as the outcome of a system of relations that determines

> who can speak, from what point of view, with what authority, and according to what criteria of expertise; it [thus] sets the rules that must be followed for this or that problem, theory, or object to emerge and to be named, analysed and eventually transformed into a policy or a plan.[22]

The argument he advances is that thinking of development in terms of discourse 'makes it possible to maintain the focus on domination—as earlier Marxist analyses, for instance, did—and at the same time to explore more fruitfully the conditions of possibility and the most pervasive effects of development'.[23] Escobar therefore explores the conditions which made it possible for so many countries to consider themselves as 'underdeveloped' and embark on the task of 'un-underdeveloping' themselves by acknowledging the need to undergo intensive restructuring of their societies.[24] Thus, to say that development started to function as a discourse is not to maintain that new ideas, dominant theories, international institutions, technological and economic processes alone produced that development enterprise whose main result would be the wholesale transformation of the 'backward' Third World societies. It is rather to say that a system of relations among these factors was established that 'systematically relates forms of knowledge and techniques of power'.[25]

[21] A Escobar, *Encountering Development: The Making and Unmaking of the Third World* (Princeton, Princeton University Press, 1995) 5.

[22] *Ibid* 41.

[23] *Ibid* 6.

[24] In looking at the main conditions which contributed to the formation of the development discourse, Escobar highlights the transformation in the structure of world power, the requirements of expansion of the capitalist system with the subsequent role that the so-called underdeveloped countries were to play, the creation of the 'population problem' and the promise of science and technology. *Ibid* 32–39.

[25] *Ibid* 10. In particular, Escobar proposes to speak of development as an 'historically singular experience, the creation of a domain of thought and action, by analysing the characteristics and interrelations of the three axes that define it: the forms of knowledge that refer to it and through which it comes into being and is elaborated into objects, concepts,

Without doubt, postwar development thinking contributed not only to the intervention of Western governments, institutions and agencies, but to the very idea that development was a necessary, as well as an inevitable, historic process to be facilitated by the 'expertise' of those countries regarded as 'developed'. Therefore, while acknowledging the pervasive effects of development, this work seeks to emphasise the fact that, at particular intersections of the world capitalist system, certain states, theories and international institutions have been and are still able to re-shape the contours of the 'science of development'. Hence, whereas at the end of the colonial period issues of access to the natural resources of the ex-colonies informed the postwar development model advocated by mainstream theories and institutions, including GATT, the crisis of the 1970s and the political reorganisation of the world capitalist system in terms of a trade-service-investment driven market integration have been central to the consolidation of neo-liberal development thinking and to the establishment of the WTO. Notwithstanding this, I do not suggest that development emanates from a unidirectional source of power.

Indeed, the second clarification regards the crucial concern that, by analysing the development dimension of the postwar international trading regime in terms of an imperial science, development ends up being conceived of in deterministic terms. Chimni, for instance, has argued that those who view 'development as a trap' neglect the fact that 'development is understood differently in different places and by different classes'.[26] As it will be seen, the 1960s and 1970s witnessed the emergence of numerous theories, policies and political struggles that challenged and decentralised the one-dimensional approach to development fostered by mainstream thinking and international institutions. For instance, by emphasising the structural imbalances of the international trading regime, developing countries challenged GATT rules and obtained a considerable degree of flexibility from its legal strictures.[27] As a result, GATT's 'flexible' development model did not substantially intrude into the domestic regulatory autonomy of its contracting parties.[28] With the neo-liberal conversion of development thinking and the establishment of the WTO, this flexibility has been noticeably reduced.[29] The shift is qualitatively different in that the

theories and the like; the system of power that regulates its practice; and the forms of subjectivity fostered by this discourse …'. *Ibid.*

[26] BS Chimni, 'The World Trade Organisation, Democracy and Development: a View from the South' (2006) 40 *Journal of World Trade* 5, 24.

[27] As will be argued in ch 2, one of the major achievements of such flexibility was the recognition that developing countries were entitled to negotiate without reciprocity.

[28] That is, beyond the obligations it posed as to their tariff policy.

[29] As the obligations deriving from the WTO agreements are made binding on all members, thereby displacing the non-reciprocity approach of GATT, such flexibility consists mainly of time-limited derogations and technical assistance.

WTO's so-called market rationality has been extended to areas previously exempted from international regulation and is accompanied by unprecedented disciplinary mechanisms to ensure compliance with the same rationality.[30] Consequently, the shift from the GATT's to the WTO's development approach has reduced not only the domestic autonomy of its members, but the space for creative contestation and alternatives.

I take this argument seriously. However, there are two observations I want to make in this respect. First, the flexibility GATT embraced owes much to the fact that it did not threaten the trade interests of the major capitalist powers.[31] Indeed, once the exports of newly-industrialised countries threatened to compete with the developed countries' industries, the economic, political and trade pressures exercised by the US and EU in particular eventually led to the withdrawal of such flexibility and the establishment of the WTO.[32] At a more fundamental level, however, the conditions that made this shift possible are to be traced back to the three-layered development framework established at the end of the colonial era. In other words, neo-liberal development linked with, while displacing, earlier approaches thanks to the permanence of the dichotomy between developed and developing countries, the reliance on economic rationality and the invocation of the help and expertise of the developed countries that constitute the premises of the 'science of development'. This is neither to adopt a mechanistic view of development nor to present 'developing countries' as a monolith. Indeed, one aim is to show that there was nothing natural or inevitable in the process that led to the creation of the WTO. However, as the focus of this work is on the modality through which the 'science of development' has operated within the international trading regime and, in this respect, the main argument is that the very idea of development cannot be separated from the three premises on which it is founded, it is my contention that any alternative to the way in which the multilateral trade regime deals with 'development' and/or 'developing

30 Chs 5, 6 and the concluding chapter will analyse the impact of the WTO agreements, in particular that of the GATS, TRIPs and TRIMs and the surveillance mechanisms they rely on, on the regulatory autonomy of WTO members.

31 Indeed, other factors made GATT's flexible approach to development possible, such as the challenges developing countries brought to the international economic and political system after decolonisation, the tension generated by the Cold War and the fact that industrialised countries themselves were experimenting with Keynesian policies.

32 The WTO approach to development is the outcome of the complex relationship between different factors, including neo-liberal theories, the end of the Cold War, the oil and debt crisis, the processes of change of the international economy and the political responses that followed to address these events. However, as will be argued in ch 3, the number of measures developed countries enacted against the exports of developing countries coincided with the increasing competitiveness of the products of the latter vis-à-vis the products of the developed countries.

countries' should be assessed in light of the three normative assumptions through which this 'science' has operated since its inception.

The aim of this book is therefore to expose the development assumptions of the international trading regime and its trade disciplines as political rather than rational, neutral and objective. In particular, this work engages with mainstream trade literature that views the shift from the GATT's so-called flexible approach to development to the WTO's neo-liberal development model in terms of a natural and inevitable historic process. Contrary to these claims, it argues that this was the outcome of a political process whose desirability needs to be seriously questioned. Consequently, it contends that the current emphasis on symmetry of rules and market access to deliver the development promise of the international trading regime implies the acceptance of the neo-liberal mindset of the WTO and, ultimately, of the normative assumptions of the 'science of development'. In this regard, any alternative to the current state of affairs needs to simultaneously challenge the three normative assumptions on which development operates and the imperial interests it serves.

III OUTLINE OF THE CHAPTERS

In chapter one, *The Bretton Woods Conference: Trade and the 'Civilising Mission' in the Postwar International Trading Regime*, I analyse the premises on which the Mandate System under the League of Nations was founded, namely: the separation between the political and economic status of the mandate territories; the establishment of a dichotomy between the advanced and the backward members of the international community; the rise of economics as the supposedly neutral terrain on the basis of which to reconcile this dichotomy; and the positioning of the 'help' and 'expertise' of the advanced members as necessary in order to achieve development. The chapter explores how the concealment of both the normative assumptions about non-Western societal organisations and the advancement of Western interests through the employment of a supposedly neutral economic rationality provided the 'extra-economic means' according to which non-Western territories could be brought within the post-war capitalist system. With respect to the international trading regime, it shows that both the 'science of development' and the capitalist interests of the imperial powers were central to the negotiating process that led to the adoption of the GATT. Hence, despite the fact that the GATT's legal edifice was informed by free-trade thought, the liberalisation of trade in goods occurred on a selective basis.

In chapter two, *The 'Science of Development' and the GATT Norm*, I explore the process through which the scientific authority of development thinking emerged and consolidated into a fixed framework in the postwar period. The focus is on the modality through which GATT's development enterprise was influenced by and interacted with this development norm. I aim to show that the most important premise GATT produced was the positioning of a 'failure' on the part of developing countries to develop their trade as fast as that of the developed countries.[33] Consequently, it established the endless need for developing countries to follow the rational trade policy prescriptions of the industrialised nations and the various groups of experts appointed to redress the 'failure'. Thus, if in the immediate postwar period the so-called failure of development was imputed to the dual economic structures of the ex-colonies so that their capitalist transformation through an interventionist state would deliver the promise of development, in the 1980s the persistence of this failure was made to rest on the adoption of erroneous economic policies and legal claims by developing countries so that market forces became the appropriate development means.

In chapter three, *The Neo-Liberal Transformation of Development Thinking and the Renewed Mission of the Multilateral Trading Regime*, I argue that despite the qualitative difference with earlier approaches to development, neo-liberal thinking linked with, while displacing, earlier development theories. As both the premise of development—that is, the representation of Third World societies as backward—and the consequent norm—namely the need for developing countries to catch up with the economic stage of developed countries—remain unaffected, the so-called neo-liberal revolution of development thinking reformulates the means through which to achieve development. By emphasising the permanence of these normative assumptions in neo-liberal arguments, the chapter aims to challenge current arguments according to which the entry into force of the WTO is the result of a rational choice for the most efficient trade policy. It concludes that these accounts are congruent with the neo-liberal turn that obfuscates important political processes under the guise of neutrality and rationality.

In chapter four, *The Uruguay Round and the Construction of the New Consensus*, I further substantiate the conclusions reached in chapter three by examining in detail the political and economic pressure exerted on developing countries from 1986 to 1994 in order to obtain their adherence to the US and EU agendas. In particular, I challenge the literature that has presented the conclusion of the Uruguay Round (UR) as the success of the US administration in resisting the pressure to abandon the multilateral system and the developing countries' rational decision to adhere to the

[33] GATT (n 14).

extensive northern agenda.[34] This will serve to contextualise the subsequent discussion on the economic and legal arguments that have been advanced to describe the WTO regime as beneficial with respect to the interests of developing countries. In short, the assumption underlying the legal arguments is that by giving up their 'Differential and More Favourable Treatment' and non-reciprocity status within GATT, developing countries are able to exert greater influence in the direction of WTO negotiations. Furthermore, a rules-based multilateral system endowed with an effective dispute settlement mechanism acts as a guarantee against the bilateral and unilateral abuses of the past. Underlying the economic arguments is an intrinsic belief in the universal beneficial role of trade liberalisation as opposed to the ineffective import substitution policies developing countries have pursued in order to industrialise.

In chapter five, *The World Trade Organisation: The Power of Transnational Capital and the Reduction of Domestic Regulatory Space*, I take the neo-liberal development framework embodied by the WTO at its face value to assess whether the shift from the GATT to the WTO has entailed the outcomes that the arguments in support of reciprocal liberalisation have posited. The chapter therefore examines whether the WTO agreements have eliminated the discrimination against the trade of developing countries and shows that, in continuity with GATT practice, developed countries continue to frustrate the export interests of developing countries. It then analyses the legal provisions of the General Agreement on Trade in Services (GATS), the Agreement on Trade Related Aspects of Intellectual Property Rights (TRIPs) and the Agreement on Trade Related Investment Measures (TRIMs) and shows that they provide the first international legal architecture for the effective protection and enforcement of foreign investors' rights and have the potential of greatly impinging upon the regulatory autonomy of WTO members.

In chapter six, *Of Failures and Promises: The Many Lives of the Doha Development Round*, I show how these agreements have provided the US and EU with the legal means to enhance the power of their transnational capital within the latest round of WTO negotiations. The Doha Development Round was launched in order to correct the imbalances of the multilateral trading regime that have hindered the trade of developing countries since 1947. Rather than removing these obstacles, however, Doha has ended up being a market access round for the US and EU capital. Its suspension in 2006 and 2008 owes much to the refusal by the developed countries to live up to the development-related trade principles whose universal beneficial validity they have promoted since the end of the

[34] See eg EH Preeg, *Traders in a Brave New World: The Uruguay Round and the Future of the International Trading System* (Chicago, The University of Chicago Press, 1995) 165.

1970s. More importantly, the analysis of the negotiating history reveals the misconceptions about the role and purpose of the WTO, in particular those concerning its multilateral nature, trade liberalisation mandate and development agenda.

First, the WTO, like the GATT, is about promoting selective free trade rather than overall liberalisation. Secondly, the US and EU tendency to revert to bilateral negotiations when their agenda is not satisfied at the multilateral level defies not only the neo-liberal assumptions about the so-called level playing field, but the possibility of multilateralism itself. More importantly, the Doha Development Round confirms the continuity of the modality through which development has operated within the international trading system since decolonisation. Its scientific authority continues to be invoked within the WTO in order to advance the interests of the major capitalist powers.

In the concluding chapter, *The Development Mission of the WTO*, I reflect on the normative assumptions on which the WTO's development enterprise rests. I show how, despite the transformation that the civilised/uncivilised, advanced/backward, developed/developing dichotomy has undergone within the multilateral trading regime, the 'civilising mission' continues to operate through powerful regulatory mechanisms. In particular, the WTO's new linkages with institution building, good governance and anti-corruption reinforce the neo-liberal assumptions about the impropriety of developing countries' political, social and institutional arrangements. By emphasising the permanence of the 'civilising mission' within the WTO's development agenda, and some of the proposals that aim to make the WTO 'more supportive of development', these concluding reflections make the case for challenges to be brought not only to its current free-trade mindset, but to the three normative assumptions that have allowed the 'science of development' to operate within the international trading regime since its inception.

1

The Bretton Woods Conference: Trade and the 'Civilising Mission' in the Postwar International Trading Regime

TRADE HAS LONG been an essential underlying element of international law. Already at the time of Westphalia, the new system of sovereign rights over mutually exclusive territories was based on the acknowledgment that future quarrels between European sovereigns were to exert no influence on the right to trade of private actors.[1] As Arrighi notes, '[t]he considerable freedom granted to private enterprises to organise commerce peacefully across political jurisdictions even in wartime … marks the birth not just of the modern inter-state system, but also of capitalism as world system'.[2] The relationship between trade and the so-called civilising mission was a crucial aspect of the colonial enterprise of European states in the non-Western world: the naturalist approach to international law relied on a universal Reason that extended to non-European peoples. Vitoria, for instance, repudiated the treatment given by the Spanish to the Indians. However, as he subsequently argued, wherever the natives were impeding a natural right, such as the right to freely trade and invest, war was correspondingly a natural response.[3] Positivist international law saw the natives as 'uncivilised'. Crucially, 'trade was an indispensable part of the civilising

[1] See G Arrighi, *The Long Twentieth Century: Money, Power and the Origins of our Time* (London, Verso, 2000) 43.

[2] *Ibid* 44.

[3] See A Anghie, 'Francisco de Vitoria and the Colonial Origins of International Law' (1996) 5 *Social and Legal Studies* 321, 321–36. See also M Sornarajah, *The International Law on Foreign Investments* 2nd edn (Cambridge, Cambridge University Press, 2004) 18–19.

mission itself; the expansion of commerce was the means by which the backward natives could be civilized'.[4]

At the beginning of the twentieth century, however, it became apparent that colonies would soon have achieved independence. This meant that their vast economic resources would no longer be under the direct control of the imperial powers. A new means which enabled the latter to continue to operate in the territory of the ex-colonies was therefore needed in order to ensure their future access to natural resources. One central argument of this book is that this means was provided by the emerging 'science of development'.[5] Although the birth of development thinking as a scientific discipline occurred officially in the postwar period,[6] its antecedents can be traced back to the Mandate System under the League of Nations. Indeed, as Anghie has pointed out, the moral repudiation of the colonial violence and political control of the past was inaugurated with the League of Nations and the establishment of the Mandate System.[7] In order to break with the colonial past of political control, the League of Nations was presented as a neutral institution fostering development on the basis of economic expertise. However, the promotion of the so-called wellbeing of natives was accompanied by another objective, that is, the utilisation by the mandatories of the economic resources of the mandate territories.[8]

Thus, drawing from Anghie's account of the Mandate System and its imperial legacy within the postwar international financial institutions, this chapter argues that this legacy was also central to the commercial side of the Bretton Woods negotiations.[9] The first part examines the premises upon which the Mandate System was founded, in particular the separation between the political and economic status of the mandate territories, the establishment of a dichotomy between the more advanced and the backward members of the international community and the rise of economics as the supposedly neutral terrain on the basis of which this dichotomy would have been reconciled. As it will be shown in the following chapters, these premises would become the unquestionable constitutive elements of the

[4] A Anghie, 'Finding the Peripheries: Sovereignty and Colonialism in Nineteenth Century International Law' (1999) 40 *Harvard International Law Journal* 1, 64. Anghie is here referring to the Berlin West Africa Conference of 1884–85 which marks a departure from earlier approaches to trade as merely a means of maximising European profits and increasing national power.

[5] This expression is borrowed from Anghie's work on the Mandate System. See A Anghie, 'Time Present and Time Past: Globalisation, International Financial Institutions, and the Third World' (2000) 32 *New York University Journal of International Law & Politics* 243, 281.

[6] The emergence of the official science of development will be discussed in ch 2.

[7] Anghie, 'Time Present and Time Past' (n 5).

[8] *Ibid* 278.

[9] The Bretton Woods negotiations were intended to put in place the international rules and institutions governing the postwar international economic regime.

development framework that was to emerge in the immediate postwar period and would inform the development-related trade activity of both the General Agreement on Tariffs and Trade (GATT) and the World Trade Organisation (WTO). The concealment of both the normative assumptions about non-Western societal organisations and the advancement of Western interests through the employment of a supposedly neutral economic rationality is possibly the most important legacy of the Mandate System within the postwar international order.

The second part of the chapter contextualises this claim by analysing the negotiating process that led to the drafting of the Charter of the International Trade Organisation (ITO) and the adoption of the GATT.[10] Between 1941 and 1948, in the middle of the restructuring of the international economy, the American and British ideas concerning international trade became the universal commercial policy that any government which aspired to qualify as economically 'rational' was to adopt. The negotiations carried out in this period introduced the two recurrent features of postwar international trade activity which, as it will be argued in the following chapters, continue to characterise current international trade practice.

First, the idea of a universally rational commercial policy became an integral part of the development apparatus of the postwar period. Despite the fact that the never ratified ITO and GATT were primarily concerned with the reduction of obstacles to trade in goods, they both contained provisions, which GATT developed further, concerning economic development. From its inception, the GATT would therefore actively participate in the constitution and transformation of the 'science of development'. Secondly, the reliance on a universal economic rationality to explain how development was to be achieved concealed the particular interests of the universal providers of trade knowledge. In this respect, the contradictions inherent in the US-UK advocacy of free trade are analysed to show how free-trade principles were employed in a selective fashion to restructure the postwar international division of labour between the so-called developed and the soon-to-be developing countries.

I THE MANDATE SYSTEM AND 'THE SCIENCE OF DEVELOPMENT'

The Preamble of the League of Nations Covenant stated that the main objective of the Organisation was 'to promote international cooperation

[10] The ITO never came into force due to the US Congress' refusal to ratify the Charter. However, the rules of trade the Charter contained were carried over in the GATT.

and to achieve international peace and security'.[11] Its work was the result of 'disinterested and technical experts' and was completely 'scientific in character'.[12] The Mandate System of the League of Nations was created after the First World War in order to bring the colonial territories of the defeated countries under the guidance of the League of Nations.[13] The moral premise of the Covenant was that these territories were to be assisted by the League in order to gain sovereignty and therefore fully participate in the international system of sovereign states. Article 22 of the League of Nations Covenant provided that

> to those colonies and territories which as a consequence of the late war have ceased to be under the sovereignty of the States which formerly governed them and are inhabited by peoples not yet able to stand by themselves under the strenuous conditions of the modern world, there should be applied the principle that the well-being and development of such peoples form a sacred trust of civilization and that securities for the performance of this trust should be embodied in this Covenant.[14]

Hence, the formal principle driving the signatories of the Covenant was the moral repudiation of the colonial past of exploitation and violence. However, as Anghie points out:

> [T]he future of the mandate territories was conceived of principally within the framework of the same goals that Lord Lugard had articulated with respect to the African colonies. In his classic on colonial administration, *The Dual Mandate*, Lugard argued that the colonies were important markets for metropolitan products. Furthermore, while 'the abundant wealth of the tropical regions of the earth must be developed and used for the benefits of mankind', colonial powers were obliged 'not only to safeguard the material interests of the natives, but to promote their moral and educational progress'. No tension was perceived between the two goals. The orderly and efficient exploitation of native resources for the 'benefit of mankind' would, in turn, benefit the native himself. Thus, humanitarianism and the expansion of international commerce were two of the basic and related principles guiding the enlightened colonial policy that mandatories were supposed to implement.[15]

Three interrelated aspects deriving from Anghie's study of the Mandate System need to be analysed in order to emphasise the permanence of the mutually reinforcing relationship between the so-called civilising mission and international commerce within the postwar international trading

[11] League of Nations, *Covenant of the League of Nations*, Art 3. www.library.northwestern.edu/govinfo/collections/league

[12] *Ibid.*

[13] Notably the territories under the Ottoman and German Empire.

[14] League of Nations, *Covenant of the League of Nations*, Art 22, para 1; quoted in Anghie, 'Time Present and Time Past' (n 5) 276.

[15] Anghie, 'Time Present and Time Past' (n 5) 278.

regime. First, the Mandate System established a dichotomy between the political status of the mandate territories, which was to change gradually in order to acquire full sovereignty,[16] and their economic status, which was based on the acknowledgement that the mandate territories would continue to provide raw materials and markets for the mandatories.[17] In particular, the achievement of political independence was intertwined with the acquisition of an economic rationality the ex-colonies did not possess and which could be provided by the more 'advanced' members of the international community.

The first outcome of this premise is therefore the reconceptualisation of the 'civilised-uncivilised' dichotomy of positivist international law.[18] Economic backwardness, rather than racial and cultural connotations, made the people of the mandate territories unable 'to stand by themselves under the strenuous conditions of the modern world'.[19] The second interrelated outcome is the crucial positioning of an unquestionable gap between the economic status of the mandate territories and that of the mandatories. As it will be argued in chapter two with respect to the GATT's development-related trade activity, this gap would be reconceptualised in terms of a failure on the part of so-called developing countries to develop their trade as fast as that of the industrialised countries. This failure would consequently establish the need for the former to catch up with the economic stage and trade policies of the latter.[20]

Secondly, the League of Nations was the first major international institution managing the relationship between European and non-European peoples. As Anghie notes, under the 'new international law' of pragmatism the League of Nations could be presented as a neutral institution as opposed to the self-interested nature of colonial powers.[21] Consequently, the need for the former colonies to overcome their failure was premised on the universality of economics. The neutral character of the League was achieved through the resort to economic rationality and the establishment of a neutral body of experts, the Permanent Mandates Commission (PMC). The Commission was given the task to gather, analyse and elaborate a vast amount of information regarding different territories

[16] Indeed, Latin American countries had achieved political independence at the beginning of the nineteenth century. However, as it will be argued in ch 2, the antecedents of the development discipline and the forms of intervention it gave rise to can be traced back to the *modus operandi* of the Mandate System analysed by Anghie.

[17] Anghie, 'Time Present and Time Past' (n 5) 279.

[18] *Ibid* 285.

[19] See above, text to n 14.

[20] As it will be argued in ch 3, the so-called failure on the part of developing countries would be re-formulated in terms of their failing economic policies and legal claims under the GATT to argue for the withdrawal of the 'Differential and More Favourable Treatment' and non-reciprocity status within the WTO.

[21] Anghie, 'Time Present and Time Past' (n 5) 283–85.

and several subject areas.[22] The result was that the PMC could claim to be able to formulate the best policies to be adopted in the so-called backward countries. In other words, a universal science based on economic rationality was born. This science was deemed to transcend social, cultural and political particularities.[23] Thus, once the failure of so-called backward societies was established in supposedly neutral terms, economic rationality was posited as the means through which mandate territories could overcome their inability to 'stand by themselves' and achieve equal status in the international community.

The third aspect of the Mandate System derives from the preceding two. Contrary to what the neutrality of economics seemed to suggest, the influence exercised by the Mandate System was not limited to the economic sphere. By relying on the scientific authority of the international experts of the PMC, the administration of the mandate territories was presented as an objective and neutral enterprise. The policies that followed appeared to be based on a scientific understanding of universal laws that unquestionably allowed for the achievement of the welfare of the native peoples.[24] Consequently, the profoundly political assumptions about non-Western societal organisations could be concealed under the neutral veil of economic laws. The ultimate result of this supposedly neutral enterprise was the 'normalisation' of the natives. As Anghie writes:

> In developing this science and, thus, such authoritative view of the 'normal'—the proper path of economic progress and the political institutions which would achieve this—the mandate sought to create new systems of disciplining the natives. Native obedience was to be achieved, not through the application of force alone, but by the formulation of a compelling and authoritative vision of society, of progress and of the individual, that would be internalized by the native and govern his actions.[25]

Thus, the development mission was not based on the use of force, or force alone, but more importantly on the creation of an 'authoritative view of the "normal"—the proper path of economic progress' which was offered by the supposedly advanced members of the international community. Concurrently, the need to 'un-underdevelop' and undergo intensive restructuring of their economic, political and social arrangements became an integral part of the development activity of the soon-to-be developing countries. As it will be seen in the context of the GATT's development-related trade activity, the need for developing countries to 'develop their trade as fast as that of the industrialised nations'[26] through the guidance

[22] *Ibid* 280.
[23] *Ibid* 280–82.
[24] *Ibid* 284.
[25] *Ibid.*
[26] GATT, Twelfth Session of the Contracting Parties (1957) BISD 6th Supp (1958) 18.

and expertise of the industrialised members would become the principle informing trade relations between developing and developed countries. Thus, the need for the assistance and guidance of the 'advanced' members of the international community would constitute the third element of the 'science of development' established in the postwar period. Once the failure was posited as unquestionable and economic rationality was invoked as the neutral terrain for overcoming it, economic experts and specialised international institutions could assist the ex-colonies in their development enterprise.

A Freedom of Transit and Equitable Treatment: The First Regulatory Attempt at a World Trade Order …

A significant part of the 'authoritative view of the "normal"—proper path of economic progress'[27] included international commercial policy. Article 23 of the Covenant made provision to 'secure and maintain freedom of communications and of transit and equitable treatment for the commerce of all members of the League'.[28] Between 1920 and 1929, four major conferences were held under the League in order to deal with specific aspects of its members' commercial policy. The 1927 Geneva World Economic Conference stated that

> [i]n view of the fact that harmful effects upon production and trade result from the high and constantly changing tariffs which are applied in many countries;
>
> And since substantial improvement in the economic conditions can be obtained by increased facilities for international trade and commerce;
>
> And in view of the fact that tariffs, though within the sovereign jurisdiction of the separate states, are not a matter of purely domestic interest but greatly influence the trade of the world;
>
> The conference declares that the time has come to put an end to the increase in tariffs and to move in the opposite direction.[29]

The conference therefore posited that the universal way forward to achieve 'improvement in the economic conditions' of the League's members was the gradual elimination of tariff barriers. The League also dealt with the technical aspects of the principle of equitable treatment by holding a series of conventions for the simplification and equitable application of customs formalities and licensing systems and the harmonisation of laws regarding

[27] See above, text to n 25.
[28] League of Nations (n 11) Art 23.
[29] Quoted in WA Brown, *The United States and The Restoration of World Trade* (Washington DC, Brookings Institution Press, 1950) 32.

bills of exchange.[30] These conventions would serve as a platform for over 100 bilateral agreements between 1929 and 1939.[31] By concentrating on the technical aspects of 'equitable treatment', the League could bypass the political significance of the principle. The principle according to which 'equitable treatment for the commerce of all members of the League' was to be secured recalled the goals Lord Lugard had articulated with respect to those resources that were to be used 'for the benefits of mankind'.[32] Despite the fact that Article 23 applied to all members of the League, the resources at issue were those of the mandate territories and the countries that would have soon achieved independence.

Article 23 of the League of Nations and the international activity it generated until 1939 represented the first attempt towards a regulatory system of trade relations on a worldwide scale. The first statement as to what constituted 'proper' international commercial policy was made: tariffs were no longer a domestic matter but needed to be regulated at the international level. Once the 'proper' commercial policy had been defined, mandate territories had to comply with the prescribed model in order to be able to 'stand by themselves'. This meant entering commercial agreements providing for the reduction of tariffs, adhering to the new customs and licensing systems and harmonising internal laws in accordance with international standards. The accomplishment of these objectives was another test the mandate territories had to undergo in order to gain access to the international community.

After the brief interruption of the Second World War, international commercial activity resumed in 1941. The United Kingdom and the United States embarked on a period of intense negotiations in order to devise the international rules and institutions of the postwar order. Negotiations were conducted exclusively between the two powers until 1946, when they presented their proposals to the rest of the world. Certainly, the majority of the countries of the world were still colonies, protectorates or mandate territories. However, the last stage of the negotiating process that led to the adoption of the GATT witnessed the participation of 13 countries, referred to as less developed.[33] The analysis of the international commercial activity between 1941 and 1948 is important in two respects. First, by assessing the underlying contradictions in the trade rationale advanced by the UK and US, it is possible to identify the commercial interests that the post-world international trade regime was intended to serve. This is important to contextualise the claim that GATT rules played a crucial role in the

[30] *Ibid* 34.
[31] *Ibid* 32.
[32] See above, text to n 15.
[33] These countries were Brazil, Burma, China, Ceylon, Chile, Cuba, Czechoslovakia, India, Lebanon, Pakistan, southern Rhodesia, South Africa and Syria.

redefinition of the imperial mission of the ex-colonial powers. Secondly, the interaction between the two powers and the so-called less developed countries, in particular the way in which the former responded to the latter's arguments concerning their economic development status, introduces the specific modality through which the 'science of development' was to operate within the postwar international order.

B ... and the Extension of Market Imperatives

The international trade rules devised in the 1940s need to be examined in the context of the new imperialist relationship between the ex-colonial powers and the ex-colonies. Meiksins Wood refers to 'capitalist imperialism' to emphasise the power of capitalism to impose its economic laws without the need for the direct political and military rule which had characterised former empires.[34] She argues that

> [c]apitalism is distinctive among all social forms precisely in its capacity to extend its dominion by purely economic means. In fact, capital's drive for relentless self-expansion depends on this unique capacity, which applies not only to class relations between capital and labour but also to the relations between imperial and subordinate states.[35]

In order to understand the 'new imperialism', it is crucial to appreciate the separation of the political and economic power of capitalism in the immediate war period. Indeed, this separation occurs with the birth of capitalism itself, in that in non-capitalist societies

> direct producers typically had non-market access to the means of production, especially land, and therefore were sheltered from the forces of the market, while appropriators relied on superior force to extract surplus labour from direct producers. In capitalism, the market dependence of both appropriators and producers means that they are subject to the imperatives of competition and accumulation and increasing labour productivity; and the whole system, in which competitive production is a fundamental condition of existence, is driven by these imperatives.[36]

However, until the twentieth century, European powers would still rely on 'extra-economic' means in the non-European world. It was with decolonisation that the detachment of the economic power from the political power of capitalism took place and, as a result, 'economic imperialism became strong enough to dispense with older, extra-economic forms of colonial

[34] E Meiksins Wood, *Empire of Capital* (London, Verso, 2005) 5.
[35] *Ibid* 12.
[36] *Ibid* 9.

rule'.[37] This detachment becomes operational when non-capitalist states are brought within the orbit of the world-capitalist economy. As a consequence of the implantation of the compulsion of the market, these economies are made vulnerable to economic imperatives and Western capital. However, the point Meiksins Wood makes is that this separation cannot sustain itself but always needs extra-economic force.[38]

As argued below, it was through the postwar international negotiations of the 1940s that the first step to separate the economic from the political power of capital was made and this was reflected in the institutional separation between public and economic international law. It was indeed the international economic rules devised by the US and UK that made the soon-to-be developing economies vulnerable to Western economic imperatives. In the context of the international trade rules embodied by the GATT, this is evident in the contradiction between free-trade principles employed to justify the liberalisation of industrial goods and raw materials and the exception to these rules applying to the products of export interest to the so-called developing economies. Thus, the role of states, and in particular that of the United Kingdom and United States, was central to the establishment of 'capitalist imperialism'.[39] Concurrently, the wholesale transformation of the so-called Third World could not have taken place without the 'extra-economic force' provided by the emerging 'science of development'. As the negotiations leading to the adoption of the GATT show, the three normative assumptions about development that the Mandate System introduced would provide the ex-colonial powers with the scientific authority for imposing the 'authoritative view of the "normal"—the proper path of economic progress'.[40]

II THE BRETTON WOODS CONFERENCE AND THE POSTWAR INTERNATIONAL ECONOMIC ORDER

The Bretton Woods Conference took place in the middle of an important transformation in world affairs. In order to understand the proposals put forward by the United States and United Kingdom with respect to the new international order, it is important to briefly refer to the factors that contributed to the transformation in the structure of world power. The US

[37] *Ibid* 45.

[38] *Ibid* 137–42.

[39] The centrality of the role of major capitalist states is evident in two specific moments in the history of the postwar world capitalist system, namely after decolonisation, as will be examined below; and, as will be examined in chs 3 and 4, after the crisis of the 1970s. With respect to the international trading regime, these two moments coincide with the establishment of the GATT in the 1940s and the WTO in the 1990s.

[40] See above, text to n 25.

had acquired an undisputed economic and military dominance in the world capitalist system, effectively supplanting that of the UK in the nineteenth century. As Arrighi notes:

> [T]he United Kingdom had been all but parsimonious in its territorial acquisitions, and empire-building in the non-Western world had been integral to its world hegemony. As for the United States, its development into the main pole of attraction for the labour, capital, and entrepreneurial resources of the world-economy was closely tied to the continental scope attained by its domestic economy in the nineteenth century ... This unprecedented domestic territorialism was wholly internal to a capitalist logic of power.[41]

The first phase of this logic began with the dispossession and occupation of the natives' lands and resources.[42] The consequent acquisition of the vast natural resources of the North American continent in addition to the co-existence of a closed-door policy with respect to foreign products and an open-door policy with respect to capital and labour made the United States' domestic market increasingly dynamic.[43] The second phase started at the beginning of the twentieth century when, as a result of European conflicts, the US came 'to enjoy a substantial "protection rent", that is, exclusive cost advantages associated with absolute insularity from the main seat(s) of inter-state conflict on the one side, and with absolute or relative proximity to the main intersection(s) of world trade on the other'.[44]

However, the insular position the US had previously adopted was to change soon. In order to support its expanding productive capacity, the US needed to find new markets abroad in which to place its products, invest its surplus capital and access cheap sources of raw materials.[45] In order for the US to secure access to the markets of the soon-to-be developing countries, the participation of the latter in its plans for a new world order was crucial. Thus, the initiative for a postwar international order was taken by the US. Two major conferences were held in the 1940s. The Dumbarton Oaks Conference was to give birth to the postwar international political institution, namely the United Nations (UN), which, established in 1945, was to be the successor of the League of Nations.[46] The Bretton Woods Conference of 1944 dealt with the establishment of the

[41] Arrighi (n 1) 59. Arrighi is arguing that the absence of territorialism abroad was due to the unprecedented territorialism at home. Whereas 'British capitalism and territorialism had cross-fertilized one another...US capitalism and territorialism were indistinguishable from one another'. *Ibid.*

[42] *Ibid.*

[43] *Ibid* 61.

[44] *Ibid* 62.

[45] See A Escobar, *Encountering Development: The Making and Unmaking of the Third World* (Princeton, Princeton University Press, 1995) 32–33.

[46] See HG Nicholas, *The United Nations as a Political Institution* 5th edn (Oxford, Oxford University Press, 1975) 1–13.

postwar international economic institutions. The International Monetary Fund (IMF) would be in charge of assisting countries experiencing short-term financial difficulties; the International Bank for Reconstruction and Development (IBRD), which later became part of the World Bank (WB), was to administer postwar reconstruction loans; and the ITO was to shape the international commercial environment.[47]

Thus, the Bretton Woods Conference and the Dumbarton Oaks Conference institutionalised an important separation between public and economic international law. This separation served to consolidate the perception that, contrary to the UN, the Bretton Woods institutions were neutral organisations based on economic rationality and, as such, capable of fostering universal economic policies. As previously seen, the precedent for insulating economics from political considerations can be traced back to the Mandate System. However, the League of Nations continued to manage both the economic and political affairs of its members. With the advent of the functionalist approach to international organisations, according to which the world's interests would be best served by organisations which specialised in their respective areas of expertise, the conceptual separation between the two areas became institutionalised.[48] This approach therefore legitimised the assumption that technocratic institutions could function on purely economic grounds unaffected by political considerations. As argued below, this separation could be relied on by the US and UK to dismiss the arguments advanced by the so-called less developed countries against the universal commercial rules the US and UK had devised. By asserting the political nature of these claims, as opposed to the economic nature of trade negotiations, 'less developed' countries' grievances with regard to the international rules of trade could be remanded to the UN as the appropriate international forum.

The negotiations carried out by the US and UK between 1941 and 1948 were therefore informed by a fictional separation between the economic and political realms that served to conceal the deeply political nature of the international economic institutions and rules of the postwar period. Indeed, from its very outset, the US administration's programme had made the political and economic sides of the negotiations mutually interdependent. In his proposals for a Stabilisation Fund and Bank, White stated:

> Just as the failure to develop an effective League of Nations has made possible two devastating wars within one generation, so the absence of a high degree of economic collaboration among the leading nations will, during the coming

[47] See R Peet, *Unholy Trinity: The IMF, World Bank and WTO* (London, Zed Books Ltd, 2003) 27.

[48] For a classical explanation of functionalist theory see D Mitrany, *A Working Peace System: An Argument for the Functionalist Development of International Organisation* (London, National Peace Council, 1946).

> decade, inevitably result in economic warfare that will be but the prelude and instigator of military warfare of an even vaster scale.[49]

International peace was therefore linked to, if not made dependent on, 'economic collaboration' and the catchphrase for accomplishing this task became multilateralism. The rules and objectives of this multilateral system were at the centre of a long period of negotiations between the US and UK which focused on both financial and commercial policy. The financial side of the negotiations ran quite swiftly with both parties agreeing on similar monetary plans to avoid exchange controls, currency disorders and economic fluctuations.[50] In order to be fully accomplished, however, the project had also to be articulated in terms of commercial policy. Thus, during the conference held in 1944 to draft the charter of both the IMF and the IBRD, it was recognised that 'complete attainment of … the purposes and objectives … cannot be achieved through the instrumentality of the funds alone' and that governments were to reach an agreement in order to 'reduce obstacles to international trade and in other ways promote mutually advantageous international commercial relations'.[51] International trade was therefore at the forefront of the negotiations between the two powers. However, a controversial issue between the US and UK was to be resolved prior to presenting a common proposal on the universal rules of trade.

A Grounding 'Non-Discrimination' and 'Equal Treatment' in Trade Relations

The crucial point advanced by the United States was 'non-discrimination' in trade relations.[52] The Most Favoured Nation and the National Treatment principles, which were to become the cornerstones of GATT and WTO legal architecture, are based on the free-trade assumption that discrimination between foreign producers and between domestic and foreign goods distorts the operation of comparative advantage. Although the United States explained the reliance on the principle of non-discrimination in terms of free-trade doctrine, there was another reason. Tariff reductions were only to be made when reciprocal benefits derived

[49] Introductory section of undated typescript, 'Suggested Plan for a United Nations Stabilization Fund and a Bank for Reconstruction of the United Associated Nations' in White papers, quoted in RN Gardner, *Sterling-Dollar Diplomacy: Anglo-American Collaboration in the Reconstruction of Multilateral Trade* (Oxford, Clarendon Press, 1956) 8.

[50] Gardner, *ibid*, 99–100.

[51] Quoted in JH Jackson, *World Trade and the Law of GATT* (New York, Bobbs-Merrill, 1969) 40.

[52] The other two issues were employment and tariff reductions. See Gardner (n 49) 104–09.

from negotiations. Furthermore, the US did not resist in principle the imposition of tariffs when domestic industries were threatened by foreign imports but made a clear distinction between these measures and other trade-restrictive measures, namely preferences.

The campaign was directed against the preferential tariffs of the British Empire. During the First World War, the United States had become a major exporter of mass manufactures and soon realised that the growth of its industrial capacity would have been impaired if its products did not have equal access to foreign markets.[53] This problem was amplified by the Ottawa Agreements of 1932 which increased the preferences given to Britain by the Empire.[54] According to the United States, the extension of the Imperial Preferences had worsened the problem faced by countries outside the British Empire to gain foreign currency in order to purchase raw materials.[55] After the outbreak of the Second World War, under-Secretary of State Welles had made clear that no peace agreement

> . . . would be valid or lasting unless it established fully and adequately the natural rights of all peoples to equal economic enjoyment. So long as any one government possesses a monopoly over natural resources or raw materials which are needed by all peoples, there can be no basis for a world order based on justice and peace.[56]

Therefore, point IV of the 1941 Atlantic Charter provided for 'the enjoyment by all states, great and small, victors and vanquished, of access, on equal terms, to the trade and raw materials of the world which are needed for their prosperity'.[57]

The similarity between point IV of the Atlantic Charter and Article 23 of the League of Nations is striking: both are reminiscent of the Dual Mandate articulated by Lord Lugard, according to which the promotion of the wellbeing of natives was to be accompanied by the utilisation of their raw materials 'for the benefits of mankind'.[58] The principle of non-discrimination was, however, advanced on both economic and moral grounds. The objective of reducing trade protection was justified by the US in order to avoid the worldwide damages caused by protectionism during the 1930s. Furthermore, the objective of eliminating distortions was justified by moral reasons, namely the eradication of the colonial system.[59]

[53] See Escobar (n 45) 32–33.

[54] See Lord Marley, 'The Empire as an Economic Unit' (1938) 9 *The Political Quarterly* 529, 533.

[55] Gardner (n 49) 18.

[56] S Welles, *Department of State Bulletin* v (1941) 75; quoted in Gardner (n 49) 19–20.

[57] Atlantic Charter, Point IV, *Department of State Bulletin* (27 September 1941) (Washington, Government Printing Office, 1941).

[58] See above, text to n 15.

[59] See RE Hudec, *Developing Countries in the GATT Legal System* (London, Trade Policy Research Centre, 1987) 9.

Thus, although the underlying issue of tariff preferences was at the centre of the reorganisation of economic power between the UK and US, the formal principle of non-discrimination was presented as universally beneficial. In 1941, therefore, tariff preferences emerged as a fundamental issue between the United Kingdom and the United States. The other controversial issue of the US commercial programme concerned quantitative restrictions. Although the US strongly opposed quotas on imports as trade-distorting measures which could not be maintained under free-trade principles, it was unwilling to change its protectionist policy in the agricultural and fishery sectors. Under section 22 of the Agricultural Adjustment Act, the President was authorised not only to impose quotas on imports, but to enact price-support schemes and export subsidies, with the result that both domestic and export agricultural prices did not reflect those prevailing in world markets.[60]

After two years of negotiations, the commercial policy programme was completed by British and American negotiators and resulted in the drafting of a convention to reduce tariffs and the establishment of an international body—the ITO— with the power to interpret this convention and settle the disputes between its members.[61] Therefore, up to 1946, negotiations were mainly carried out on Anglo-American terms with substantially no other members entering the negotiating stage. The issues of interest to the US and UK were access to raw materials necessary to maintain domestic productive capacity, the reduction of import barriers to place their industrial products in foreign markets and a protective environment abroad for their investments. Although these three objectives were integral to the post-colonial reorganisation of power, they were advanced on universally beneficial terms. The first documented appearance of the so-called less developed countries within the ITO-GATT scene is to be found when their adherence to the already formulated trade principles was sought during the London conference in 1946.[62]

[60] See Gardner (n 49) 20–21. As discussed below, agricultural protectionism would become a contentious issue between the US and the less developed countries during the final stage of the negotiations and would continue to remain controversial throughout GATT and WTO history.

[61] See Gardner (n 49) 161–62.

[62] The official call for the conference was made by the newly created Economic and Social Council of the United Nations. The countries appointed as members of the Preparatory Committee were Australia, Belgium, Brazil, Canada, Chile, China, Cuba, Czechoslovakia, France, India, Lebanon, Luxemburg, Netherlands, New Zealand, Norway, South Africa, the USSR and the United States. See Gardner (n 49) 269.

B The Draft Charter and the London Conference: Of Rules and Exceptions

The ITO Charter contained four rules of conduct which the Preparatory Committee was supposed to discuss with other countries and finally approve. The first substantial principle concerned the obligation to grant general Most Favoured Nation treatment (MFN) to the trade with other countries.[63] There was full agreement between the United States and United Kingdom under Article VII of their mutual Aid Agreement as to the inclusion of the principle within the Charter. The only exception admitted was in favour of established trade preferences which had to be gradually eliminated.[64] This issue was closely connected to the second principle consisting of the obligation not to increase preference margins. The US and UK had already settled their controversy on preferences by agreeing that these would have been gradually eliminated by way of negotiations.[65]

The first confrontation between the US and UK and the 'less developed' countries participating in the conference concerned both the principle of MFN and the obligation not to increase preference margins. Arguing that their economic development stage placed them at a competitive disadvantage with the industrialised economies, Chile, Brazil and Lebanon sought to obtain an exception that allowed 'less developed' countries to conclude preferential arrangements among themselves. By placing their industrial products in markets where similar economic conditions prevailed, preferential tariff regimes would have provided the foreign exchange needed in order to industrialise.[66] At a more general level, however, they criticised the Charter's emphasis on equal treatment. This principle, complemented by MFN, tilted the balance in favour of industrialised economies as it privileged countries already having preferential treatment and locked 'less developed' economies into a role of suppliers of raw materials. However, the US and the UK rejected both arguments on the ground that it made no 'economic sense' to provide such an exception when negotiations were clearly heading towards progressive multilateral negotiations for the elimination of old preferences.[67] The only concession made was that new preferences could be granted only if approved by two-thirds of the Organisation.

The last two substantial principles advanced by the US and the UK concerned the obligation to negotiate substantial tariff reductions on a

[63] Countries would therefore be required to extend any trade privilege, favour or advantage conferred to one party to all members of the ITO.

[64] Brown (n 29) 72.

[65] Therefore, the UK kept the Imperial Preferences in place but undertook the obligation not to increase tariff margins and reduce them over time.

[66] Brown (n 29) 72.

[67] *Ibid* 73.

MFN basis and that of eliminating Quantitative Restrictions (QR).[68] Despite the 'less-developed' countries' argument that flexibility in their import tariffs regime was essential to pursue industrialisation programmes, the US refused to accept any general exception and the issue was settled in Havana where it was restated that any exception for so-called economic development reasons could take place only on the Organisation's two-thirds approval. India, China and Lebanon also opposed the prohibition of QR, arguing that these measures represented an important tool for carrying out national plans of development.[69] The US response was seemingly based on liberal trade principles: since QR were the most restrictive and discriminatory forms of trade regulation, they could not be maintained under the new multilateral system which aimed at the reduction and gradual elimination of the obstacles to international trade.[70]

However, as already mentioned, the liberal trade rationale was not to apply to two US-sensitive sectors, namely agriculture and fisheries.[71] The main argument underlying the elimination of QR was that system quotas distorted market forces, thereby preventing the efficient allocation of worldwide resources. Therefore, it was striking that the US could maintain agricultural and fisheries protection on the same economic grounds 'less developed' countries were advocating with respect to their sensitive sectors, namely industry. The other substantial exception negotiated between the US and UK aimed at granting relief from the prohibition of QR and bound tariffs for balance of payments purposes. This exception, unlike the economic development exceptions examined above, did not require prior approval by the organisation.

Two additional procedural exceptions were drafted by the US and UK. The first one, known as the 'escape clause', applied to both QR and tariffs. The suggested Charter provided that if, as the result of the obligations taken under the Charter, increased imports caused or threatened to cause serious injury to domestic producers, members could withdraw tariff concessions or use quotas on the import concerned.[72] In addition, the

[68] *Ibid.*

[69] See Jackson, *World Trade and the Law of GATT* (n 51) 628.

[70] Brown (n 29) 76.

[71] This was to become GATT Art XI: 2(c), according to which quantitative restrictions on agricultural products were permitted only if necessary for the enforcement of domestic programmes which restricted the output or marketing of similar domestic products. In addition to this, they were supposed not to operate in a way that would have reduced 'imports relatively to domestic production as compared with the proportion prevailing in a previous representative period'. However, the first condition was set aside in 1955, when the US, under the threat of abandoning GATT, obtained a waiver from GATT Art XI:2(c) in order to maintain its otherwise GATT-inconsistent legislation. As for the second requirement, the complexity inherent in assessing the conditions prevailing in absence of such restrictions made this provision extremely difficult to enforce. See JH Jackson, *The World Trading System: Law and Policy of International Economic Relations* (Cambridge, The MIT Press, 1997) 57–58.

[72] The so-called safeguard clause was to be incorporated in GATT Art XIX.

Charter provided that although consultations with members affected by the measure were to be carried out, members were free to adopt it even without an agreement. The 'less developed' countries' proposal to extend the application of this procedural exception to imports that threatened the development of a new industry was, however, rejected.[73] The other procedural exception formulated by the US and UK was to apply in cases where a country believed the action by another state had produced the so-called nullification and impairment of any objective of the commercial policy chapter.[74]

C The Free-Trade Contradictions of the Charter: Structuring the International Division of Labour

Once these exceptions had been agreed on, the United States made clear during the Havana Conference that it would not negotiate further on the unlimited use of QR: QR for economic development reasons would be admissible only if approved by the Organisation.[75] Cuba's statement is worth quoting at length as it represented the mood of the so-called less developed countries by the end of the Geneva Session in 1947:

> We are here, like one of the other bad boys of this Conference, who have dared to raise a voice before our elder brothers, and have come into the room where the big Civilised Nations ... [are] drafting the Charter of a new economic order. We must confess though, that we will be very glad with the liberty of the jungle, if the kind of Charter which is going to come out of this work goes in the way that is shaped at this moment, because sometimes the liberty of the jungle is healthier than the very sophisticated and civilised world. We are very much at a loss, because we had thought that we were struggling for liberty, and instead we have been spanked the whole afternoon because we were restricting business. If we come to analyse the Charter, do we find that Chapter V is full of restrictions from the beginning to the end proposed by the underdeveloped, almost 'uncivilised' countries? No, they have been proposed by the 'experienced' nations ...
>
> The principle against Q.R. is good, but then follow, I do not know how many, but no less than one and a half pages of exceptions. So, if the highly experienced peoples have found the necessity for inserting here one and a half pages of exceptions, we too would offer one little exception. Just one more ... the Cuban exception proposes that where they talk of important restrictions on agricultural and fisheries products, we simply want to add one word, that is, to include here, also, the industrial products. And this is our big crime; for that we have received

[73] Brown (n 29) 98.

[74] According to the US interpretation, this meant that if there was a violation of a general or specific obligation under the Charter, the state suffering the violation could retaliate against the injuring one. See Brown (n 29) 91.

[75] *Ibid* 154.

> all sorts of admonitions to-day ... We think that if the London and New York Drafts were to continue, we would be freezing the actual economic status of the different countries of the world. The agricultural countries would continue to be agricultural. The monoproducer countries would continue to be monoproductive, and the more developed countries would continue selling type-writers, radios, etc. to those nations that are still trying to produce the primitive tools.[76]

This statement highlighted the contradictions inherent in the US/UK position. As mentioned, the spirit of the Charter was explained in terms of free-trade doctrine. The underlying rationale was that trade liberalisation contributes to the augmentation of wealth and therefore can be a valuable means of economic development. However, the Charter was far away from the contemplation of a free-trade order. Contrary to pure free-trade principles, the Charter reflected the emerging postwar consensus that trade liberalisation was beneficial when coupled with appropriate public intervention in the economy. This is the underlying rationale for the inclusion of the so-called escape clause in addition to the 'contractual' type of tariff reduction. However, requiring 'less developed' countries to comply with the obligations to reduce tariffs and eliminate QR on industrial products while permitting protection with respect to the trade in agriculture and fisheries defied both free-trade principles and the emerging consensus around state intervention.

As dependency theories would later argue, the international division of labour operated under colonialism had made the economies of the colonies dependent on the production of raw materials, primary commodities and agriculture.[77] Thus, the 'equal treatment' rules devised by the US and UK did not take into account the difficulties that non-industrialised economies would have faced in competing with the industrial products from the developed countries. In addition, one of the fundamental sectors in which 'less developed' countries were, according to the logic of international specialisation, expected to gain from trading with the industrialised countries was exempted from liberal trade principles. In this respect, whereas industrialised countries could rely on the sensitive nature of agriculture and fisheries as a valid ground for departing from free-trade principles, the same rationale could not apply to the 'less developed' countries' sensitive issue, namely industrialisation. However, the contradiction between free-trade principles seemingly informing the international trade regime and

[76] Quoted in Brown (n 29) 633–35.

[77] Dependency thinking will be discussed in ch 2. One of the important insights that dependency thinkers offered to the development debate within GATT was that concerning the unequal trade relationship between the industrialised and the developing countries. Focusing on the inelastic demand for raw materials and primary commodities from the industrialised countries, and, conversely, on the elastic demand for industrial goods from developing countries, they argued that the developing countries were at a competitive disadvantage vis-à-vis the industrialised nations.

actual selective free-trade practice can be accounted for in terms of the imperial reorganisation of the postwar capitalist order operated by the US and UK.

Furthermore, the ITO negotiations revealed a fundamental attitude the US and UK would adopt in their interaction with the so-called less developed countries. As the Cuban statement shows, the exceptions to the prohibition of QR the US and UK had drafted with respect to their sensitive sectors could not be invoked when other countries' sensitive sectors were at issue. The result was not just a system based on selective free trade, but a specific modality for dealing with the opposition by the so-called less developed countries. Positions which did not conform to the universal view on commercial policy, that is, the US and UK's, were simply dismissed on the basis of lack of economic expertise. This attitude is perhaps best expressed by Clair Wilcox[78] with the following words:

> None of these proposals was accepted. They serve, however, to reveal an attitude that is widely shared. Enthusiasm for industrial development is accompanied by little interest in the conditions that must be satisfied if such development is really to be achieved. The basic importance of natural resources, of agriculture, and other extractive industries, and of power, transportation, and communication is lost from sight; attention is centered on manufacturing .... *The obstacles to industrialisation inherent in social and religious patterns*, in lack of health and education, and *in political instability and corruption* are never mentioned; the fact that increasing population may cancel increasing output is ignored. These things are fundamental; their correction will take time. The underdeveloped countries seek industrialisation by some quick and easy routes. By obtaining large loans with no strings attached and by offering enterprises a monopoly of local markets, they hope to build new factories overnight. *They do not believe that they must creep before they walk*[79] (emphasis added).

Economic expertise was not only the ground for advancing certain views, but the means through which other views and knowledge could be rationally excluded. This attitude was evident in the way the US and UK dealt with the 'less developed' countries' concerns regarding their 'economic development'. The major alteration of the suggested Charter introduced during the London conference was the recognition of the economic development principle, which came to be known as the London compromise.[80] It is important to note that when the first concerns about development were raised during the ITO negotiations, the US refused to

[78] Clair Wilcox served as chairman or vice-chairman of the US delegation during the ITO–GATT negotiations from 1946 to 1948.

[79] C Wilcox, *A Charter of World Trade* (New York, The MacMillan Company, 1949) 143.

[80] This principle was to appear in Art 13 of the Havana Charter.

consider the particular concerns of 'less developed' countries, arguing that these should have been addressed within the Economic Development Sub-Commission of the United Nation Economic and the Social Council. As Hudec observes, it was as a result of the anxiety to include newly independent countries within the international trading system that the US and UK accepted the provision on 'economic development', subject, however, to the approval of the Organisation.[81] The basic position of the US in response to the various arguments for more flexibility was that industrial development was not to be achieved by way of protectionism and that the methods of promoting economic development had to be consistent with the Charter's purposes.[82]

D The Investment Provisions: Protecting Capital Abroad

The United States' recipe for economic development was therefore based on open markets and capital investments.[83] These development ingredients were inextricably linked with the US and UK need for new markets in which to obtain raw materials, place industrial products in excess of domestic demand and invest surplus capital. The rules on international trade examined so far created a favourable climate for achieving the first two objectives. The rules on capital investments derived from the debate concerning the access to the means of economic development. India and Brazil had asked for the Charter to include a specific provision stating that capital and materials should be supplied on terms that were reasonable to the receiving countries. Significantly, the Charter provided that developed countries were to co-operate on these issues through appropriate international agencies.[84] However, the reverse of this debate concerned the obligations of the capital-receiving countries. The US proposal on investments aimed at inserting within the chapter on Economic Development the recognition of the importance of private and public international capital. Furthermore, the proposal contemplated that one of the purposes of the Charter should be 'to encourage the international flow of capital for productive investments through measures designed to assure fair and equitable treatment of the legitimate interests of investors'.[85]

[81] Hudec (n 59) 16–18. Thus, the generic formula adopted under Art 13 of the Charter allowed for some measures of protection subject to the prior approval of the two-thirds of the Organisation.

[82] Brown (n 29) 99–102.

[83] See Hudec (n 59) 15–16.

[84] Brown (n 29) 100. This meant that their concerns were remanded to the specialised agencies of the United Nations.

[85] *Ibid* 102.

Contrary to the hortatory language of the obligation on the developed countries' part, the Charter was to include three specific principles. First, National Treatment was to be granted to foreign investments except in cases where the country had given prior formal notice of the different treatment. Secondly, MFN was to apply without qualifications. Thirdly, in the event of expropriation, states were to grant full compensation in convertible currency.[86] Due to the opposition by the 'less developed' countries, the compromise consisted in a generic formula declaring observance of international obligations in this field and, at the same time, abstention from undertaking actions injuring the interests of capital-supplying members.

On the foreign investment proposal as a whole, India and Czechoslovakia opposed any provision laying down detailed rules for the treatment of foreign investments that would have allowed foreign investors to get an economic and political hold on their national lives.[87] The confrontation between the United States on one side—supported by the United Kingdom, the Netherlands, Belgium, Canada and Sweden—and India and the Latin American countries on the other, came to the fore during the Havana Conference. The American delegation made clear

> that the only great reservoir of long-term foreign investment was the private capital market of the United States, that this capital would not go abroad if it could find better return at home, that the United States government would not compel its citizens to invest and that there was no real pressure on them to do so because of the vast accumulation of investment opportunities at home.[88]

The final draft of the Investment Chapter was in US-favourable terms. Against the threat of expropriation and the international recognition of this right, the Investment Chapter considered an obligation of the members to grant 'adequate security' to existing and future investments. Adequate security included the fact that expropriation had to occur on 'just' terms. Although no definition of the term 'just' was agreed on, its inclusion meant that the US could resort to the 'nullification and impairment' procedure in case of unjust expropriation.[89] Thus, had the Chapter come into force, the US would have secured for its existing and future capital abroad adequate return through the threat of possible trade retaliation.[90] On the other

[86] *Ibid.*

[87] *Ibid.*

[88] *Ibid* 152.

[89] *Ibid* 153.

[90] However, according to Dattu, the fact that the Charter provided for the right of each state to 'determine whether and to what extent and upon what terms it will allow future foreign investments' played an important role in the US Congress' refusal to ratify the Charter. See R Dattu, 'A Journal from Havana to Paris: the Fifty-years Quest for the Elusive Multilateral Agreement on Investments' (2000–01) 24 *FORDHAM International Law Journal* 275, 283.

hand, all requests for capital to be supplied on more favourable terms taking into consideration the historic, political and economic contexts of 'less developed' countries were to be deferred to appropriate international agencies, such as the UN.

E The Outcome of the ITO Negotiations

The ITO negotiations ended with a formal recognition of the 'Economic Development' principle.[91] The crucial issue concerned the right to protect infant industries for development purposes by raising bound tariffs, using quantitative import restrictions and obtaining preferential tariffs from other developed or developing countries.[92] The substance of the principle, however, was limited by the procedural requirements attached to it. Each of these measures had to be subject to prior approval of both the Organisation and the party specifically affected by the measure. It is worth reiterating that these requirements did not apply to the exceptions advanced by the United States and the United Kingdom. In the case of the Balance of Payment exception (Articles 21 and 23 ITO), escape clause exception (Article 40 ITO), agricultural quantitative import restrictions (Article 20(2) ITO) and export subsidies on primary products (Article 27 ITO), members were not required to obtain the Organisation's approval and no veto on the part of the affected country was contemplated.

In short, the Economic Development Chapter was a compromise the US was prepared to make in order to encourage participation by newly independent states to a multilateral system whose terms it had drafted. What prevailed in the end was the US idea of the 'proper' commercial policy which would enable all countries to achieve economic development. The universal keys to development were, according to the US, capital investments and (selectively) open markets. Therefore, the exceptions 'less developed' countries were allowed to rely on were mere exceptions to the general principles of commercial policy and their adoption was made conditional on the approval by the Organisation. In continuity with the League of Nations' attitude towards the mandate territories, the US and UK acted as universal providers of development-related commercial policy for the so-called less developed countries. Economic expertise was invoked in order to obtain participation by developing countries in a system whose intellectual underpinnings they could not challenge.

[91] United Nations Conference on Trade and Employment, 'Havana Charter for an International Trade Organization, Final Act and Related Documents' (New York, Lake Success, April 1948) Art 13.

[92] *Ibid* Art 15.

III THE GENERAL AGREEMENT ON TARIFFS AND TRADE (GATT)

The blueprints of international commercial policy were therefore laid down during the Havana Conference. The ITO Charter never came into force due to the US Congress' refusal to ratify it.[93] The trade-policy provisions of the ITO, however, were carried over from the Havana Charter to the General Agreement on Tariffs and Trade concluded in 1947 in order to implement a round of tariff reductions before the ITO came into force.[94] Although the infant industry exception provided for in the Charter (Article 13 ITO) survived in GATT (Article XVIII), the provision allowing for new trade preferences (Article 15 ITO) was withdrawn by the United States.[95] Other ITO provisions about the supply of capital funds and other facilities for economic development purposes as well as the investment provisions were left out of the GATT.[96] Crucially, capital investments did not receive the protection of a multilateral treaty that capital-exporting countries and the US in particular were adamant to obtain.[97]

In comparison with the ITO Charter, however, the GATT 1947 seemed even closer to the original US proposal based on the principles of equal treatment and non-discrimination. It is worth re-emphasising that their universal appearance concealed the political nature of the interests these principles served: with strategic US economic sectors exempted from the GATT's obligations and the exceptions provided in order to protect domestic industries from harmful imports, the free trade the US and Britain promoted was an atypical one. As Hudec has eloquently illustrated, the principle of reciprocity which was carried over from the ITO to the GATT implied a concept of 'payment' according to which something must be gained in order to negotiate.[98] As it will be argued in chapter two, the GATT's rules and the trade liberalisation practice of its developed-country members prevented the 'development' process GATT purported to promote.

The GATT came into force on 1 March 1948. Although the GATT policy towards so-called less-developed countries in the first seven years

[93] Brown (n 29) 14.

[94] During the 1946 London Session, the US submitted a draft for a General Agreement on Tariffs and Trade which was to contain the rules for the reduction of tariffs by each participant country. Thus, through the adoption of a Protocol of Provisional application, the commercial policy of the Charter was to survive the US refusal to ratify the ITO Charter. See Jackson, *The World Trading System* (n 71) 40.

[95] Brown (n 29) 242–43.

[96] KW Dam, *The GATT Law and International Economic Organisation* (Chicago, University of Chicago Press, 1970) 226.

[97] As will be argued in ch 5, this objective would be pursued by the US half a century later in the course of negotiations that led to the establishment of the WTO.

[98] See Hudec (n 59) 17.

remained unchanged, GATT practice encouraged their participation. The original contracting parties of the GATT were 23, of which 13 were 'less developed' countries (Brazil, Burma, China, Ceylon, Chile, Cuba, Czechoslovakia, India, Lebanon, Pakistan, Southern Rhodesia, South Africa and Syria). A few years later, China, Lebanon and Syria withdrew from the GATT while the Dominican Republic, Ghana, Haiti, Malaysia, Nicaragua, Uruguay, Indonesia, Peru and Turkey entered the Agreement. It was during the 1960s, however, that the majority of 'less developed' countries acceded to the GATT, a large number of which became contracting parties according to a special procedure. GATT Article XXVI5.(a) provided that governments with overseas territories had accepted the Agreement not only for their metropolitan territories, but for their overseas customs territories.[99] Under GATT Article XXVI.5(c) such territories could, on reaching independence, automatically become contracting parties 'upon sponsorship through a declaration by the responsible contracting party establishing the above-mentioned fact'.[100]

Colonies and mandate territories were therefore GATT contracting parties as a result of being under the 'international responsibility' of the metropolitan territories. Once they achieved independence, which in the terms of the above Article meant that metropolitan countries had declared so, they would carry this status unless otherwise specified by the new state through the so-called 'de facto application' of the Agreement.[101] Thus, new states became contracting parties according to the terms and conditions previously accepted by the metropolitan government on behalf of the territory in question and they were bound by any tariff concession made by the sponsoring contracting party.

CONCLUSIONS

The documents produced by the United States and United Kingdom between 1941 and 1948 presented the objectives of the postwar economic order. The IMF was concerned with short-term lending to countries experiencing financial difficulties. The IBRD was to administer loans for postwar reconstruction and the never-ratified ITO was to shape the

[99] 'Each government accepting this Agreement does so in respect of its metropolitan territory and of the other territories for which it has international responsibility, except such separate customs territories as it shall notify to the Executive Secretary to the CONTRACTING PARTIES at the time of its own acceptance'.

[100] 'If any of the customs territories, in respect of which a contracting party has accepted this Agreement, possesses or acquires full autonomy in the conduct of its external commercial relations and of the other matters provided for in this Agreement, such territory shall, upon sponsorship through a declaration by the responsible contracting party establishing the above-mentioned fact, be deemed to be a contracting party'.

[101] Dam (n 96) 346.

international trade environment. The underlying character of the Bretton Woods Institutions was their non-political nature as opposed to that of the UN. From a strictly legal perspective, GATT could not be considered an international organisation. However, as GATT executive secretary White pointed out with respect to the Agreement's provisions for joint action and decision, it 'had the potentiality to become, and has in fact become, an international "organisation" for trade co-operation between the signatory States'.[102] Thus, GATT was presented as an international mechanism for multilateral reduction of tariff barriers to trade in goods. In this respect it shared with the IMF and the IBRD some aspects of the functionalist approach to international organisations. First, the underlying rationale that specialised organisations can best serve the world community by performing specific functions. Secondly, the assumption that economic and technical matters can be effectively separated from politics. Under these assumptions, the Bretton Woods Institutions were separated from the UN and secured the appearance of economic neutrality in carrying out their activities.[103]

In 1947, the GATT had already defined the contours of 'proper' commercial policies. Trade liberalisation was the way forward, and the achievement of economic development had to be consistent with GATT's purposes.[104] However, as it will be argued in the following chapters, it is exactly the assumption that the postwar international trade activity can be separated from politics that needs to be challenged. Indeed, the rules of trade that GATT embodied cannot be explained, at least not entirely, in terms of free-trade doctrine. The contradictions examined, however, can be explained in terms of the strategic position the 'less developed economies' occupied within the expanding world capitalist system with the US in its dominant position. Access to the raw materials of the soon-to-be developing countries was secured through both the prohibition of QR and the reduction of tariffs on exports. The obligation to lower tariffs on imports was to serve the need to place industrial products in the market of the ex-colonies, and both the MFN principle and the prohibition of new preferential arrangements ensured non-discrimination as between countries competing for such outlets. If free-trade theory could be employed to give the appearance of economic neutrality to these rules, the agricultural and fishery exceptions entirely defied the comparative advantage rationale.

[102] Quoted in Dam (n 96) 335. However, at no point did the Agreement refer to GATT as an organisation, or mention membership.

[103] Anghie, 'Time Present and Time Past' (n 5) 264–65. See also L Claude, *Swords into Plowshares: the Problems and Process of International Organisation* (New York, Random House, 1971) 384.

[104] Brown (n 29) 99–102.

Thus, despite the fact that economic neutrality was invoked to confer universal validity to non-discrimination and equal treatment in trade relations, these principles and their carefully drafted exceptions concealed the political nature of the postwar trading order and the international division of labour it reinforced. If the functionalist approach to international organisations gave authority to the separation between the UN and the Bretton Woods Institutions, the antecedents have to be traced back to the Mandate System and in particular the modus operandi inaugurated by the PMC. By granting economic neutrality to technocratic organisations, a new system emerged. This system, based on the analysis and elaboration of information collected worldwide, would allow for a 'new science of intervention' to be employed in the ex-colonies once they achieved independence. In this respect, Anghie argues, the contemporary 'science of development' is the progeny of the 'science of colonial administration'.[105] Indeed, as Escobar writes:

> [I]f during World War II the dominant image of what was to become the Third World was shaped by strategic considerations and access to its raw materials, the integration of these parts of the world into the economic and political structure that emerged at the end of the war grew more complicated.[106]

In other words, once Western countries sought the participation of the ex-colonies in the postwar international system, the positions of the latter had somehow to be taken into consideration. Thus, to the request of a more flexible system that took into account the specific contexts of 'less developed' countries, the industrialised countries responded with various reforms that modified the rules of GATT so as to grant a certain degree of autonomy for 'economic development' reasons. Chapter two will examine the premise, nature and scope of such flexibility.

105 Anghie, 'Time Present and Time Past' (n 5) 281.
106 Escobar (n 45) 31.

2

The 'Science of Development' and the GATT Norm

AS SEEN IN chapter one, the antecedents of the modern 'science of development' can be traced back to the Mandate System established under the League of Nations.[1] In particular, the relevance attributed to economic rationality in analysing the continuous flow of information collected from the mandate territories provided the basis on which experts could devise and employ supposedly neutral policies for the benefit of the natives. Simultaneously, this 'civilising' mission was closely linked to the commercial interests of the colonial powers.

However, as the twentieth-century decolonisation process would put an end to the political presence of European countries in non-European territories, the old colonial powers would no longer be able to exert their economic influence 'by means of "extra-economic" coercion, by military conquest and often direct political rule'.[2] The detachment of economic power from direct forms of coercion thus required a new means of control over the ex-colonies and this was soon to be provided by the emerging 'science of development'.

The first part of this chapter therefore explores the process through which the scientific authority of development thinking emerged and consolidated into a fixed framework in the immediate postwar period. In particular, development economics with its specific focus on the economies of developing countries signals the moment in which development starts to function as a 'science'.[3] The so-called backwardness of Third World

[1] A Anghie, 'Time Present and Time Past: Globalisation, International Financial Institutions, and the Third World' (2000) 32 *New York University Journal of International Law & Politics* 243, 281.

[2] E Meiksins Wood, *Empire of Capital* (London, Verso, 2005) 12.

[3] For an overview of development economics, see A Escobar, *Encountering Development: The Making and Unmaking of the Third World* (Princeton, Princeton University Press, 1995) 55–89. See also MS Haque, *Restructuring Development Theories and Policies: A Critical Study* (Albany, State University of New York Press, 1999) 53–79. In what follows,

countries came to be neutrally theorised and new forms of intervention based on economic rationality were made possible. At a more general level, however, the 'science of development' established as early as the 1950s would set the terms within which it became possible to think about, speak of and reformulate 'development'. This framework borrowed and further elaborated the three normative assumptions examined in the context of the Mandate System.[4] Posed as unquestionable, these assumptions became the constitutive elements of the 'science of development' and would continue to operate despite the subsequent transformation and reformulation of development thinking. The exploration of this framework is therefore crucial to analyse both the development-related trade reforms adopted within GATT and the theoretical and practical shifts this framework has entailed.

Hence, the second part of this chapter examines the process through which GATT's legal structure became officially involved in the development apparatus that emerged in the postwar period. The argument is that, from its inception, GATT was influenced by and greatly affected the production of development knowledge and policies. The area of international trade law and policy that GATT promoted and disciplined relied on the prevailing theories and conceptions of development formulated in the immediate postwar period. Concurrently, GATT contributed to the formation of trade-related development knowledge. The most important premise it produced in this respect was the positing of a 'failure' on the part of developing countries to develop their trade as fast as that of the developed countries.[5] Consequently, it established the endless need for developing countries to follow the 'rational' trade policy prescriptions of the industrialised nations and the various groups of experts appointed to redress this 'failure'.

This endless need is the most crucial production of the postwar international trading system: as it will become clear from the discussion in chapter three on the neo-liberal transformation of development thinking, the so-called failure of the trade of developing countries as opposed to the success of that of the industrialised nations would be a fundamental factor in the shift from the GATT's approach to development to the WTO's approach, coupled with new representations of Third World societies.

however, the discussion is limited to the works of two of its exponents, namely J Lewis and RR Rostow, in order to analyse the premise that development economics established for the development framework of the postwar period.

[4] See above, ch 1, I.

[5] GATT, 'Trends in International Trade: A Report by a Panel of Experts' (Geneva, GATT Publications, 1958). This, as discussed below, was the development norm produced by the Contracting Parties with the commissioning of the Haberler Report. Hereafter, the Haberler Report.

I THE EMERGENCE OF THE DEVELOPMENT ENTERPRISE

> [T]he notions of underdevelopment and Third World were the discursive products of the post-World War II climate. These concepts did not exist before 1945. They emerged as working principles within the process by which the West — and, in different ways, the East—redefined themselves and the rest of the world. By the early 1950s, the notion of three worlds—the free industrialised nations, the Communist industrialised nations, and the poor, non-industrialised nations, constituting the First, Second and Third World respectively—was firmly in place.[6]

It is important to qualify the reasons according to which Escobar places the birth of the development enterprise in the postwar period. There were significant antecedents that paved the way to its emergence. First, although the transformation of pre-modern capitalist societies into market economies occurred in and related to a particular historical and geographical context, its significance was interpreted as universal and extended worldwide with the establishment of the colonies and foreign trade. As Gray writes, all classical thinkers believed in 'the creation of a single worldwide civilization in which the varied traditions and cultures of the past were superseded by a universal community founded on reason'.[7] In the name of this reason, the other was regarded as the 'barbaric non-European' and Western intervention was advocated in order to lead the way to 'civilization'.[8] In this sense, the very concept of development was first shaped by the colonial encounter: it was possible to conceive of development only in terms of its opposition to a condition of underdevelopment characterising non-European societies. Secondly, the Mandate System under the League of Nations reformulated this idea by considering the people of the mandate territories 'not yet able to stand by themselves under the strenuous conditions of the modern world'[9] and in need of assistance by the more advanced members of the international community. Concomitantly, the dichotomy of civilised–uncivilised that characterised much of the language of positivist international law was being replaced by that of advanced–backward which was supposed to rely on a more objective ground, namely economic expertise.[10]

[6] Escobar (n 3) 31.

[7] J Gray, *False Dawn: The Delusions of Global Capitalism* (London, Granta, 1998) 2.

[8] See Anghie (n 1) 275–76.

[9] League of Nations, *Covenant of the League of Nations*, Art 22, para 1; quoted in Anghie (n 1) 276.

[10] The dichotomy between advanced and backward societies would be replaced with that between developed and less-developed or developing countries. This furthered the appearance of an objective and neutral evaluation of societies based on economics. See Anghie (n 1) 285. Notwithstanding the problematic nature of the assumptions these definitions embody, the terms 'backward', 'less-developed' and 'developing' countries are referred to, in what follows, as employed by the literature examined.

For Escobar, the connection between the decline of the colonial rule and the launching of the development enterprise can clearly be seen in Africa.[11] In the settler states of southern Africa, 'preoccupations with questions of labour and food supplies led to strategies for the modernisation of segments of the African population ... at the expense of Afrocentric views of food and community defended by women'.[12] The rise of the development enterprise in Latin America was different, however, as these countries had achieved independence at the beginning of the nineteenth century. The decline of European influence was coupled by the ascendancy of that of the United States. With the 'big stick policy' and the 'good neighbour principle' characterising US foreign policy in the region until the 1930s, the US aimed to achieve 'ideological as well as military and economic hegemony and conformity, without having to pay the price of permanent conquest'.[13] This situation was to change during the Second World War, when the US military and economic interests were challenged by Latin American interests in the pursuit of economic and social goals.[14]

Although the differences in the historic processes of the various ex-colonies are important, it is possible to speak of the birth of the official development thinking in the postwar period. The new structure of world power with the United States in the dominant position, the expansion of the world capitalist system, the search for new markets and the Cold War were among the most important factors that explained the strategic relevance of the soon-to-be developing countries.[15] Independence would have greatly affected the interests of metropolitan territories since the ex-colonies were to gain sovereignty over their natural resources. For the so-called advanced countries to argue that their intervention could still be beneficial, it was crucial to rely on the well-established idea of backwardness and build on it the great promise of its overcoming as a necessary and desirable historic process. In other words, development thinking had to become a 'proper' science in order to explain 'neutrally' how economic development was to be achieved in 'backward' or 'underdeveloped' countries. Nothing better than economic expertise, whose neutrality had been established with the Mandate System and which happened to be the privileged domain of the industrialised countries, could have facilitated this supposedly inevitable historic process.

[11] Escobar (n 3) 26.

[12] *Ibid* 27.

[13] P Drake, *From Good Men to Good Neighbours: 1912–1932*; quoted in Escobar (n 3) 28.

[14] For an account of the controversy between the US and Latin American countries which arose in the context of the international legality of expropriation and compensation, see M Sornarajah, *The International Law on Foreign Investments* (Cambridge, Cambridge University Press, 2004) 37–38 and 347–48.

[15] See Escobar (n 3) 32–33.

A The 'Professionalisation' and 'Institutionalisation' of Development

It was at this point that development acquired its 'scientific' authority, which would allow for endless forms of intervention to take place in the so-called Third World. What Escobar refers to as the 'institutionalisation' and 'professionalisation' of development recalls the modus operandi Anghie has emphasised with respect to the Mandate System. The work of the Permanent Mandate Commission (PMC) was based on the collection of a vast body of information regarding different subject areas and mandate territories which would have been elaborated by experts in order to formulate policies applicable to different cultural, social and political contexts.[16] The experience of the PMC therefore posited the premise for the so-called professionalisation of the development apparatus in the 1950s. Furthermore, the League of Nations had been the first international institution which, through the work of supposedly neutral experts, had claimed the disinterested character of its activity, introducing the institutionalisation of the development field.[17] Both features of the Mandate System were to become the crucial mechanisms through which the development enterprise was to operate. As Escobar notes:

> The concept of professionalisation refers mainly to the process that brings the Third World into the politics of expert knowledge and Western science in general. This is accomplished through a set of techniques, strategies, and disciplinary practices that organise the generation, validation and diffusion of development knowledge … in other words those mechanisms through which a politics of truth is created and maintained, through which certain forms of knowledge are given the status of truth … an unprecedented will to know everything about the Third World flourished unhindered, growing like a virus … The professionalisation of development also made it possible to remove all problems from the political and cultural realms and to recast them in terms of the apparently more neutral realm of science … Like the landing of the Allies in Normandy, the Third World witnessed a massive landing of experts, each in charge of investigating, measuring, and theorising about this or that little aspect of Third World societies. The invention of development necessarily involves the creation of an institutional field from which discourses are produced, recorded, stabilised, modified and put into circulation. This field is intimately imbricated with processes of professionalisation; together they constitute an apparatus that organises the production of forms of knowledge and the deployment of forms of power, relating to one another.[18]

Although the so-called institutionalisation and professionalisation of development involved different levels, from international organisations and

[16] See Anghie (n 1) 280.
[17] *Ibid* 284.
[18] Escobar (n 3) 45–46.

national planning agencies to non-governmental organisations and academics in Third World countries, the terms of the debate were set between the 1940s and 1950s. As discussed below, the basic underpinnings of the development framework were that the economic growth and progress experienced by industrialised countries were both desirable and inevitable. It was therefore a matter of identifying the most appropriate means in order to achieve the result, namely the replication of the industrialised countries' experience. Borrowing from the experience of the Mandate System that claimed to do away with the political interests of the mandatories, the privileged terrain from which to articulate the development mission was that of economics.

Thus, the first preoccupation of development experts in the early 1940s was to overcome the fact that traditional economics was unable to explain the conditions of underdevelopment characterising many Third World countries.[19] This new approach came to be known as development economics and the theories that followed analysed the roots of the so-called backwardness and proposed models and strategies which were to be employed by the postwar international institutions. It is crucial to emphasise, as Escobar does, that development theories and practice went far beyond the economic analysis and recommendations they produced and aimed at the transformation of all social relations in Third World societies.[20] Hence, the need for such transformation was made indisputable and became the development 'norm'.[21] It is equally important to acknowledge that a crucial objective of the transformation that development theories and practice aimed to accomplish was the incorporation of developing countries within the world capitalist system, as the following analysis of development economics' main tenets shows.

B Development Economics' 'Growth' and 'Progress'

The common theme these theories reflected was the centrality of notions such as growth and progress which qualified development as the desirable transition from backward, traditional to advanced, modern societies. Lewis and Rostow were among the most prominent scholars of development economics. They both qualified development in terms of economic growth

[19] Haque (n 3) 68.

[20] Escobar (n 3) 1–12.

[21] To talk of 'normalisation' in the context of the emerging development discipline is to say that for whatever theory, policy, view or position to be taken into consideration, it had to conform to the said truth, namely the need for the underdeveloped to develop. This need would permeate even dependency theories which, as discussed below, have challenged many assumptions on which development economics was based.

and underdeveloped economies in terms of their economic gap with the stage of growth characterising advanced societies. Lewis was to argue that

> communities in which the national income per head is not increasing invest 4 or 5 per cent of their national incomes per annum or less, whilst *progressive* economies invest 12 per cent per annum or more. The central problem in the theory of economic growth is to understand the process by which a community is converted from being a 5 per cent to a 12 per cent saver—with all the *changes in attitudes, in institutions and in techniques which accompany this conversion*[22] (emphasis added).

Therefore, unlike the so-called advanced countries, so-called underdeveloped societies were characterised by the co-existence of labour surplus and lack of capital with the consequent shortage of both savings and investments.[23] This was due, according to Lewis, to the co-existence of two different models in Third World economies; a traditional sector based mainly on agriculture with poor productivity, low income and surplus of labour and a capitalist sector characterised by technological innovation, labour demand and capital expansion.[24] In order to catch up with the advanced economies, underdeveloped countries were to pursue the conversion of their economies so that savings and investments could run from 5 per cent to 12 per cent of their national economies:

> If profit is the major source of saving, the conversion of an economy from a 5 to a 12 per cent saver must be explained by an increase of the share of profits in the national income. How does this come about? One obvious answer is: by the growth of the capitalist sector of the economy, relatively to the rest, resulting from the continuous reinvestment of capitalist profits ... If the process of converting an economy from a 5 to 12 percent saver is essentially dependent upon the rise of profits relatively to national income, it follows that the correct explanation of why poor countries save so little is not because they are poor, but because their capitalist sectors are so small.[25]

Thus, primacy was to be accorded to the creation of the conditions for capitalist expansion. This, in turn, would have absorbed the labour surplus from the traditional sector by offering higher wages. Eventually the capitalist sector would have replaced the traditional one. Therefore, the central fact of economic development became rapid capital accumulation and this was to be pursued through the creation of the conditions for a capitalist sector. Essential to the initial stage of this process was the reliance on foreign investments.[26] In agreement with Lewis, Rostow considered

22 WA Lewis, *The Theory of Economic Growth* (London, Allen & Unwin, 1955) 225–26.
23 *Ibid* 200–25.
24 *Ibid* 233.
25 *Ibid* 233, 236.
26 *Ibid* 244–45, 264–74.

capital accumulation as the driving force of development.[27] He maintained that, in accordance with the experience of the advanced countries, each society undergoes five stages of economic growth.

The stages are: the stage of 'traditional society', characterised by an agricultural economy; the 'preconditions for taking off', where higher rates of capital accumulation are stimulated by a national government; the 'take off', determined by an industrial revolution registering rapid economic growth; the 'drive to maturity', featuring the enhancement of technologies; and the final stage of 'mass consumption', characterised by the presence of a structured social welfare.[28] Of the five stages, Rostow emphasised the relevance of the 'take off' phase in order to promote development. This stage was successfully achieved when the rate of productive investments corresponded to 10 per cent of the national income. This, in turn, had to be ensured by a stable institutional framework able to generate continuous growth through massive injections of foreign capital and technologies. Foreign investments were necessary in order to overcome the lack of enterprise spirit and domestic savings.[29]

C Development Economics' Normative Assumptions

The framework within which it was possible to think of development had therefore been drawn at this early stage. A number of assumptions in Lewis and Rostow's analysis are worth emphasising. The assumption that development coincided with modernisation, the transition from backward and traditional to advanced and modern societies implied a reading of this process as a natural, linear, inevitable and desirable historic phenomenon. The point is not so much that of qualifying in absolute terms urbanisation and industrialisation but, as Escobar points out, that of realising that these constructions 'equate tradition with backwardness, a burden to be disposed of and a part of the economy with nothing to contribute to the process of development'.[30] In other words, development economics contributed to hierarchically ordering different societal organisations by assuming Western capitalist economies and societies as the universal term of reference for determining whether a given society could be considered developed or underdeveloped. Consequently, this hierarchical ordering

[27] WW Rostow, *The Process of Economic Growth* (New York, WW Norton & Co., 1962) 80–108.
[28] *Ibid.*
[29] *Ibid.*
[30] Escobar (n 3) 78.

disqualified all other economic relations by positing them as failing economic arrangements and therefore in need of replacement. This point is best described by Lewis' own words:

> We find a few industries highly capitalised, such as mining or electric power, side by side with the most primitive techniques ... We find the same contrast also outside the economic life. There are one or two modern towns, with the fine architectures, water supplies, communications and the like, into which people drift from other towns and villages which might almost belong to another planet. There is the same contrast even with people; between the few highly westernised, trousered, natives, educated in western universities, speaking western languages, and glorifying Beethoven, Mills, Marx or Einstein, and the great mass of their countrymen which live quite in other worlds ... Inevitably what one gets are very heavily developed patches of the economy, surrounded by economic darkness.[31]

The result of this representation of the so-called Third World was that the economic, social and cultural 'darkness' was to be replaced by new forms of societal organisation which, in turn, were to be incorporated into the expanding world capitalist system. Therefore, Lewis and Rostow provided the first means of the development strategy of the postwar period, namely capital accumulation, intensive industrialisation, development planning and foreign aid. These principles were to become the theoretical basis for the enactment of the credit-based development launched by Truman with his well known Point-Four Programme in 1949 which relied on capital, science and technology to promote the wholesale transformation of Third World societies.[32] Once the objective had been established and made indisputable, the means for achieving it could be open to challenge.

The credit-based development ideology, for instance, was soon to be criticised by Milton Friedman, who refuted the basic propositions characterising the programme.[33] The credit-based development programme was grounded on the assumptions that economic development depended on the availability of capital and that underdeveloped countries lacked such capital. Furthermore, central planning was considered essential for achieving economic development. Friedman emphasised that the issue was not the availability but rather the incentive and proper use of capital. So-called backward countries needed the right circumstances to make capital available, such as the protection of property against private and public

[31] A Lewis [1954] 1958. *Economic Development with Unlimited Supply of Labor*; quoted in Escobar (n 3) 78.

[32] H Truman, Public papers of the President of the United States: Harry S Truman, 1949 (Washington DC, US Government Printing Office, 1964).

[33] See M Friedman, *Why Government is the Problem* (Stanford, California, Hoover Institution on War, Revolution and Peace, 1993); M Friedman, *Foreign Economic Aid, Means and Objectives* (Stanford, California, Hoover Institution on War, Revolution and Peace, 1995).

seizure.[34] Furthermore, they needed a market for their products in order to extend agricultural cultivation and therefore increase the production of capital, savings and investments. For Friedman, the fact that these countries were not able to attract foreign investments was explained by the lack of institutional arrangements needed to encourage private property and free enterprise.[35] What Friedman most opposed was the idea that development had to be achieved through central planning structures. He argued that the transfer of capital in the form of grants and loans would have retarded the development of the recipient country since governments would have spent them in wasteful projects.[36] As will be examined in chapter three, central planning, or the so-called dirigiste dogma, would indeed become the first target of the neo-liberal transformation of development thinking.[37]

On these premises, Friedman posed the case for the abolition of economic aid and the establishment of global free trade. Referring to US policies, he strongly criticised the practice of erecting trade barriers and imposing quotas on imports and dumping exports in order to protect domestic production: these policies were counterproductive as they prevented the most efficient allocation of resources from taking place both at home and abroad. He therefore maintained the need to abolish such barriers as 'The new opportunities afforded by the expansion of world trade and the more efficient use of resources involved therein, would benefit many more than were harmed'.[38] Although Friedman was critical of US double standards with respect to commercial policy, his view on development shared Lewis and Rostow's core assumptions. The underlying belief was that developing countries had to catch up with the economic stage of the industrialised economies. This meant the restructuring of their economies by replacing the agricultural sector with a capitalist one and the establishment of institutions that supported such a process, namely private property and free enterprise.

Thus, the policy recommendations that followed were based on either foreign investments accompanied by state planning as argued by Rostow and Lewis, or, as in Friedman's case, market openness with a state limiting itself to grant and support private property and free enterprise. In the immediate postwar period, Lewis and Rostow's prescriptions prevailed

[34] Friedman, *Foreign Economic Aid*, ibid 7.

[35] *Ibid* 8.

[36] *Ibid* 9–10.

[37] Lal, for instance, would argue against the dirigiste dogma that posits the state as the principal provider of economic and social goods and services. See D Lal, *The Poverty of 'Development Economics'* (London, Institute of Economic Affairs, 1983) 5.

[38] Friedman, *Foreign Economic Aid* (n 33) 14–15.

over Friedman's recommendation of global free trade.[39] Capital accumulation and industrialisation through central planning were to be accompanied by liberal trade in accordance with the GATT rules established in 1947.

D Reformist Dependency Theories and the Development Matrix: The Structuralist School of Thought

As early as the 1960s, the decolonisation of the Third World engendered a new flow of ideas and concepts which challenged the one dimensional approach to development.[40] In the international trade arena, the GATT's intellectual underpinnings were to be called into question by a group of theorists who challenged the foundations of the system of international relations and related underdevelopment to the working of these forces. The theories which adopted this approach came to be known as dependency theories.[41] Most of them derived from the experience gained by some scholars within the UN Economic Commission for Latin America and influenced the development debate within GATT from the late 1950s to the early 1980s. Among them, Raul Prebisch argued that there were structural forces within the international trade system that constrained the economic growth of countries specialising in the production and exports of primary commodities.[42]

The argument focused on a perennial trend to inequalities between the so-called centre of the trading system, consisting of the developed capitalist economies specialising in the production of industrial goods, and the so-called periphery, consisting in turn of the underdeveloped countries that

[39] As it will be seen in ch 3, the neo-liberal transformation of development thinking relied on the critique of development economics that Friedman had already articulated in the 1950s.

[40] See Haque (n 3) 81–102.

[41] The subsequent discussion does not aim to comprehensively cover dependency thought. It presents a brief overview of the Structuralist School of Thought and the policy recommendations that followed in order to highlight their contribution to the GATT's development activity between the 1960s and 1980s. Therefore, the analysis is necessarily a limited one. For instance, the theoretical insights into the working of the world capitalist system offered by radical dependency theories and world-systems theories, which challenged the claim that underdevelopment was a social reality that had nothing to do with political and economic exploitation, are left out. For the most relevant works of radical dependency theorists, see AG Frank, *Capitalism and Underdevelopment in Latin America: Historical Studies of Chile and Brazil* (New York, Monthly Review Press, 1967) and S Amin, *Imperialism and Unequal Development* (Hassocks, Harvester Press, 1977). For an exposition of world-systems thought, see I Wallerstein, *The Capitalist World Economy: Essays* (Cambridge, Cambridge University Press, 1979).

[42] R Prebisch, *Economic Development of Latin America and its Principal Problems* (New York, United Nations, 1950). See also R Prebisch, 'Commercial Policy in the Underdeveloped Countries' (1959) 49 *The American Economic Review* 251, 251–73 and R Prebisch, *Towards a Dynamic of Development Policy for Latin America* (New York, United Nations, 1963).

had specialised in the production of primary commodities. Prebisch further argued that such inequalities were reflected in the deterioration of the terms of trade between the centre and the periphery. He took into consideration the consequences that followed from an increase of income in both developed and underdeveloped countries in order to explain this phenomenon. An increase of income for underdeveloped countries usually translates into an increase in the demand for the industrial goods produced by advanced countries. However, if the advanced countries' income were to increase, the excess income did not translate into greater demands for raw materials due to the slow growth of the international demand for primary commodities.[43]

Prebisch emphasised that the same principle applied in terms of productivity and prices. If the productivity or supply of raw materials increased, their prices decreased as the producer countries had to deal with the growing competition among them. Because of the inelastic demand for raw materials from the advanced countries and the need to acquire currency in order to repay the imported capital, developing countries were induced to lower prices and force production to the limit.[44] However, if the centre's productivity increased, the prices of industrial goods did not decrease. This was due to the elastic demand of the 'periphery' for industrial goods, the political power of industrial monopolies and the pressure exercised by the unions.[45]

Due to these structural imbalances, which in turn were the consequence of the division of labour operated under colonialism, trade could not function as an engine of growth. In order to overcome the permanent subordination of Third World countries in the international trading system, Prebisch suggested the employment of import substitution policies. The internal production of industrial goods previously imported from industrialised countries would have a positive effect on the balance of payments, thus stimulating autonomous growth. Prebisch's enquiry into the structural imbalances of the international trading system as the primary cause of underdevelopment was followed by Sunkel and Furtado. Sunkel identified the main reason for underdevelopment as the infiltration of transnational capitalism that introduces capital-intensive technologies and imposes consumption patterns.[46] This in turn results in the subordination of national capital and the destruction of indigenous development. Furtado argued that, influenced by the external demand, export firms adapt their

[43] Prebisch, 'Commercial Policy' *ibid*, 253.

[44] The price elasticity of demand concerns the relationship between demand for goods and services and their respective prices. In general, the demand for goods and services is rigid or inelastic when the quantity demanded does not change noticeably with a change in prices.

[45] Prebisch, 'Commercial Policy' (n 42) 253.

[46] O Sunkel, 'National Development Policy and External Dependence in Latin America' (1969) 6 *Journal of Development Studies* 23, 29–31.

production to the requirements of international markets, while internal production tends to satisfy the demand of the high income groups. As a result of this tendency, local firms depend on the import of capital-intensive technologies from advanced countries.[47]

It is worth noting that Prebish, Sunkel and Furtado also identified development with economic growth, capital accumulation and industrialisation. However, their analysis of the structural imbalances of the international trade system would provide the background for advocating broader reforms both within the periphery and in their relationship with the centre. Internally, Sunkel[48] suggested agrarian reforms and industrial reorganisation in order to reach marginal groups and ensure their participation in the decision-making process, whereas Furtado advocated central planning to resolve the problem of underdevelopment.[49] In line with the need for internal reforms, the International Labour Organisation (ILO) recommended the employment of different strategies aimed at the redistribution of national income in favour of the low-income classes.[50] Their increased income would be spent on consumer goods and, as these goods required labour intensive techniques, their increased demand would generate more employment. Furtado also argued for a comprehensive reform of the international trading system. This reform would contemplate the reduction of the fluctuations of primary commodity prices and the need for the industrial goods of less-developed countries to access the markets of developed countries on a preferential basis and without reciprocity.[51]

Therefore, these theories provided the basis for the demands developing countries were to articulate within the United Nations Conference on Trade and Development (UNCTAD) in the following years. An instance of this was the series of proposals advanced by the so-called Group of 77 within UNCTAD known as the New International Economic Order (NIEO).[52] With regard to the terms of international trade, they requested the stabilisation of commodities prices through agreed levels under which prices could not fall.[53] They also proposed the negotiation of a Preferential

[47] C Furtado *Development and Underdevelopment* (Berkeley, University of California Press, 1964) 141–71.

[48] Sunkel (n 46) 35–36.

[49] C Furtado, 'Underdevelopment: To Conform or Reform' in GM Meier *et al* (eds), *Pioneers in Development* (New York, Oxford University Press, 1984) 225.

[50] ILO, 'Employment, Growth and Basic Needs: A One World Problem'. Report of the Director General of the International Labour Office to the Tripartite World Conference on Employment, Income Distribution and Social Progress, and the International Division of Labour (Geneva, ILO, 1976).

[51] C Furtado, *Teorie dello Sviluppo Economico* (Bari, Laterza, 1970) 338.

[52] See J Gelinas, *Freedom from Debt* (London & New York, Zed Books, 1998) 11–12.

[53] With regard to the 18 commodities whose price it was agreed to stabilise with the adoption of the Integrated Programme for commodities during the UNCTAD IV Negotiations, only the agreement on rubber was negotiated. An existing agreement on cocoa became inoperative, and the one on tin and sugar failed. *Ibid.*

System of Tariffs to grant southern commodities better access to northern markets and requested the use of protectionist trade measures to safeguard infant industries. In relation to their financial instability, they advanced the proposal for the establishment of a Fund for Economic Development controlled by the United Nations and requested more stable exchange rates, debt relief and financial assistance.[54] These demands were to influence the so-called north–south debate which unfolded within GATT and gave rise to the reforms that aimed at making GATT mechanisms more favourable to developing countries.

Dependency theories, as well as the NIEO's strategies, provided the development discipline with new perspectives. The range of arguments varied from income redistribution, primary needs and international relations to unequal exchange, indigenous development and economic subordination. Thus, reformist dependency theories and the strategies they inspired did not aim at subverting the international order but at making its principles less unfavourable to the interests of developing countries. They would therefore animate the debate within different international institutions, including the GATT, and produce a certain degree of reforms. Notwithstanding this, development was still identified with economic growth, capital accumulation and industrialisation or, in other words, with the need for developing countries to catch up with the economic stage of the industrialised countries. Whereas development economics amplified what Haque terms 'excessive empiricism, indifference to ethical and moral values, analytical reductionism, Eurocentric bias and claim of universalism', reformist dependency theories also employed empiricist parameters such as primary necessities, trade relations and unequal exchange to define development.[55]

As Haque points out, all growth theories based their assumptions on economic criteria such as production and accumulation while considering political and social issues as constants.[56] For their part, the Structuralist School of Thought and the NIEO strategies omitted to consider the diversity of political and social contexts characterising the many 'satellite' countries.[57] More importantly, dependency theories shared the matrix of the 'science of development', notwithstanding the important challenges they brought to the assumptions about the unproblematic nature of the international order. As its normative assumptions, namely the unquestionable dichotomy between developed and underdeveloped societies and the

[54] Most developed countries withdrew from the NIEO, which silently disappeared in the early 1990s. *Ibid.*

[55] Haque (n 3) 133.

[56] *Ibid* 133–38.

[57] *Ibid.*

reliance on economics as the neutral terrain on which to achieve development, remained firmly in place, they already contained the premise for the neo-liberal transformation of development thinking.

II THE GATT DEVELOPMENT MISSION

When the GATT entered into force, its Economic Development provisions reflected the postwar climate on development. The original proposal submitted by the United States during the ITO negotiations did not contemplate any different treatment for those countries referred to as less-developed economies. The US view on commercial policy was based on universal rules of conduct including Most Favoured Nation, National Treatment, the obligation not to increase preference margins or create new preferences, the progressive negotiations of tariff reductions and the gradual elimination of quantitative restrictions.[58] Initially the US had maintained that any issue of concern for the less-developed economies had to be addressed within the Economic Development Sub-Commission of the United Nations Economic and Social Council.[59] However, confronted with the opposition of the 13 less-developed countries who argued that the universal rules of trade did not take into account their specific concerns, the US compromised during the London Conference. As a result, GATT Article XVIII provided for some measures of protection, namely quantitative restrictions on imports in order to assist the establishment of infant industries until they were able to compete at the international level.[60] However, these measures were to be subject to the prior expert scrutiny and approval of the Contracting Parties. With the exception of Ceylon, Cuba, Haiti and India, less-developed countries never relied on this complex Article.[61] Unlike Article XVIII, the Balance of Payments exception provided for in GATT Articles XII and XIV did not require prior approval and less-developed countries resorted to the use of these provisions rather than to the infant industry exception.[62]

By the late 1940s, development within the GATT system had thus been qualified as a universal concept based on economic growth to be achieved through industrialisation by means of liberal trade. Development economics and the interpretation of Third World societal organisations it articulated provided the theoretical support for these assumptions and the exceptional character of GATT Article XVIII was consistent with this view.

[58] See ch 1, II B.
[59] See ch 1, II and III.
[60] This measure was to be carried over from Art 13 of the never ratified ITO Charter.
[61] KW Dam, *The GATT Law and International Economic Organisation* (Chicago, University of Chicago Press, 1970) 228.
[62] See ch 1, III.

However, as increasingly more colonies and mandate territories achieved independence and dependency theories provided new insights into the structural imbalances of the international trading regime, their discontent grew with respect to the GATT's theoretical underpinnings and the legal provisions that adversely affected their international trading position. First, notwithstanding the US and UK rhetoric about the beneficial impact of trade liberalisation, GATT was never completely engaged with free-trade theory. Agriculture and fisheries were in actual fact exempted from the prohibition of quantitative restrictions, clearly benefiting the United States and EEC.

This meant that the trade of developing countries was not only penalised in terms of the inelastic demand for their products; industrialised countries also discriminated against one of the sectors in which, according to the logic of international specialisation that sustains trade liberalisation, developing countries had a strong export interest.[63] In addition to this, the mechanisms for negotiating tariff reductions reinforced the view that access to a market was a gain that had be paid for.[64] As noted by Tussie, the principle of reciprocity implied that a country would grant a tariff reduction in exchange for a corresponding concession by a trading partner.[65] That is to say that tariff reductions would occur when countries had something to offer in exchange. This issue was closely connected to the so-called Principal Supplier rule, according to which negotiations for the reduction of tariffs on particular products, the so-called product-by-product negotiations, began in a bilateral fashion with the request made by the largest exporter of a particular product to the larger importer.[66] Since liberalisation of agriculture had been de facto singled out, the product-by-product negotiations carried out under the Principal Supplier rule meant that negotiations focused almost entirely on industrial products and were conducted on a de facto bilateral basis between the industrialised countries. Only if and when an agreement was reached between the interested parties, could developing countries benefit from an extension of the negotiated concession due to the application of the Most Favoured Nation (MFN) clause. The result was that developing countries were largely excluded from the negotiating process.[67]

[63] See ch 1, II C.

[64] The idea of tariff reduction as a 'payment' that must be paid for has been analysed by Robert Hudec. See RE Hudec, *Developing Countries in the GATT Legal System* (London, Trade Policy Research Centre, 1987) 17.

[65] D Tussie, The Less Developed Countries and the World Trading System: A Challenge to the GATT (London, Pinter, 1987) 23–24.

[66] See MJ Trebilcock and R Howse, *The Regulation of International Trade* (London; New York, Routledge, 2005) 179.

[67] As Trebilcock and Howse point out, this was the case during the first four rounds of GATT negotiations, namely the Geneva (1947–48), Torquay (1949), Annecy (1950–51) and Geneva (1956) Rounds. *Ibid.*

Arguing against the imbalances of the GATT regime, developing countries set out to reform its rules. The challenges they brought to the development assumptions underlying the GATT legal structure resulted in the amendments of some of its original provisions. As discussed below, the outcome was the recognition that, by virtue of the difficulty developing countries encountered in the international trading environment, they were entitled to some degree of flexibility from GATT legal strictures. However, it is also important to acknowledge the fact that, notwithstanding the positive language of the commitments developed countries undertook in this respect, they continued to discriminate against the trade of developing countries. Hence, in what follows, the nature, scope and content of such initiatives is analysed in order to emphasise the contradictions inherent in the four decades long development-related trade activity of the GATT.

A The GATT First Review Session: Positing Developing Countries' Failure

The first review of the GATT's substantive provisions was carried out by the Contracting Parties in 1955. With the spreading out of the Cold War, the United States aimed to attract as many developing states as possible.[68] Therefore, the Review Session altered GATT's discipline regarding less-developed countries in two respects. First, there was a formal recognition within Article XVIII that 'economic development' was not an exception but an integral part of the GATT's objectives.[69] This was contrary to the early US position which had considered the concerns of less-developed countries outside its scope, namely that of universal provider of commercial policy. GATT was now officially involved in the promotion of trade-related development knowledge. Another change made by the 1955 Review Session concerned a provision contained in Article XXVIII (*bis*) according to which developed countries were to take into consideration the particular situations of less-developed countries and were therefore not to insist on reciprocity when negotiating tariff concessions.[70] In practice, as Hudec notes, this meant that each country was to make a decision as to the adequacy of reciprocity so that there was no substantial commitment on the part of developed countries.[71]

[68] See Hudec (n 64) 26.

[69] Furthermore, a specific provision concerning Balance of Payments exceptions for developing countries was introduced under Art XVIII(B). However, the fact that prior approval was retained meant that no fundamental changes to the infant industry exception were made. The only developing country to invoke the infant industry exception after the review session was Ceylon. See Dam (n 61) 228.

[70] See Hudec (n 64) 26.

[71] *Ibid*.

The second initiative taken by GATT Contracting Parties followed the appointment of a panel of experts which was supposed to study the reasons for 'the *failure* of the trade of less-developed countries to develop as rapidly as that of industrialised countries' (emphasis added).[72] Significantly, development had become an integral part of the GATT's objectives and was here defined in terms of the failure of less-developed countries to develop their trade as fast as that of the developed countries. As argued below, this principle set the framework within which all successive GATT initiatives would be taken. Development had already been identified with rapid economic growth within a capitalist economy. Consequently, trade had entered the development discourse as its necessary and beneficial engine. The trade-related development policies that the GATT pursued until the 1980s would carry this legacy: the need for developing countries to develop, through trade, as rapidly as the developed countries.

B The Haberler Report and Committee III: Tracing Discrimination

Thus, the Haberler Report, published in 1958, limited itself to this mandate and focused on the Contracting Parties' compliance with GATT rules of conduct in order to explain the so-called failure of less-developed countries.[73] However, the report produced an important result. Among the other problems that less-developed countries were facing, including their insufficient effort to liberalise trade, the report crucially exposed the agricultural protectionism practised by developed countries, the effects of regional trading blocs and the instability of commodity prices.[74] GATT Contracting Parties reacted by launching a Programme for Trade Expansion within which a committee was to be established in order to study the developed countries' measures restricting less-developed countries' exports. Committee III produced a detailed account showing that developed countries were actively hindering the trade of less-developed countries—both traditional exports and exports of manufacture—by way of tariffs, quantitative restrictions, internal taxes, state trading and import monopolies. Less-developed countries also faced high tariffs on their major exports, especially in respect to vegetable oil, coffee, tea, cocoa products, jute products, cotton products, sporting goods and leather goods.[75]

Furthermore, Committee III emphasised that developed countries were discriminating against less-developed countries' exports on the basis of

[72] GATT, Twelfth Session of the Contracting Parties (1957) BISD 6th Supp (1958) 18.

[73] GATT, 'Trends in International Trade' (n 5).

[74] JH Jackson, *World Trade and the Law of GATT* (New York, Bobbs-Merrill, 1969) 642–43.

[75] Dam (n 61) 229.

origin and the degree of processing. Committee III focused on these two kinds of discrimination, highlighting that tariff rates for processed products were much higher than those for raw materials, thereby representing a serious impediment to less-developed countries' industrialisation process.[76] The discrimination on the basis of origin derived mainly from the arrangements entered by the EEC with some of its ex-colonies.[77] As for quantitative restrictions, Committee III found that developed countries were using them against less-developed countries' exports of vegetable seeds and oil, coffee, raw cotton, tobacco, tropical timber, jute manufactures, cotton manufactures and sewing machines. Again, discrimination on the basis of origin and processing degree was found. The result was that less-developed countries were locked into the pattern of producers of raw materials.[78] In addition to tariffs and quantitative restrictions, a high rate of internal taxes was levied by developed countries on coffee, tea and cocoa while state trading and import monopolies were found in many cases to be a surrogate of quantitative restrictions.[79] The result of the report was that many developed countries' restrictions to less-developed countries' exports were GATT-inconsistent. Developed countries not only maintained the double standards in respect to the sectors to be liberalised, namely agriculture and fisheries, but were also contravening the GATT's rules and spirit. The discrimination against the exports of less-developed countries amounted to a material impediment of that development process industrialised countries were alleging to promote.

The response of GATT Contracting Parties to the alarming report of Committee III demanding greater access for the exports of less-developed countries came to be known as the Action Programme. The Action Programme was intended to create greater access by means of unilateral trade liberalisation by developed countries and trade negotiations to be held in 1960. Neither of the two objectives were met. Although several recommendations were formally made and accepted, there were no legally binding commitments on the part of developed countries.[80] The Dillon Round negotiations made no progress regarding the reduction of the tariff barriers that Committee III had denounced, even though developed countries had accepted the Committee's view that less-developed countries could not be expected to make progress through negotiations on tariff reductions involving reciprocity.[81]

[76] *Ibid* 230.
[77] *Ibid.*
[78] *Ibid* 232.
[79] *Ibid* 232–33.
[80] See Hudec (n 64) 42–44; see also Jackson (n 74) 644–46.
[81] The Dillon Round was the fifth Round of GATT negotiations held between 1960 and 1962.

C The GATT Part IV: Discharging Responsibility

The 1963 Ministerial Meeting which had agreed on the establishment of the Action Programme also produced a statement according to which ministers 'recognised the need for an adequate legal and institutional framework to enable the Contracting Parties to discharge their responsibilities in connection with the work of expanding the trade of less developed countries'.[82] A committee was therefore charged with the task of drafting the amendments to the GATT texts and its outcome became Part IV of the GATT. This was a reaction to the preparation of the 1964 UNCTAD that threatened to become a permanent organisation representing the interests of developing countries.[83] The first secretary of UNCTAD was Raul Prebisch whose enquiry into the structural imbalances of the international trading system had called into question the GATT's intellectual underpinnings. Thus, reinvigorated attention to development was required to avoid the consequence that countries critical of GATT would have opted out of its legal framework. However, as Hudec has pointed out, Part IV was a proverbial example of the attitude that developed countries would employ towards less-developed countries throughout the history of GATT negotiations, namely that of using impressive statements to give the illusion of legal commitments without undertaking 'definable legal obligations'.[84]

The two core provisions that formed Part IV of the GATT were Article XXXVI on 'Principles and Objectives' and Article XXXVII on 'Commitments'. Article XXXVI specified that developed countries did not expect reciprocity for the commitments they made during trade negotiations. In theory this Article set aside the GATT principle according to which concessions must be paid for. The practical relevance of this was to be tested during the Kennedy Round.[85] However, the most important provision was Article XXXVII because it was to state the legal obligations of developed countries. It recalled the language used in the 1963 Action Programme in respect to the 'reduction and elimination of barriers to products currently or potentially of particular export interest to less-developed countries, including custom duties and other restrictions which differentiate unreasonably between such products in their primary and processed forms'.[86] It also provided for the standstill on the introduction

[82] GATT, Twenty-first Session of the Contracting Parties (1963) BISD 12th Supp (1964) 36.

[83] See Hudec (n 64) 39–40.

[84] Hudec (n 64) 56.

[85] The Kennedy Round was the sixth round of GATT negotiations held between 1963 and 1967.

[86] GATT Art XXXVII.1(a).

or increase of 'customs duties or non-tariff import barriers on products currently or potentially of particular export interest to less-developed country parties'.[87]

This was to be seen as the response of developed countries to the analysis and suggestions made by Committee III with regard to the measures hindering less-developed countries' exports. However, these commitments were highly qualified by the words 'to the fullest extent possible—that is, except when compelling reasons, make it impossible'.[88] Thus, developed countries were committed 'to the fullest extent possible [to] accord high priority' to the reduction or elimination of such tariff barriers. The same formula was employed with respect to the standstill on the introduction or increase of custom duties or non-tariff import barriers. Developed countries committed 'to the fullest extent possible' to refrain from imposing new fiscal measures on products 'wholly or mainly produced in the territories of less-developed contracting parties'.[89] This provision was supposed to deal with the problem of fiscal measures affecting tropical products. Here, the commitment 'to accord high priority' to the 'fullest extent possible' was further limited by the fact that the standstill agreement concerned only 'new fiscal measures' and did not apply to the existing ones. In addition, the reduction of internal taxes on these products was to take place only in the context of 'any adjustment of fiscal policy' by a contracting party. As Hudec points out, 'the text of part IV contained no definable legal obligations'[90] and specific proposals by less-developed countries concerning the reform of agricultural protection and the granting of preferences were rejected.[91]

The 1964 Kennedy Round negotiations on tariff reductions highlighted the same technique. Formal engagements with less-developed countries were made but no legal obligations resulted from them. Following Committee III's suggestion that less- developed countries could not be expected to engage in full reciprocal concessions, developed countries had given formal recognition to the non-reciprocity rule through Article XXXVI. In principle, less-developed countries could benefit from all concessions made by developed countries through negotiations according to the MFN obligation, even when they had not made reciprocal concessions. In reality this did not mean that less-developed countries could obtain concessions on the products of interest to them. As Hudec observes, once developed countries had dealt with the 50 per cent tariff cut on products of interest to

87 GATT Art XXXVII.1(b).
88 GATT Art XXXVII.1.
89 GATT Art XXXVII.1(c).
90 Hudec (n 64) 56.
91 See Dam (n 61) 241.

them, they dealt with less-developed countries' requests for liberalisation by simply accepting or refusing their requests with no negotiations to be carried out.[92]

Therefore, many products of interest to less-developed countries, such as cotton textiles and agricultural products, continued to be excluded from tariff reduction.[93] Both Part IV and the Kennedy Round were supposed to provide some answers to the recommendations made by the Haberler Report and Committee III. These recommendations did not imply any revolutionary vision of international trade. They both highlighted the need for eliminating those GATT-inconsistent measures which were hindering the trade prospects of less-developed countries. All Committee III asked of developed countries was that they respected the system they had created. Part IV did not translate into any legal obligations, and the Kennedy Round did nothing to reduce those tariff barriers that most impeded less-developed countries' access to the markets of the developed countries.[94] However, developed countries followed one recommendation made by Committee III on the need to limit the growing number of quantitative restrictions on textile exports from less-developed countries. The Contracting Parties agreed to study the so-called market disruptions in this sector. Oddly enough, the study of market disruption would become the platform for the Multi-Fibre Arrangement (MFA) established in 1973.[95] Thus, the only legally binding agreement reached on the basis of the report would be one which legalised quantitative restrictions on one of the greatest export sectors for developing countries.

D Enabling Non-Reciprocity

The dissatisfaction of less-developed countries with the conventional GATT approach was expressed during the second UNCTAD Conference, which prepared the ground for the launching of the NIEO strategies.[96] Thus, the US embrace of the preferences issue shortly after the Kennedy Round might be explained by the need to avoid the possibility that less-developed country members critical of the GATT could opt out of its legal regime. Only one year after the close of the Kennedy Round where

[92] Hudec (n 64) 46.

[93] *Ibid.*

[94] A procedural outcome of the Kennedy Round was the establishment of the Committee on Trade and Development, charged with the task of addressing the issue of technical assistance in favour of developing countries.

[95] Hudec (n 64) 43. The MFA, formally the Agreement Regarding International Trade in Textiles, was negotiated and concluded under the GATT between textile-exporting and importing countries to manage trade in textile products through a system of quotas imposed on imports.

[96] Hudec (n 64) 17.

developed countries had rejected proposals for the establishment of a system of tariff preferences by India and Chile, the United States changed its position and agreed to support a Generalised System of Preferences (GSP).[97] According to this system—proposed during the 1968 UNCTAD Conference—developed countries were to grant tariff preferences to several products coming from developing countries without reciprocity. As Hudec has noted, the US also used its support for the GSP in order to get the European Community to abandon the preference system granted to some African and Mediterranean countries. The US specifically aimed to obtain the dismissal of the so-called reverse preferences the European Community was obtaining from former colonies.[98] The issue between the US and the EEC seemed finally to have been settled under the so-called Casey-Soames Understanding of August 1973, where the European Community abandoned the reverse preferences in exchange for the US commitment not to challenge the legality of the Lome Convention.[99]

In order for the GSP to enter the General Agreement, it was necessary to amend GATT Article I, which was not effected until the Tokyo Round of 1979.[100] In 1971, however, GATT Contracting Parties adopted two waivers. The first was a 10-years' waiver casting aside the Most Favoured Nation clause in order to permit the establishment of the Generalised System of Preferences. The second waiver allowed for tariff preferences to be exchanged between developing countries subject to review after 10 years. Although this was presented as a victory for developing countries which, after two decades, had managed to obtain recognition of the right to negotiate preferential tariffs,[101] the effectiveness of the system was limited in several respects. First, instead of a Generalised System in favour of all developing countries, as UNCTAD had envisaged, each developed country adopted a different scheme. Secondly, the feature common to all schemes was that the system was 'permissive and non-mandatory'.[102]

This meant that preferential concessions were accorded as well as withdrawn by the preference giving country with no recourse mechanism available to the recipient country. The developed country would therefore decide whether to give preferential access, select the recipient country as well as the products to cover and fix the ceiling limitations on either the volume or the value of the product imported on a preferential basis.[103]

[97] Dam (n 61) 241; Hudec (n 64) 62.

[98] Hudec (n 64) 63.

[99] *Ibid* 68, fn13.

[100] The Tokyo Round was the seventh round of GATT negotiations held between 1973 and 1979.

[101] The argument for trade preferences was first made by the less-developed countries during the London Conference. See ch 1, II B.

[102] Hudec (n 64) 64.

[103] Tussie (n 65) 31.

Developing countries soon lamented the insecure status characterising GSP and tried to obtain legal reforms during the Tokyo Round.[104] The only outcome of the Tokyo Round negotiations was that a waiver would no longer be required by developed countries granting preferences to less-developed countries or by less-developed countries negotiating preferences among themselves.

E A 'Differential and More Favourable Treatment'?

This agreement was put together in the form of an 'Enabling Clause' which allowed developed countries to provide 'Differential and More Favourable Treatment' to less-developed countries without extending such treatment to other contracting parties—which amounted to a de facto amendment of the MFN in Article I.[105] Such differential treatment was meant to cover the Generalised System of Preferences as well as the following aspects of less-developed countries' trade: the use of non-tariff measures to protect the home market; the granting of mutual preferences within regional or global trade arrangements between less-developed countries; and special treatment for the least-developed countries. However, security of access under preferential cover was not attained, nor was an amendment to make preferential concessions binding introduced.[106]

In exchange for these concessions, however, the United States obtained the recognition of the so-called Graduation Principle it had sought for some time. According to this principle,

> [l]ess-developed contracting parties expect that their capacity to make contributions or negotiate concessions or [to] take other mutually agreed action ... would improve with the progressive development of their economies and improvement in their trade situation and they would accordingly expect to participate more fully in the framework of rights and obligations under the general agreement.[107]

The graduation text had been accepted by the US Congress as the condition that justified accepting the other, pro-developing-countries framework text.[108] As for the implementation of the GSP, the US 1974 legislation provided a series of reasons for excluding individual developing

[104] Brazil, for instance, contended that since preferences entirely depended on the discretion of the developed countries, they were not a solid basis for long-term investments. It therefore argued that in order to create a more favourable investment climate, it was necessary to bind preferential concessions on a MFN basis. See GA Maciel, *The International Framework for World Trade: Brazilian Proposals for GATT Reform* (London, Trade Policy Research Centre, 1977) 8.

[105] This principle is commonly referred to as Special and Differential Treatment.

[106] Hudec (n 64) 64.

[107] GATT, BISD 26th Supp (1980); quoted in Hudec (n 64) 86.

[108] Hudec (n 64) 86.

countries from the system. Among these, the US denied the scheme benefits to countries 'dominated or controlled by international terrorism, members of the Organisation of Petroleum Exporting Countries (OPEC) or similar commodity cartels which engage in actions that, inter alia, raise prices to an unreasonable level, countries that expropriate US property without paying prompt, adequate and effective compensation, [and] countries that fail to cooperate with US narcotics law'.[109] The President was required to authorise or deny the benefits to these countries, and moreover, in designating a country as a beneficiary of the system, he had to take into account 'the extent to which such country has assured the United States it will provide equitable and reasonable access to the markets and basic commodity resources of such country'.[110] Not only had the GSP been emptied of any content, it was also increasingly becoming a means through which developed countries, and the US in particular, could unilaterally push for more market openness in developing countries.

This strategy was pursued even further with the Trade Act of 1984. This extended the list of countries disqualified with respect to the GSP by including countries which expropriated US intellectual property rights without adequate compensation and those which did not grant adequate protection to internationally recognised workers' rights. The lists of criteria that a country had to satisfy before the US granted the benefits was extended in order to take into consideration

> the extent to which a country has assured the US it will refrain from unreasonable export practices, especially copper exports; the extent to which the country protects the intellectual property rights of businesses in the US, especially against counterfeiting; the extent to which the country has acted to (i) liberalize foreign investments and (ii) liberalize trade in services; and the extent to which the country has acted to recognize workers' rights.[111]

As Hudec recounts, the 1984 Trade Act included another significant objective. It provided a very elaborate mechanism for inducing developing countries to accept reciprocal obligations. First, the President was given authority to limit GSP benefits under the 'competitive need' standard, and secondly, he could waive these limitations whenever he found that the country in question was 'providing reasonable access to its markets and to its commodities or is providing adequate and effective protection of intellectual property rights'.[112] Therefore, the US aimed to use the GSP as leverage to achieve its graduation objective. As the Report of the Ways and Means Committee in the House of Representatives plainly put it, 'the

[109] US Trade Act 1974, s 502(b); quoted in Hudec (n 64) 114.
[110] US Trade Act 1974, s 502(c) 4; quoted in Hudec (n 64) 114.
[111] *Ibid* 115.
[112] *Ibid*.

purpose of granting the President this waiver authority is to provide him with additional tools to achieve US trade interests with Beneficiary Developing Countries, such as greater market access for United States exports'.[113]

F Assessing the GATT's Flexibility

Notwithstanding the fact that the industrialised countries actively discriminated against the trade of developing countries, it is important to acknowledge that under the GATT the latter managed to retain a considerable degree of autonomy in their tariff regimes to pursue industrial policy programmes.[114] This was the result of a complex relationship between political, economic and historic factors. The political struggles of newly independent countries in the 1960s and 1970s and the emergence of dependency theories challenged the Western dominant view on the universal beneficial impact of liberal trade. Although most theories did not dispute the core assumptions of the development framework, they served as the theoretical complement for developing countries' requests for more flexibility within GATT. This idea was also to succeed because of the rise to prominence of Keynesian theories, the concomitant experience with public intervention in Western economies and the Cold War with the tensions it generated with respect to the geopolitical influence on the so-called Third World. Part IV of the GATT and especially non-reciprocity, the so-called Enabling Clause, the Generalised System of Preferences and other initiatives can be seen in this context.

Although the significance of the autonomy to pursue industrial policies cannot be underestimated, the fact that this flexibility applied insofar as it did not challenge the interests of the major capitalist powers cannot be overlooked. As seen before, the consolidation of US economic and military dominance in the immediate postwar period was dependent on the ability to secure markets abroad in which to extract raw materials, place its output and invest surplus capital.[115] Although the GATT's rules did not deal with the protection of foreign capital, they accomplished the other two US objectives.[116] As a consequence of the activity of developing countries within GATT, and in particular the legal reforms leading to

[113] *Ibid.*

[114] D Rodrik, 'Globalization, Social Conflict and Economic Growth', Prebisch Lecture delivered at UNCTAD, Geneva, 24 October 1997 www.unctad.org/en/docs/prebisch8th.en.pdf

[115] See Escobar (n 3) 32–33.

[116] As seen in ch 1, this was achieved through the prohibition on quantitative restrictions and the obligations to reduce tariffs, apply national treatment and grant most favoured nation to the products of GATT Contracting Parties.

non-reciprocity, the US had to compromise on the degree of openness achieved with respect to its output in developing markets.[117] However, it is also important to emphasise that non-reciprocity and the More Favourable and Differential Treatment applied so long as developing countries' products did not threaten developed countries' industries. Indeed, as soon as developing countries' industrial exports became competitive, the latter responded with mounting and aggressive protectionism.

This issue came to the fore during the Tokyo Round negotiations. In addition to the discrimination denounced by the Haberler Report and Committee III, the new discrimination focused on areas such as anti-dumping duties,[118] selective application of the safeguard clause,[119] agricultural subsidisation[120] and the so-called grey area measures, namely voluntary export restraints (VERs) and the MFA,[121] which the United States and the European Community were trying to extend to sectors other than textiles.[122] Despite the fact that many of these measures were overtly targeting the competitive exports of developing countries and were therefore inconsistent with both the GATT's provisions and its spirit, namely the promotion of development through liberal trade, no solution emerged during the Tokyo Round. As will be argued in chapter three, the eradication of the old and new forms of discrimination would be a crucial factor behind the acceptance of the WTO agreements by developing countries.

[117] Thus, the result of non-reciprocity was that developing countries could protect their industries against northern manufactures while enjoying the tariff concessions negotiated by developed countries.

[118] Anti-dumping was disciplined under GATT Art VI. It allowed countries to impose additional duties on imports (so-called anti-dumping duties) provided that there was a difference between the normal value (domestic value) and the export price of the product, and this was causing serious injury to the domestic industry of the importing state. Significantly, the US did not need to undergo the injury test in order to impose anti-dumping duties as it had 'grandfathered', that is exempted from GATT rules, its 1937 legislation. This provided the US with a useful mechanism against the competitive exports of developing countries. See Trebilcock and Howse (n 66) 233.

[119] Since GATT Art XIX did not explicitly state the non-discriminatory character of the safeguard clause, this was used, especially by the US and EC, against developing countries' exports. See Trebilcock and Howse (n 66) 302–04.

[120] Thus, in addition to the fact that unlike industrial trade, trade in agriculture had not been liberalised, the increase of agricultural subsidies in the US and EC, followed by Canada and Japan, greatly affected developing countries' competitive position both abroad and at home. See Trebilcock and Howse (n 66) 321–25.

[121] This issue was closely linked to that of the safeguard clause. As Trebilcock and Howse note, since the issue of selectivity was controversial under GATT Art XIX, the US and EC resorted to de facto bilateral pressure to induce competitive exporting countries to adopt the so-called voluntary export restraints (VERs). This notwithstanding the fact that the legal conformity of these measures with GATT Art XI and the MFN was also doubted. See Trebilcock and Howse (n 66) 301.

[122] See United Nations Conference on Trade and Development (UNCTAD), *Beyond Conventional Wisdom in Development Policy: An Intellectual History of UNCTAD 1964–2004* (New York and Geneva, United Nations, 2004) UNCTAD/EDM/2004/4 28.

CONCLUSIONS

From its inception, GATT practice contributed to the formation and transformation of the 'science of development' while also being influenced by this 'science' itself. The development norm that was being articulated in the field of development studies, namely the need for developing countries to catch up with the economic stage of the developed economies, was received within and reinforced by the international trading system. In other words, the GATT contributed to the formation and consolidation of this norm by positing the endless failure of developing countries to trade as efficiently as the industrialised nations.[123] In turn, this provided the framework within which the GATT's development-related trade reforms were to be carried until the 1980s. It is possible to look at GATT's development experience from the late 1940s to the 1980s from two different but interrelated perspectives.

Reasoning from within the GATT's development framework set up in the immediate postwar period implies an engagement with the terms of this framework without challenging its inherent assumptions. This means accepting the assumptions about economic growth and industrialisation to be achieved through liberal trade, in addition to capital investments, at their face value. From this perspective, over 30 years of development-related policies within GATT have produced numerous initiatives, declarations, reports and amendments that have made GATT legal disciplines more flexible. Thus, it is important to qualify the content of such flexibility. As the Haberler Report and Committee III had shown, developed countries were not abiding by the GATT rules and were seriously hindering the chances less-developed countries had to industrialise and therefore develop.

Declarations of principle and GATT amendments followed, giving the appearance that the situation would be corrected. However, hardly any measure contained legally binding commitments by developed countries. Hence, developed countries continued to hinder developing countries' trade by (a) exempting from trade liberalisation agriculture, fisheries and textiles; (b) imposing higher tariffs on manufactures than those applied to raw materials; (c) subsidising their agricultural production and exports; (d) using trade remedies such as anti-dumping and countervailing duties; and (e) inducing countries to impose VERs. The United States even managed to circumvent the scope of measures such as the GSP and to use them to its own advantage. In other words, GATT practice towards developing countries violated the very principles it claimed to promote, namely economic growth and industrialisation by means of liberal trade.

123 See above, text to n 72.

However, there is another angle from which it is possible to evaluate the GATT's development agenda, namely that which looks at the constitutive elements of the framework established at the end of the colonial era. From this perspective, GATT activity can be considered consistent with the general development norm that originated in the 1940s. The theories elaborated by Rostow, Lewis and Friedman during the 1950s would represent the two variants the science of development endorsed following its inception within the international trading system. In the immediate postwar period, mainstream development theories and practices rejected the free market strategies embodied in Friedman's position and considered the state the prime agent for achieving rapid economic growth. However, what these two development criteria share is the intrinsic and undisputed assumptions about development that form its core framework.

First, the representation of Third World societies as backward is presented as neutral rather than political. Secondly, the contraposition of backward economies to the advanced stage of industrialised countries posits the need for the former to catch up with the economic stage of the latter. Thus, economic rationality is relied on as the neutral terrain for bridging this 'gap' and achieving progress. Thirdly, the help and expertise of the more advanced members of the international community and their experts is invoked to explain the reasons for this 'failure' and consequently advocate appropriate reforms.

The GATT fully participated in this enterprise by establishing the undisputed need for the trade of less-developed countries to 'develop as rapidly as that of the industrialised countries'. This would become the norm for thinking of, debating and reformulating development within the international trading regime. This norm would persist and become even stronger in the 1980s, when the new development theories and the political decisions made to address the processes of change of the international economy were to produce the neo-liberal transformation of the development mission and the establishment of the WTO.

3

The Neo-Liberal Transformation of Development Thinking and the Renewed Mission of the Multilateral Trading Regime

CHAPTER TWO HAS examined the process through which the scientific authority of development thinking emerged and consolidated into a fixed framework in the immediate postwar period. This chapter engages with the theoretical shifts in development thinking that took place in the 1980s. The first part shows how, despite the qualitative difference from earlier approaches to development, neo-liberal thinking linked with—while displacing—earlier development theories. The nexus is to be found within the terms of the 'science of development' set up at the end of the colonial era. As both the premise of development, that is, the representation of Third World societies as backward, and the consequent norm, namely the need for developing countries to catch up with the economic stage of developed countries, remained unaffected, the so-called neo-liberal revolution of development thinking reformulated the means through which to achieve development.

What neo-liberal scholars, therefore, reconsider is the appropriate role for the state and the market in pursuing the adequate level of development. Thus, if in the immediate postwar period state-based development prevailed over market-based development, the latter gained centre stage in the 1980s. The reconceptualisation of Third World societies, however, was essential in order to replace earlier approaches to development with neo-liberal development. In this respect, the modus operandi of the Mandate System was re-enacted to explain the reasons for developing countries' persistent 'failure' within the international economic and trading system and, consequently, to build on the universality of neo-liberal laws the promise of its overcoming. The uncovering of neo-liberal assumptions about Third World societal organisations is essential for two reasons: first, to emphasise the continuity of the development mission in neo-liberal claims even when they seem to repudiate the paternalistic attitude of early development approaches and secondly, to appreciate the theoretical background against which the collapse of developing countries' coalition and their acceptance of the WTO agreements have occurred.

The second and third parts of this chapter therefore analyse the process through which the neo-liberal transformation of the science of development was received within and influenced by the GATT legal structure and practice. The neo-liberal shift in development thinking provided the theoretical basis for such a transformation. However, the policy responses that followed need to be assessed by complementing these theoretical insights with the changes that occurred within the international political and economic system in the 1970s and 1980s. These changes greatly affected the position of both developing and developed countries on the eve of the Punta del Este meeting.[1] The aim is to offer a different understanding of the neo-liberal turn of the international trade regime from the accounts provided by the majority of trade scholars. In short, a common thread in these accounts is that developing countries have acknowledged the failure of their past economic policies and legal claims, recognised the rationality of the market and hence opted for a market-based development agenda. The argument made in this chapter is that this shift was the result of political decisions made with respect to particular events and therefore cannot be accounted for in terms of a logical, desirable and inevitable historic process.

I THE NEO-LIBERAL CONVERSION OF DEVELOPMENT THINKING

Neo-liberalism is a very complex system of thought whose origins and significance cannot be limited to the field of development thinking and the interaction between the developed and developing worlds. Indeed, there were various historic, political and economic conditions that led to its ascendancy and which cannot be relegated to a single determining agenda.[2]

[1] The Punta del Este Ministerial Meeting of 1986 launched the eighth round of GATT negotiations, namely the Uruguay Round, which resulted in the establishment of the World Trade Organisation. As argued below, it signals both the break-up of the developing countries' coalition within GATT and the neo-liberal transformation of the international trading regime.

[2] Harvey's enquiry into the history of neo-liberalism is interesting in that it shows how the worldwide acceptance of neo-liberal intellectual underpinnings and policy prescriptions varied according to the different places in which it occurred, thereby producing different outcomes. However, his argument is that despite the different factors and conditions contributing to its emergence, its effects can be evaluated in terms of the restoration of class power that has taken place around the world. See D Harvey, *A Brief History of Neo-Liberalism* (Oxford, Oxford University Press, 2005).

The world economic recession that first affected the industrialised countries in the 1970s, the decline of the postwar Keynesian consensus, the OPEC oil price increase and the debt crisis of the 1980s are some of the factors that contributed to the intellectual acceptance of neo-liberal thinking. Also, as various scholars have pointed out, the theoretical framework that neo-liberalism entails, especially with regard to its political and economic rationales, is not always consistent.[3]

In what follows, however, the discussion focuses on a particular aspect of early neo-liberal theories, namely the way in which their economic analysis of development intersected with political representations of Third World societal organisations. The point is that these representations are central to the replacement of early development approaches with neo-liberal development. Neo-liberal analysis strongly rejected the underlying assumptions of development economics with respect to Third World economies and individuals. However, neo-liberal scholars simultaneously re-enacted a new and powerful construction of developing countries' backwardness to advance their universal model of economic development. The international trade arena, which had previously been influenced by development economics and the dependency school of thought, was soon to be affected by the neo-liberal transformation of development thinking.[4]

Development economics had been challenged by dependency theories which had argued against the assumption that trade liberalisation on a Most Favoured Nation (MFN) basis would automatically lead to greater growth and development for all countries.[5] Most of these theories hardly questioned the fundamental assumption that development was the necessary and inevitable result of a natural and linear historic process. However, they argued that the imbalances deriving from historical trading relationships greatly limited the trade prospects of developing economies. Consequently, developing countries had been able to obtain within GATT formal recognition of their entitlement to maintain some flexibility in their tariff regimes. For instance, they obtained legal amendments of the GATT rules

[3] Harvey, for instance, argues that 'the scientific rigour of its neo-classical economics does not sit easily with its political commitment to ideals of individual freedom, nor does its supposed distrust of all state power fit with the need for a strong and if necessary coercive state that will defend the right of private property, individual liberties, and entrepreneurial freedom'. Harvey (n 2) 21. For another account of the discrepancies between neo-liberal theory and neo-liberalisation practices, see HJ Chang, *Globalisation, Economic Development and the Role of the State* (London & New York, Zed Books, 2003).

[4] The discussion of neo-liberal development thinking presented here is therefore a limited one: it focuses specifically on those works that have argued against development economics and dependency thought to explain the 'failure' of development in the postwar period.

[5] Prebisch's analysis into the so-called unequal terms of trade between the developed and the developing countries, for instance, had counteracted the claim that trade liberalisation was beneficial to developing countries. See ch 2, I D.

in order to apply quantitative restrictions for balance of payments purposes, participate in multilateral negotiations on a non-reciprocal basis and create regional and global trading arrangements.[6] There were certainly conditions, other than the theoretical challenges to development economics, that contributed to such an outcome. These included the increasing Keynesian consensus in dominant economic circles, the concomitant experience of industrialised countries with state intervention and the high rates of economic growth they experienced in the 1950s and 1960s, the struggle of newly independent countries within the United Nations and UNCTAD in particular,[7] the geo-political balance sought during the Cold War and the fact that GATT's flexible approach to development did not threaten the postwar interests of the major capitalist powers.

However, this situation started to change at the end of the 1970s when the economic recession of industrialised countries, the oil and debt crisis, the end of the Cold War and new development theories produced the neo-liberal transformation of the development mission. By the mid-1980s, the so-called counter-revolution in development thinking had arrived. Writers such as Lal, Bauer, Balassa and Krueger refuted the basic assumptions underlying development economics and dependency theories.[8] As argued below, despite their differences, these authors shared several themes. First, the universality of rational economic behaviour was employed as the basis for arguing against the assumption that policy prescriptions deriving from neo-classical economics could not be extended to developing countries. Secondly, inefficient or failing institutional arrangements were identified as important factors precipitating their crisis. Thirdly, a set of propositions was put forward to argue that inward-oriented policies and over-extended public sectors were the causes of the economic inefficiency of developing countries. Finally, a series of comparative studies was used in order to assess the successes and failures of contrasting development policies employed by different developing countries.

[6] As discussed in ch 2, the actual gains deriving from the formal recognition of the principle of Preferential and More Favourable Treatment were limited since developed countries often circumvented the scope of these provisions and adopted several GATT inconsistent measures contradicting the spirit of the development agenda they claimed to promote. See ch 2, II.

[7] See eg, the Resolution on Permanent Sovereignty over Natural Resources, UNGA Res 1803 (XVII) (adopted 14 December 1962); the Charter of Economic Rights and Duties of States, UNGA Res 3281 (XXIX) (adopted 12 December 1974) and the Resolution on the New International Economic Order, UNGA Res 3306 (XXIX) (adopted 14 December 1974).

[8] D Lal, *The Poverty of 'Development Economics'* (London, Institute of Economic Affairs, 1983); PT Bauer, *Equality, the Third World and Economic Delusion* (London, Methuen, 1981); B Balassa, *Development Strategies in Semi-Industrialised Countries* (Baltimore, Johns Hopkins University Press, 1982); AO Krueger, *Political Economy of Policy Reform in Developing Countries* (Cambridge, The MIT Press, 1993).

A Rational Choice-Based Approach …

Development economics, as well as the dependency school of thought, had assumed that the existence of structural differences between developed and developing countries undermined the validity of neo-classical economic theories. Development economics had attributed these differences to the dual domestic structure of developing countries, whereas the dependency school had focused on the structural imbalances of the international trading system. Consequently, albeit for different underlying reasons, they all supported the central role of the state. These assumptions would become the target of the neo-liberal transformation of development thinking. In his pamphlet published in 1983, Lal argued that

> the major element of the dirigiste Dogma is that price mechanism, or the working of a market economy, needs to be supplanted (and not merely supplemented) by various forms of direct government control, both national and international, to promote economic development … (and) that classical 19th century liberal case for free-trade is invalid for developing countries, and thus government restriction of international trade and payments is necessary for development.[9]

Therefore, the so-called dirigiste dogma, namely the belief in the active role of the government in promoting development, derived from the erroneous assumption that the differences in the structures of developing economies required separate economic analysis and policies from those applicable to the developed economies.[10] The means on which Lal relies to show the fallacy of this assumption are the price mechanism and rational economic behaviour. The price mechanism is the principal organiser of economic activity, therefore the neo-classical analysis of human economic behaviour is not limited to agents operating in developed countries. Hence, the fallacy of the dirigiste dogma consists in denying the universality of rational economic behaviour. This flaw derives from

> the paternalist attitude born of a distrust of, if not contempt for, the ordinary, poor, uneducated masses of the Third World … It is easy to suppose that these *half-starved, wretched and ignorant masses* could not possibly conform, either as producers or consumers, to the behavioural assumption of orthodox neo-classical economics that people would act economically; when the opportunity of an advantage was presented to them they would take it[11] (emphasis added).

This passage is relevant in that it seems to tackle the civilising attitude towards so-called backward societies when, in actual fact, it is constructing

[9] Lal (n 8) 5.

[10] This recalls the argument with which Friedman had opposed the main tenets of Development Economics as early as the 1950s. See ch 2, I C.

[11] Lal (n 8) 104.

a new vision of backwardness that extends beyond economics to include institutional and social arrangements. Lal denounces the paternalist attitude of development economics which had conceived of the 'masses of the third world' as irrational economic agents. Simultaneously, according to Lal, these so-called uneducated masses are still in need of assistance in order to overcome their 'political and emotional resistance' to sound economic policies. As he points out:

> [T]he major benefit the developing countries derive from ... the multilateral trade institutions ... is the technical assistance built into the process of transferring the aid money to the recipient countries. Though often sound on general economic grounds, their advice is nevertheless resented for political and emotional reasons.[12]

The reformulation of the premises underlying the Mandate System is therefore fully accomplished. As seen in chapter one, the Mandate System, borrowing from the science of colonial administration, was based on the assumption that the inhabitants of the ex-colonies were 'not yet able to stand by themselves' and therefore needed guidance in order to pursue their material as well as moral and educational progress.[13] The result was the creation of a science of development able to formulate universal policies by relying on the neutrality of economics. In the immediate postwar period, development economics would carry over precisely these assumptions, namely that (a) 'backward societies' were characterised by an economic stage which was different from that of the advanced economies; (b) reliance on economic rationality would have paved the way to their development; and (c) this process would be facilitated through the assistance and guidance of the 'advanced' members of the international community. Lal seems to distance himself from the paternalist attitude of development economics by invoking the universality of rational economic behaviour. However, far from being removed, these assumptions are reformulated in his analysis.

First, non-Western societies are still characterised as backward although, in contrast to the analysis of development economics, they do not require different economic analysis and policy prescriptions. The modus operandi of the Mandate System based on the collection, analysis and elaboration of a vast body of information from the mandate territories continues to operate. As Lal writes, 'there is by now a vast body of empirical evidence from different cultures and climates which shows that uneducated peasants

[12] *Ibid.*

[13] See A Anghie, 'Time Present and Time Past: Globalisation, International Financial Institutions, and the Third World' (2000) 32 *New York University Journal of International Law & Politics* 243, 276.

act economically as producers and consumers. They respond to changes in relative prices much as neo-classical economic theory predicts'.[14]

Secondly, reliance on neo-classical assumptions about rational economic behaviour and the price mechanism provides the premise for the replacement of development economics with the universality of neo-liberal economic laws. Therefore, the universality of neo-classical economics is invoked to argue for the applicability of market-based policies in developing countries. In other words, the means invoked to achieve development is once again the neutrality of economic laws, this time neo-liberal laws.

Thirdly, developing countries are still in need of assistance in order to achieve development. The formal argument is that despite the fact that individuals in the developing world conform to the neo-classical model of rational utility maximisers, their social and institutional arrangements are such that they will resist sound economic reforms. Lal is here referring to the second failure he imputed to development economics, namely the overemphasis on physical capital formation as opposed to human capital formation. The latter needs to be encouraged through appropriate institutional arrangements both domestically and at the international level. Thus, it is necessary to make foreign aid conditional on the adoption of sound, rational policies prescribed by the donors.[15]

B ... and Failing Institutional Arrangements

Lal's analysis can be read in conjunction with similar studies that emerged in the 1980s. Bauer, for instance, had already claimed that 'emergence from poverty [in the Third World] does not require large-scale capital formation'.[16] He was also sceptical of human capital formation, since his researches into the economic growth of the Malayan, West African and Indian economies had convinced him that their different economic performances could not be explained in 'terms of differences in human capital formation'[17] but in terms of people's 'personal preferences, motivations and social arrangements'.[18] Thus, whereas Lal would argue for technical assistance and conditional aid in opposition to the overemphasis on physical capital formation, Bauer had anticipated the idea that institutional and social reforms in developing countries were necessary to stimulate growth. The theoretical basis for both, however, was a discourse about the Third World's societal organisations, which was presented as neutral,

[14] Lal (n 8) 105.
[15] See above, text to n 12.
[16] Bauer, *Equality* (n 8) 248.
[17] PT Bauer, *Reality and Rhetoric: Studies in the Economics of Development* (London, Weidenfeld & Nicolson, 1984) 7.
[18] *Ibid.*

rational and technical rather than political. Despite the highly normative assumptions underlying neo-liberal interpretations of developing countries' societal organisations, neo-liberal reforms were presented as the result of an inevitable, rational and desirable historic process.

The relevance of these theoretical constructions would gradually increase as their acceptance extended beyond traditional economic sectors. North, for instance, would argue that

> transferring the formal political and economic rules of successful western market economies to Third World and Eastern European economies is not a sufficient condition for good economic governance ... [a]s it is the informal norms that provide the essential legitimacy to any set of formal rules ... it is essential to change both the institutions and the belief systems for successful reform since it is the mental models of the actors that will shape choices.[19]

Technical assistance and conditional aid, together with institution building, would become crucial tools in the development arsenal of the international economic institutions for radically transforming institutional and social arrangements in developing countries.[20] Thus, the neo-liberal transformation of the 'science of development' set out to operate a radical alteration of economic, political and social arrangements beyond the market, or, in other words, to reconceptualise in market terms all spheres of human interaction. The beginning of this shift can be traced in Lal's and Bauer's works, where all individuals are intrinsically rational economic agents able to seize any economic opportunity. It follows that radical reforms are necessary for abolishing previous policies based on false economic assumptions such as those of development economics and dependency theories. Hence, the 'science of development' is transformed with regard to the means necessary to achieve the undisputed result, namely catching up with the economic stage of the developed economies, so that the market, rather than the state, is posited as the crucial engine of development.

C Outward-Oriented Policies and Government Controls

By positing the price mechanism as the principal organiser of human behaviour and economic activity, Lal defines direct government controls both at the national and international level as the major dogma of development economics. According to Lal, the economic crises developing

[19] DC North, 'The New Institutional Economics and Development' (Smithian Forum, Working Paper, 1993) 6 www.nju.edu.cn/cps/site/NJU/njuc/dep/shangyuan/2.doc.

[20] As it will be shown in the concluding chapter, the WTO's adoption of the language of technical assistance, institution building and good governance to promote development is informed by the political representations of Third World societies advanced by neo-liberal theories.

countries experienced during the 1980s were the result of distortions induced by the economic policies pursued by their own governments. The major causes of the alleged distortions were to be found in the over-extended public sectors and the inward-oriented policies developing countries had adopted in order to industrialise. Lal cites the studies conducted by Little, Scitovsky and Scott on the poor craftsmanship of developing countries' economic controls as 'an impressive empirical validation of the case against protection, that, even though laissez-faire may be not justifiable, free trade remains the best policy for developing (and developed) countries'.[21]

The general arguments against protection are those advanced by the neo-classical case for free trade. The ineffectiveness and counter-productiveness in achieving policy objectives, the production of unintended consequences and excessive costs are some of the most relevant.[22] Balassa would also argue that restrictions of imports in existing systems of trade controls were responsible for the balance of payments' constraint on the economic growth of developing countries. Contrary to Lal, Balassa does not advocate the elimination of all government controls. However, he suggests that governments should operate within a system which is the closest possible to a 'neutral state of affairs in which there is no discrimination among economic activities or between foreign and domestic markets'.[23]

The tendency in analysing the economic crisis of developing countries in the 1980s is one that identifies the causes of the crisis in the adoption of the wrong development policies by developing countries. Integral to this tendency is the fact that the incidence of exogenous factors is greatly underestimated. Not only do the insights into the structural imbalances of the international trading system gradually disappear from the development debate, but the impact of external phenomena such as the critical shortage of foreign exchange, the oil shock and the debt crisis is believed to have been magnified by the adoption of erroneous policies. For instance, in a comparative study on Argentina, Brazil, Chile, Mexico and Venezuela, Jaastad, Almansi and Hurtado argue that the origins of the debt crisis in Latin America preceded the inability of the Mexican government to service

[21] Lal (n 8) 27.

[22] In particular, governments adopting ISI (Import Substitution Industrialisation) are believed to forgo the gains from liberal trade obtained from international specialisation according to the law of comparative advantage. Secondly, given the limited size of their economies, they are said to end up protecting monopolist and oligopolist industries that produce at sub-optimal efficiency levels. Thirdly, given the low rates of interests artificially imposed by ISI, they are thought to cause lower savings, which exacerbate unemployment and income inequality. See Chang (n 3) 28.

[23] Balassa, *Development Strategies* (n 8) 9.

its debt in August 1982.[24] They admit the presence of external factors such as falling world demand due to economic recession in industrialised countries, the rapid growth of external debt with the shortening of its maturity structure, the sudden rise in dollar interest rates accompanied by worldwide dollar deflation in industrialised countries and a consequent decline in the export capacity of developing countries.[25]

However, the main problem is made to rest on the over-ambitious public investment programmes which led to uncontrolled and growing fiscal deficit and to trade policies with a bias against exports and domestic savings. Krueger, for instance, has argued that 'those countries that were unable to adjust and resume growth were those whose economic policies had been highly detrimental to growth'.[26] Balassa also links the adoption of outward-oriented policies to the improvement in the income distribution of developing countries. In other words, the price mechanism in a liberal trade regime would not only contribute to an increase of growth, but would concomitantly work as an automatic mechanism of wealth distribution. He relies again on comparative studies to assert the following:

> Available information pertaining to the 1960s indicates that outward-oriented countries were better able to increase employment, raise wages, and improve the income distribution than countries applying an inward-oriented strategy. This is because exporting permitted resource allocation according to comparative advantage, involving specialisation in labour-intensive products, with demand for labour increasing further as a result of the rapid economic growth export expansion has engendered and because outward orientation has been more favourable to agriculture where much of the poor are. These conclusions were reconfirmed in the subsequent period of external shocks. Outward-oriented countries were better able to withstand the external shocks they suffered and avoided excessive reliance on foreign borrowing while regaining earlier growth rates. In turn, inward-oriented countries borrowed extensively abroad but the policies applied did not permit the efficient use of borrowed funds, leading to a large external indebtedness.[27]

Therefore, despite the recognition of various exogenous factors, the neo-liberal interpretation of the causes underlying the economic crisis of the 1980s attributes the 'failure' to the development models adopted by developing countries. This is done through the invalidation of the theoretical underpinnings of development economics, as well as dependency

[24] A Jaastad, A Almansi and C Hurtado, 'The Debt Crisis in Latin America' in D Lal and M Wolf (eds), *Stagflation, Savings and the State: Perspectives on the Global Economy* (Oxford & New York, Oxford University Press, 1986) 131–79.

[25] *Ibid.*

[26] Krueger, *Political Economy of Policy Reform* (n 8) 3–4.

[27] B Balassa, *New Directions in the World Economy* (Basingstoke, The Macmillan Press, 1989) 95–96.

theories and by means of various comparative studies on different developing economies. Thus, the neo-liberal policy prescriptions that follow are based on the transformation of inward-looking, state-based economic structures into market-oriented economies, accompanied by reforms of their institutional and social arrangements.[28]

These analyses were to exert an enormous influence during the 1980s and 1990s, especially within the World Bank and the International Monetary Fund. The 1985 World Development Report focusing on Latin American countries would identify the causes of their economic crisis with their excessive expansionary fiscal and monetary policies impeding a sustainable external balance, overvalued exchange rates reducing the competitiveness of their exports and the low levels of savings during periods of high investments and consumption, leading to high external debt.[29] Similarly, in identifying the main areas on which scholars, politicians and technocrats of the international financial institutions in Washington agreed that developing countries needed immediate reforms, Williamson pointed to 'prudent macro-economic policies, outward-orientation and free-market capitalism'.[30] The prescription put forward by the so-called Washington Consensus would become the template for policy reforms carried out throughout the 1980s and 1990s in the so-called developing world. By relying on the authority of the World Bank and International Monetary Fund, these reforms aimed at the complete restructuring of the economic and institutional frameworks of developing countries.

II THE NEO-LIBERAL TRANSFORMATION OF THE INTERNATIONAL TRADING REGIME

The result of 30 years of GATT's development agenda was the recognition that some flexibility from the GATT's legal rules was appropriate in order to allow its developing country members to reach the advanced stage of their economies. More specifically, developing countries gained formal recognition of their need to improve the terms of trade, reduce dependency on exports of primary commodities, correct balance of payments deficits

[28] For a critical engagement with neo-liberal accounts of the failure of developing countries' policies, see Chang (n 3) 28.

[29] World Bank, *World Development Report 1985* (Oxford & New York, Oxford University Press, 1985) 6–7.

[30] J Williamson 'What Washington means by Policy Reform' in J Williamson (ed), *Latin American Adjustment: How Much Has Happened?* (Washington DC, Institute for International Economics, 1990) www.iie.com/publications/papers/paper.cfm?ResearchID=486.

and industrialise through infant industry protection and export subsidies.[31] In other words, developing countries formally enjoyed until the 1980s a certain degree of flexibility from the GATT's legal obligations through the provisions in Article XVIII, low levels of tariff bindings, Part IV, the Enabling Clause and the Generalised System of Preferences (GSP).[32]

However, there was a fundamental incoherence between the GATT's formal and actual commitments to the stated development agenda: no substantial liberalisation was achieved in the sectors where developing countries had the most comparative advantage, namely agriculture, fisheries and textiles; Part IV and the principle of non-reciprocity did not translate into the reduction of tariffs on the products of interest to developing countries and higher tariffs were imposed on their manufactures as opposed to their raw materials; the GSP was used in a way that circumvented its purpose; and new forms of protectionism were increasingly enacted against the competitive industrial products of developing countries.[33] In other words, industrialised countries actively discriminated against the trade interests of developing countries.

Notwithstanding this, the GATT's provisions granting non-reciprocity and Differential and More Favourable Treatment conceded that, in order to correct the inequalities of the international trading system, developing countries were entitled to non-reciprocal commitments, formal enhanced market access, regulatory autonomy and policy discretion in their own economies. Hence, the GATT legal structure provided for the freedom of states to decide about the optimal degree of intervention and trade liberalisation and, most importantly, did not substantially regulate other dimensions of its members' domestic policy.

The 1980s, however, signalled the reversal of this rationale. Theories which, in the 1960s and 1970s, had challenged the Western dominant view on development were discredited in light of their alleged failure to understand the rationality of the market. With neo-liberal theories, the market mechanism and rational economic behaviour exhumed from neoclassical economics were used to explain the failure of the state-based development which had prevailed for three decades in both developing and developed countries.[34] However, the neo-liberal transformation of the international trading regime cannot be explained solely in terms of the concepts advanced by these theories, however powerful their intellectual influence has been.

[31] C Michalopoulos, *Developing Countries in the WTO* (Basingstoke, Palgrave, 2001) 24–30.

[32] See ch 2, II.

[33] See ch 2, II F.

[34] Lal (n 8) 5.

Their relevance rests on the fact that they provided a powerful theoretical ground on which political decisions concerning particular events that took place in the 1970s and 1980s could be made and presented as rational choices. Emphasising the political nature of these decisions is important for two reasons. First, as argued below, to counter the argument that the abandonment by developing countries of their previous legal claims and economic policies represented their 'rational choice' for the most efficient trade policy. Secondly, to introduce the argument, further developed in chapters four to six, that neo-liberal development theories and the new international trading regime represented by the WTO intervened at a particular moment in the restructuring of the world capitalist system, serving the interests of US and EU transnational capital in particular.

A The World Recession and the Restructuring of the International Economy

The industrialised world had experienced a period of sustained and steady growth during the 1950s and 1960s.[35] Western states had actively participated in this process, domestically, by promoting a careful balance between the state and the market, and internationally, by establishing the Bretton Woods system in order to promote financial stability and trade in goods under a system of fixed exchange rates. The Bretton Woods system had two essential features. First, by anchoring the dollar to a fixed price against gold and requiring other countries to establish the price of their currencies against the dollar, it ensured a stable environment for economic operators to trade across the borders. Secondly, states retained considerable control over their financial sectors. Private finances were allowed to move funds for financing trade and productive investments abroad but, beyond that, could not freely transfer money around the world.[36]

However, both features of the Bretton Woods system were to be called into question under the Nixon Administration. By the early 1970s, the United States was experiencing a serious structural deficit in its external payments due to its ambitious military project that culminated in the Vietnam War and its massive capital exports to the European states.[37]

[35] P Armstrong, A Glynn and J Harrison, *Capitalism since World War II: The Making and Break up of the Long Boom* (London, Fontana, 1984) 167–92.

[36] As Gowan points out, 'such repression then meant that investment resources would be "home grown" within states. And it also meant that money-capital had to confine its royalty-seeking operations to these activities which its nation state would allow. In other words, states were given the right to dominate and shape the activities of their financial sectors in ways that would suit the state's economic development goals'. P Gowan, *The Global Gamble: Washington's Faustian Bid for World Dominance* (London, Verso, 1999) 17.

[37] *Ibid.*

Confronted with the difficulty of complying with the dollar's free convertibility into gold, the US responded with the unilateral abandonment of the fixed-parity system. As for the second feature, the oil shock of 1973 provided the US with the opportunity to reverse the so-called financial repression of the two previous decades. The recycling of petrodollars from the Gulf region was followed by the abolition in 1974 of the controls on capital flows from and into the United States. The new role of private finance and its relation to the dollar cannot be overestimated. As Gowan writes:

> The new international arrangements gave the United States government far more influence over the international monetary and financial relations of the world than it had enjoyed under the Bretton Woods rules. It could freely decide the price of the dollar. States would become increasingly dependent upon developments in Anglo-American financial markets for managing their international monetary relations. And trends in these financial markets could be shifted by the actions (and words) of the US public authorities, in the Treasury Department and the Federal Reserve Board ... Because the dollar has been the dominant world currency, the great majority of states would want to hold the great bulk of their foreign currency reserves in dollars, placing them with the American financial system (or in London). Similarly, because many central commodities in the world economy were priced in and traded for dollars, those trading in such commodities would wish to raise their trade finance in New York and London ... At the same time there was feedback the other way. The strength of Wall Street, as a financial centre, reinforced the dominance of the dollar: for anyone wanting to borrow or lend money, the size and strength of a financial system is a very important factor. The bigger a financial market's resources and reach, the safer it is likely to be, and the more competitive its rates for borrowers.[38]

The new 'dependency' that these monetary and financial arrangements engendered within the international economy was to be tested in the context of the economic recession that hit the industrialised countries in the 1970s. Confronted by an unprecedented rise of inflation and unemployment (that is 'stagflation'), the United States and Britain abandoned macroeconomic demand management and embraced monetarist solutions to reduce inflation.[39] Monetarist policies were accompanied by drastic deregulation and privatisation, which effectively marked the end of the postwar welfare state.[40] The repercussions of the neo-liberal turn in the

[38] *Ibid* 24.

[39] See Chang (n 3) 25.

[40] As Harvey writes, 'After the implementation of neo-liberal policies in the 1970s, the share of national income of the top 1 per cent of income earners in the US soared, to reach 15 per cent (very close to its pre-Second World War share) by the end of the century. The top 0.1 per cent of income earners in the US increased their share of the national income from 2 per cent in 1978 to over 6 per cent by 1999, while the ratio of the median compensation of workers to the salaries of CEOs increased from just over 30 to 1 in the 1970s to nearly 500 to 1 by 2000'. Harvey (n 2) 16.

US, however, were soon to be felt at the international level. The Volcker shock of 1979 with its sudden increase in interest rates, meant that countries that had previously borrowed from the New York Investment Banks, found themselves unable to repay their debts.[41] The rescheduling of their loans was in turn made conditional on the acceptance of the neo-liberal reforms dictated by the International Monetary Fund and the World Bank.[42]

Furthermore, the restructuring of the US economy along neo-liberal lines was to create new investment opportunities abroad. As noted by Harvey, the deregulation of airlines, telecommunication and finance in the US

> opened up new zones of untrammelled market freedoms for powerful corporate interests. Tax breaks on investments effectively subsidised the movement of capital away from the unionised North-East and Midwest and into the non-union and weakly regulated South and West. Finance capital increasingly looked abroad for higher rates of return. De-industrialisation at home and moves to take production abroad became much more common. The market, depicted ideologically as the way to foster competition and innovation, became a vehicle for the consolidation of monopoly power.[43]

The new market opportunities that deregulation, privatisation and liberalisation opened up for Western corporate interests were magnified by the rise in technological innovation in the 1980s, based mainly on the information technology sector and later, the biotechnology sector. The reduced costs of communication deriving from the application of technological innovation were seen as an enormous incentive for corporate strategies to operate on a much wider scale.[44] Between 1980 and 1993, international direct investments among the three industrial poles, namely Western Europe, North America and east Asia, increased by over 11 per cent per year. Corporate alliances, joint ventures and marketing arrangements for technology-intensive industries grew exponentially.[45]

Whereas world trade in agricultural products and non-agricultural raw materials had gradually declined since the 1960s, trade in manufactures and services became increasingly preponderant.[46] As a result of this new

41 Paul Volcker was the chairman of the US Federal Reserve Bank under President Nixon.

42 See Armstrong, Glynn and Harrison (n 35) 361–64.

43 Harvey (n 2) 26.

44 See MJ Trebilcock and R Howse, *The Regulation of International Trade* (London; New York, Routledge, 2005) 349–50.

45 Preeg maintains that technology cooperation agreements in the biotechnology, information technology and new materials sectors increased from 317 in 1975–79 to 2629 in 1985–89. See EH Preeg, *Traders in a Brave New World: The Uruguay Round and the Future of the International Trading System* (Chicago, University of Chicago Press, 1995) 12.

46 By the early 1990s, world trade in agricultural products accounted for 10 per cent, non-agricultural raw materials for 3 per cent, mineral fuels for 7 per cent, manufactures for 58 per cent and services for 22 per cent. See Preeg, *ibid*, 13; see also Armstrong, Glynn and Harrison (n 35) 371–76.

relationship between finance, international trade, investment and technology transfer, corporate strategies and government policies became more deeply interrelated. Policy responses followed the corporate pressure to internationalise, first on a bilateral and regional scale and later at the multilateral level.[47] The first stage of integration occurred within and among the three main industrial poles. As multinational companies established their commercial presence within and across the three regions, the European Union (EU), the North American Free Trade Agreement (NAFTA) and the Association of South East Asian Nations (ASEAN) provided the policy framework for the integration process.

Simultaneously, the so-called vertical integration between high wage industrialised countries and low wage developing countries meant that greater economic gains could flow from the deepening of markets integration. In other words, for multinational corporations to benefit more efficiently from international economies of scale, it was necessary to provide a multilateral legal framework that enabled them to operate beyond the three regions. The international monetary and financial system had already been deregulated. However, for these new opportunities to materialise fully, the international trading regime, until then concerned predominantly with trade in goods, was to be radically reformed.

B Towards a Trade-Service-Investment Driven Market Integration: Enter the 'New Issues'

The policy framework required to encourage the new market opportunities was to be based on the liberalisation of services and investments in addition to goods on the one hand, and the protection of intellectual property rights on the other.[48] GATT legal disciplines, however, were insufficient to deal with the requirements posed by the new trade-service-investment driven market integration promoted in the three industrial poles. Despite the fact that the Tokyo Round had adopted a code on government procurement, the industrialised participants had excluded all service sectors from its coverage, while developing countries had opted out of the code.[49] More importantly, GATT disciplines were too general with

[47] See Preeg (n 45) 13.

[48] The contradiction between these two trends, namely liberalisation and protection, is only apparent. If one looks at the maximisation of corporate profits that greater flows of investments and revenues from the transfer of technology generate, it makes perfect business sense.

[49] Trebilcock and Howse (n 44) 293.

respect to foreign investments[50] and absent with respect to the international protection of intellectual property rights.[51]

The relationship between trade and services was the first to be taken into account in analysis conducted both in Europe and the United States. Already in 1972, the report of the Organisation for Economic Co-operation and Development (OECD) concerning trade in services stated that 'the service sector, like the industrial sector, is experiencing a measure of internationalisation' and therefore 'action should be taken … to ensure liberalisation and non-discrimination in the service sector'.[52] In the early 1980s, the American Enterprise Institute carried out research published in seven volumes covering aviation, banking, construction and telecommunications, arguing for the inclusion of trade in services within the international trading system.[53] Finally, the service issue emerged within GATT as part of a comprehensive study published by the Secretariat observing the increasing relevance of services in world trade.[54]

The intellectual property issue arose out of the debate in the United States concerning the inadequate protection that developing and newly industrialised countries afforded to patents, trademark and copyrights. According to the US Trade Commission, US industries were facing considerable profit losses due to the lack of appropriate protection.[55] The arguments put forth were that developing countries and newly industrialised countries tolerated the sales of pirate music and videos as well as the theft of trademarks, granted shorter periods of patent protection and that both their patent granting process and the enforcement of patent protection lacked transparency. Therefore, the protection of intellectual property rights in an increasingly liberalised world market represented a crucial source of profits for multinational enterprises and the realisation of these profits was overtly connected to the markets of developing countries. The existing standards of protection provided for by the Paris and Berne

[50] GATT Art III:4, by prohibiting discrimination against imports and in favour of like domestic products, was the only provision referring to investments in that it made local content or sourcing requirements not permitted.

[51] The only provision concerning IP was GATT Art XX(d) which provides for a general exception to the obligations of the Agreement in case of 'measures necessary to secure compliance with laws or regulations which are not inconsistent with the provisions of this Agreement, including those relating to … patents, trade marks and copyrights, and the prevention of deceptive practices'. Therefore, it did not entail any international standard of protection.

[52] OECD, 'Report by the High Level Group on Trade and Related Problems' (Paris, OECD, 1982); quoted in Preeg (n 45) 37.

[53] American Enterprise Institute, *International Trade in Services: An Overview and Blueprint for Negotiations* (Washington DC, AEI, 1988) 295–322; quoted in Preeg (n 45) 37.

[54] GATT, *International Trade 88–89* (Geneva, GATT, 1990) 43.

[55] US International Trade Commission, *Foreign Protection of Intellectual Property Rights and the Effect on US Industry and Trade*, Publication 2065 (Washington DC, ITC, February 1988) 63.

Conventions were administered by the World Intellectual Property Organisation (WIPO), which, however, could not make binding decisions and provided no sanction mechanism.[56] A reform of the international trading system to remedy this deficiency was of paramount importance for US interests.

This issue had long been pursued by the United States through unilateral means. First, the US had used section 337 of the US Tariff Act 1930, as amended, to exclude imports of goods whose production involved the violation of intellectual property rights of US citizens or entities under US domestic law.[57] As seen before, the US Trade Act 1984[58] had also made the granting of the GSP conditional, among other factors, on the recipient country's adequate standards of protection of US intellectual property rights. Furthermore, section 301 of the Trade Act provided for sanctions against countries that had practised 'unfair' or 'unreasonable' trade, which included inadequate protection of intellectual property rights.[59] However, these three instruments did not go as far as to ensure that the intellectual property rights of US entities were comprehensively protected outside US territory. Thus, as Trebilcock and Howse have pointed out, the US, backed by the EU and Japan, had three clear goals to achieve at the multilateral level. First, to obtain a set of international rules to ensure that American investors' rights were as extensive and as effectively enforced abroad as they were in the US. Secondly, to make sure that an effective dispute settlement system at the international level could grant the compliance with those rules. Thirdly, to ensure that its approach to the protection of new, technology-based forms of innovation, such as biotechnology, would set the international standards for the future.[60]

[56] Paris Convention for the Protection of Industrial Property (20 March 1883) 828 UNTS 305 www.wipo.int/treaties/en/ip/paris/trtdocs_wo020.html; Berne Convention for the Protection of Literary and Artistic Works (9 September 1886) 1161 UNTS 3 www.wipo.int/treaties/en/ip/berne/trtdocs_wo001.html

[57] As Trebilcock and Howse note, the exclusion of these imports from the US market following a positive finding of violation was not subject to a requirement of injury to the American product, and, providing for an actual ban rather than a duty to offset the alleged unfair trade advantage, implied the extra-territorial application of US domestic law on intellectual property rights rather than a counter to unfair trade advantage. See Trebilcock and Howse (n 44) 407.

[58] See RE Hudec, *Developing Countries in the GATT Legal System* (London, Trade Policy Research Centre, 1987) 115.

[59] As with s 337, the application of s 301 consists of the extra-territorial application of US domestic law, since any level of intellectual property protection lower than that applied in the US is deemed to be an unfair trade practice. Although s 301 has been used mainly to 'name and shame' countries which were not providing adequate protection of IP rights to US citizens, such as Japan, India and Brazil, it has also been used as 'a weapon to convince Developing Countries that their interests lie in the a multilateral solution to intellectual property disputes at the WTO'. See Trebilcock and Howse (n 44).

[60] Trebilcock and Howse (n 44) 409–10.

Therefore, the liberalisation of services and investments and the strengthened protection of intellectual property rights were the main issues Western countries, especially the United States, were determined to bring within the international trading system. In other words, the GATT system had to be broadened in order to include trade in services, trade-related aspects of intellectual property rights and trade-related investment measures. The 1980s would witness an intense struggle between developed and developing countries over the nature and scope of the international trade regime. In the early 1980s, developing countries stood firm in objecting to the inclusion of the so-called new issues within GATT. By the end of 1986, however, the historical coalition of developing countries within GATT had collapsed, paving the way for the establishment of the WTO in 1994. The next section focuses on the crucial period of GATT negotiations between 1982 and 1986 and draws from the work of US diplomat and trade negotiator, Ernest Preeg, who has thoroughly documented the events that shaped the formation of the new 'consensus'.[61]

C Setting the Scene for the New Mandate

The first step towards a broadened international trade regime was made by the United States during the 1981 OECD Ministerial Meeting. The US trade representative, William Brock, referred to the mounting protectionist pressures due to high inflation and economic stagnation to call on the OECD to 'address the trade issues of the future' in order to resist any protectionist outcome.[62] The American call for a new GATT Ministerial Meeting was supported by OECD members. Hence, in 1982, the GATT Council decided to hold its next session at a ministerial level. The Ministerial Meeting did not mention a new round of GATT negotiations. However, it was agreed that a study-and-action programme on several subjects would be carried out in the following two years. In addition to the outstanding issues from the Tokyo Round which, as seen in chapter two, developing countries were most eager to see addressed, namely safeguards, anti-dumping, textiles and agriculture, a tenuous reference to trade in counterfeit goods and services was made for the first time.[63]

The study-and-action programme represented a compromise between the United States, pressing for debate on the so-called new issues, and the

[61] Preeg (n 45).

[62] W Brock, Statement at the June 1981 OECD Ministerial Meeting; quoted in Preeg (n 45) 30.

[63] The GATT Council was instructed to determine 'the appropriateness of joint action in the GATT framework on the trade aspects of commercial counterfeiting' and the Contracting Parties were invited to exchange information regarding their service sectors. See GATT, Ministerial Declaration adopted on 29 November 1982. GATT, BISD 29th Supp 29S/11.

developing countries, opposing new negotiations on services, investment and intellectual property and insisting on the swift removal of the obstacles to their trade. Speaking on behalf of the developing countries, the Uruguayan delegate urged the industrialised countries to withdraw their GATT-inconsistent measures, to use restraint in countervailing measures and anti-dumping procedures and to liberalise imports of textiles and clothing. Such steps, he said, 'amount to no more than fulfilling previously accepted commitments', and until such steps were taken 'any initiative such as a new round of tariff negotiations would be lacking in credibility and devoid of relevance particularly for developing countries'.[64] In 1982, the position of developing countries was therefore clear: no new round of negotiations would take place until the discrimination against their trade was effectively addressed.

Although the Ministerial Meeting did not call for a new round of negotiations, let alone the inclusion of the three new issues on the negotiating agenda, the events that took place in the following four years radically changed this situation. The decision to launch a new round of negotiations was made by the industrialised countries during the OECD meetings and the more discreet meetings between the Quad members.[65] The United States, however, was still facing a unified opposition from developing countries to a round of negotiations dealing with the three new issues. Thus, in July 1985, the US called for a postal ballot of GATT members in order to initiate a Ministerial Meeting adopting a negotiating mandate for the next round. As Preeg recalls:

> A majority would initiate the meeting in September, and if Brazil and India wanted to stay at home, so be it. US ambassadors around the world received instructions to urge their host governments to get their ballots in the mail. The pressure tactic worked, and all GATT members participated in the meeting of September 30, 1985, which followed by a week the announcement of President Reagan's new tough trade policy.[66]

President Reagan had concurrently launched before the Congress his campaign to eliminate 'unfair trade practices' abroad, mainly through unilateral actions based on section 301 of the 1974 Trade Act. As for the new round of GATT negotiations, Reagan made clear that 'if these negotiations are not initiated or if insignificant progress is made, I am instructing our trade negotiators to explore regional and bilateral agreements with other nations'.[67] The pressure tactic therefore worked, and delegates from all countries agreed to establish a Preparatory Committee

[64] GATT, Document L/5647 (4 May 1984); quoted in Preeg (n 45) 52.
[65] Namely, the United States, Japan, the European Community and Canada.
[66] Preeg (n 45) 54.
[67] R Reagan, from a speech at the White House to business and Congressional leaders on 22 September 1985; quoted in Preeg (n 45) 51.

with the aim of formulating a negotiating mandate to be adopted at a Ministerial Meeting in September 1986. Between January and July 1986, the Preparatory Committee held nine meetings in order to discuss the subject matters for the new round, including the issues of interest to developing countries, namely a safeguards agreement, clear procedures on anti-dumping and countervailing duties and the liberalisation of agriculture and textiles.[68] In exchange for the inclusion of these negotiating objectives, the US insisted on discussing not only counterfeit goods, but the protection of patents, trademarks and copyrights within the subject matter of intellectual property rights.

D Punta del Este: A Divisive Strategy

The decisive moment in the collapse of the developing countries' coalition was marked by the Punta del Este Ministerial Meeting. By the end of the 1986 meeting, the coalition of developing countries had split. India, Brazil, Argentina, Cuba, Nicaragua and Peru were among the group of ten developing countries opposing the inclusion of services, intellectual property and investment in the new round of negotiations.[69] However, Chile, Colombia, Jamaica, Mexico, Trinidad, Tobago, Uruguay, Bangladesh, Indonesia, South Korea, Malaysia, Pakistan, the Philippines, Singapore, Sri Lanka and Thailand joined the group of countries supporting the US agenda for the broadening of the negotiating mandate, forming the so-called block of 48 countries.[70] These countries opted for a compromise that would allow the outstanding issues from the Tokyo Round to be dealt with in the next round of negotiations in exchange for the inclusion of the three 'new issues' within the negotiating mandate.

Thus, the G-48 mandate draft provided for the liberalisation of textiles and tropical products; an agreement on safeguards; a so-called standstill and rollback commitment by industrialised countries not to adopt new restricting measures inconsistent with the GATT, which also referred to the growing use of informal import quotas and 'voluntary export restraints' against developing countries' exporters; the improvement of existing GATT rules on subsidies and countervailing duties; a strengthened dispute settlement system; and the formal provision of Special and Differential Treatment (SDT). A third bloc of countries was also formed around a proposal for substantial trade liberalisation in the agricultural sector. The six initial countries, Australia, Chile, Colombia, Thailand, New Zealand

[68] Preeg (n 45) 51.
[69] *Ibid* 58.
[70] *Ibid* 59.

and Uruguay were joined by Argentina, Brazil, Canada, Fiji, Hungary, Indonesia, Malaysia and the Philippines to form the so-called CAIRNS group.[71]

Hence, despite the opposition of India and Brazil to the new issues in the GATT, the G-48 draft was adopted and trade ministers from 96 countries agreed to launch a new round of GATT negotiations, the Uruguay Round (UR). In addition to the issues of interest to developing countries, the negotiating mandate was to include services, investment and intellectual property rights. The Punta del Este Ministerial Declaration provided that negotiations in the area of services

> shall aim to establish a multilateral framework of principles and rules for trade in services, including elaboration of possible disciplines for individual sectors, with a view to expansion of such trade under conditions of transparency and progressive liberalisation and as a means of promoting economic growth of all trading partners and the development of developing countries.[72]

As for intellectual property, the declaration provided that negotiations 'shall aim to develop a multilateral framework of principles, rules and disciplines dealing with international trade in counterfeit goods, taking into account work already undertaken under GATT' and, with regard to other trade-related aspects of intellectual property rights, 'to elaborate as appropriate new rules and disciplines'.[73] The text also called for negotiations in the area of trade-related investment measures and provided that 'Following an examination of the operation of GATT Articles relating to the trade restrictive and distorting effects of investment measures, negotiations should elaborate, as appropriate, further provisions that may be necessary to avoid such adverse effects on trade'.[74]

i The Uncertain Future of the Special and Differential Treatment

Therefore, by the end of the Punta del Este meeting in 1986, the three 'new issues' had been brought within the mandate for the eighth round of GATT negotiations. The other fundamental issue for the United States was that concerning the inclusion of the SDT[75] within the agreements laying down the international rules on services, investment and intellectual property rights. If developing countries were allowed to continue with the exemptions provided for by the SDT and the non-reciprocity principle, US

[71] *Ibid* 60–62.

[72] GATT, Punta del Este Ministerial Declaration, App B (adopted 20 September, 1986) BISD 33S/19.

[73] *Ibid.*

[74] *Ibid.*

[75] This is a reformulation of the principle of Differential and More Favourable Treatment. Hereafter, the term 'Special and Differential Treatment' will be adopted.

interests in the markets of developing countries would be compromised. Hence, in 1987, the United States established an interagency group with the aim of formulating a strategy for developing countries in the Uruguay Round. The secretary of the interagency group, Peter McPherson, criticised the development approach of many developing countries and described the use of import substitution policies as based on 'false economic assumptions'.[76]

This recalls the argument that neo-liberal scholars were advancing with respect to the economic policies inspired by development economics and dependency theories. As seen, neo-liberal scholars rejected the idea that neo-classical economics, based on the price mechanism and rational economic behaviour, could not be applied to developing countries due to their different economic structures. In their view, government restrictions on international trade were not conducive to economic development.[77] Drawing from this argument, McPherson opposed the use of SDT provisions and the principle of non-reciprocity and pointed to the fact that they reduced the incentives of industrialised nations to trade with developing countries. Following McPherson's suggestion to arrive at the Uruguay Round with a strong and uncompromising position with respect to the developing countries' status, the US called for a change in the GATT system with respect to the dual legal status of developed and developing countries.[78] By the end of the Uruguay Round, SDT would be conceptually and practically transformed.

Therefore, five years after the 1981 OECD meeting, the United States had managed to achieve its initial objective of broadening the scope of the international trading system. Although an agreement was by no means secure in 1986 and it took eight long years of negotiations for the WTO agreements to come into force, the US had been successful in getting developing countries to agree to negotiate on services, investment and intellectual property rights despite their initial unified opposition. The United States used its political and economic leverage to get developing countries around the negotiating table, and the pressure continued throughout the Uruguay Round negotiations.[79] As argued below, the collapse of the developing countries' coalition within GATT was the result of a complex relationship between the economic crisis of the 1970s, the new interests of the capitalist powers in a trade-service-investment driven market integration, the oil and debt crisis and the Structural Adjustment

[76] Quoted in Preeg (n 45) 73.
[77] See Balassa, *Development Strategies* (n 8) 9.
[78] See Preeg (n 45) 73–74.
[79] The pressure strategy employed throughout the Uruguay Round will be analysed in ch 4.

Policies (SAPs) that followed, the increasing frustration with GATT practice and the rise to dominance of neo-liberal development theories that provided a partial and biased account of these events.

III DEVELOPING COUNTRIES' REALIGNMENT: REVISITING THE STORY

The breakdown of developing countries' cohesion was a crucial moment in the negotiating history of the GATT and one of the determining factors leading to the adoption of the Uruguay Round agreements. Furthermore, it represented an important shift in the development rationale developing countries had adopted since the inception of the GATT. The majority of trade scholars have given an almost unanimous account of this shift, an account premised on both economic and legal grounds. According to the former, developing countries appear to have acknowledged the failure of their inward-oriented policies and, consequently, to have opted for a market-oriented development agenda.[80] This position relies on the burgeoning comparative studies that showed how economies that had pursued outward-oriented policies were experiencing faster growth than those relying on import-substitution industrialisation. As previously seen, these studies were part of the growing literature that, in the 1980s, rejected the so-called dirigiste dogma of development economics and dependency theories and replaced it with the centrality of the market and rational economic behaviour. In other words, this position assumes that the split among developing countries represented the rational choice for the most efficient trade policy.

On the legal side of the argument, developing countries are shown to have recognised that the benefits deriving from reciprocal negotiations are far greater than the gains they could obtain from insisting on unilateral actions by developed countries. The thrust of the argument is that the majority of GATT development provisions were drafted in hortatory rather than mandatory language and, as a result, developing countries were unable to enforce them. In addition to this, the non-reciprocity position meant that developing countries did not have sufficient bargaining power to negotiate access to the developed countries' markets for the products of interest to them. Conversely, only by entering negotiations on a reciprocal

[80] See Michalopoulos, *Developing Countries* (n 31) 30–32; Preeg (n 45) 55–59; AO Krueger, 'The Political Economy of Rent-Seeking Society' (1974) 64 *American Economic Review* 291; AO Krueger, 'Agricultural Incentives in Developing Countries: Measuring the Effects of Sectoral and Economic-wide Policies' (1988) 2 *World Bank Economic Review* 255; J Bhagwati, *Anatomies and Consequences of Exchange Control Regimes* (New York, National Bureau of Economic Research, 1978); M Matsushita, TJ Schoenbaum and PC Mavrodis, *The World Trade Organisation: Law, Practice, and Policy* (Oxford, Oxford University Press, 2003) 378–81.

basis could developing countries obtain meaningful commitments by the industrialised members.[81] Developing countries were thus presented with the choice between continuing to require unilateral obligations by industrialised countries or competing on an equal footing with them.[82] As with the economic argument, the legal argument assumes that developing countries have recognised the failure of their former legal strategy and opted for a multilateral trading system based on reciprocal and binding commitments for all members.

Notwithstanding the fact that these arguments reflect important aspects of the developing countries' position within the international trade regime, the situation is much more complex. By privileging the incidence of certain factors while overlooking or downplaying the importance of others, these representations end up viewing the shift in terms of a logical, rational and inevitable process. What is argued is that if one looks at the historic, political and economic contexts in which the realignment of developing countries took place, the inevitability and desirability of this process might be called into question.

A From the Oil and Debt Crisis to the Structural Adjustment Policies

It is widely acknowledged that the deterioration of the economic positions of many developing countries reached a dramatic stage after the oil shocks of 1973 and 1979 and the debt crisis announced by Mexico in 1982.[83] Most scholars, however, have seen the oil and debt crisis as events that have magnified their already precarious conditions.[84] At best, these events are viewed as accelerating an economic decline that was underway and

[81] See Hudec (n 58); Matsushita, Schoenbaum, Mavrodis (n 80) 373–93; Michalopoulos, *Developing Countries* (n 31) 30--33; BM Hoekman and MM Kostecki, *The Political Economy of the World Trading System: From GATT to WTO* (Oxford, Oxford University Press, 1995) 239–40. Preeg (n 45) 55; TN Srinivasan, 'Trade and Development: Developing Countries in the World Trading System, 1947–1999' (Yale University, Department of Economics, 1999) 5–8 www2.cid.harvard.edu/cidtrade/Issues/srinivastad.pdf.

[82] A related argument is that developing countries have opted for a ruled-based multilateral system in order to put an end to the unilateral threats and bilateral pressures by the most powerful members. M Michalopoulos, 'The Role of Special and Differential Treatment for Developing Countries in GATT and the World Trade Organisation' (World Bank Working Paper, 2000) 13 wbln0018.worldbank.org/research/workpapers.nsf/0/f427de05fa00793885256913006 52b9f/$FILE/WPS2388.pdf.

[83] For a concise account of the developing countries' debt crisis and the various initiatives that followed, see Trebilcock and Howse (n 44) 488–90.

[84] For instance, Jaastad, Almansi and Hurtado had argued that the crisis in Latin America preceded the inability of governments to repay their loans and owed much to the over ambitious public investments of the 1960s and 1980s. See Jaastad, Almansi, Hurtado (n 24) 131–79. Krueger also argues that countries adopting outward-oriented policies survived the crisis whereas those practicing Import Substitution Industrialisation (ISI) failed in comparison. See Krueger, *Political Economy of Policy Reform* (n 8) 3–4.

whose causes have to be found elsewhere, particularly in the adoption by developing countries of import substitution policies and failing institutional arrangements. Consequently, the crucial role these two events played in the economic crisis of developing countries and their subsequent position within the international economic system are obfuscated. In other words, what has been left out by mainstream accounts is the complex relationship between the world recession of the 1970s, the oil and debt crisis and the political response devised by the United States in each of these instances.

The crisis of 'stagflation' hit the industrialised countries with an unprecedented rise of inflation and unemployment in the early 1970s. However, the United States was the first country to experience a serious structural deficit by the end of the 1960s. As seen, the US responded to its structural deficit with the abandonment of the fixed system of exchange rates in 1971. This was, however, not an automatic response following the crisis. As Gowan argues, there were

> obvious solutions to this problem under the Bretton Woods rules: either the US could undertake the necessary economic adjustments to bring its deficit under control— cutting back on external military expenditure and reducing imports, perhaps through domestic deflation—or it could devalue the dollar against gold, thus ensuring that the surplus countries could buy less gold with their surplus dollars. But the Nixon Administration was not prepared to take either of these steps: it preferred to break up the Bretton Woods regime instead.[85]

The breaking up of the Bretton Woods regime has to be seen in the context of the other decision the Nixon Administration took in the aftermath of the oil shock of 1973. The oil shock produced large trade deficits for most oil importing countries, precipitating their economic position. However, at the same time, the majority of petrodollars from oil exporting countries were deposited in Western banks, especially the New York commercial banks, which began to look for profitable places in which to invest their surpluses. The situation at home was not promising since Western governments refused to expand borrowings to stimulate internal demand. Economic recession had kicked in and the abandonment of the Keynesian consensus had started. Thus, in 1974, Nixon took the important step of removing controls on US capital accounts and actively encouraged US banks to lend abroad by eliminating the ceiling for the maximum amount that could be lent to a borrower.[86] The other important decision made by President Carter in the attempt to increase exports of US manufacture was

[85] Gowan (n 36) 17.
[86] *Ibid* 22.

the devaluation of the dollar that, between 1975 and 1979, lost a quarter of its value against the mark and the yen.[87]

These events were soon to exert their pressure on developing countries. As Rodrik points out, between the 1950s and 1970s, the countries of the south overall experienced high rates of growth through state intervention.[88] However, as a result of the economic recession in the north and the dollar deflation inaugurated by Carter, developing countries started to face a decline of their export earnings and a critical shortage of foreign exchange that compromised their current accounts. The countries experiencing balance of payments difficulty had two choices: either borrowing from the commercial banks whose operations had been deregulated or embarking on structural adjustments of their economies by restricting fiscal policies and devaluing their currencies.[89]

With commercial banks eager to invest their petrodollars in a deregulated financial environment, the Middle East, Latin America, Poland, Hungary and the former Yugoslavia chose the former route.[90] What happened next was to have profound consequences for these countries. The Volcker shock of 1979, engineered in the US in order to curb inflation, caused the sudden rise in dollar interest rates and the shortening of the debt maturity structure. Thus, the Mexican government was the first developing country in 1982 to declare its inability to repay the debt. Since the nine largest US banks had lent almost their entire capital to Mexico and Brazil alone,[91] if these countries defaulted the banks would have been in serious financial difficulties. Thus, as Armstrong, Glynn and Harrison presciently wrote in 1984:

> [S]omeone has to foot the bill. There are three candidates. One is the banks. If loans are simply written off then banks shareholders suffer, with the attendant risk of a collapse of the international credit system. If governments bail out the Banks then Western taxpayers pay. The only other possibility is for the LDCs to depress their economies enough … in other words to make the Third World masses pay.[92]

The third option was the way out of the crisis offered by the World Bank and the International Monetary Fund through the SAPs that would lead to

[87] *Ibid* 39.

[88] D Rodrik, 'Globalization, Social Conflict and Economic Growth', Prebisch Lecture (Geneva, UNCTAD, 24 October 1997). In Gowan (n 36) 48.

[89] Rodrik, *ibid.*

[90] 'Between the close of 1973 and 1981 LDCs debt to Western governments and international agencies such as the World Bank rose about three times, while that to private banks rose nine times. It had reached around US$ 400 bn by early 1983'. Armstrong, Glynn and Harrison (n 35) 361–62.

[91] *Ibid* 363.

[92] *Ibid* 364.

the overall transformation of the economic structure of borrowing countries.[93] Despite the crucial role these exogenous factors played, the main causes of the economic crises that affected developing economies in the 1980s are still made to rest on the adoption of erroneous economic policies by their governments. This is not to qualify inward-oriented policies in universal terms although, as Rodrik writes, Import Substitution Industrialisation 'brought unprecedented economic growth to scores of countries in Latin America, the Middle East and North Africa, and even in Sub-Saharan Africa'.[94] It is rather to assert that the representation by neo-liberal scholars of the crisis of developing economies in the 1980s offers a partial account of the complex climate in which outward-oriented policies emerged and gradually consolidated into the prevalent trade strategy in most developing countries.

B The Challenge of Increasing Discrimination

One important consequence of the debt crisis was the dissemination of SAPs throughout the developing world in the 1980s with their consequent economic restructuring. In exchange for the rescheduling of the debt of developing countries, the rescue package required the conversion of quantitative restrictions into tariffs, tariff reductions, the phasing out of export subsidies and the liberalisation of foreign exchange markets.[95] Thus, when developing countries met at Punta del Este, many of them had already embarked on substantial liberalisation of their trade regimes with their economic structures increasingly dependent on the export sector. However, their enhanced interest in export markets was frustrated by the obstacles posed by the developed countries on the products of interest to them. Therefore, on the eve of Punta del Este, many developing countries found themselves in the ambiguous situation of having their market-oriented economic policies adversely affected by the obstacles posed by the discriminatory practices of GATT developed members.

Despite GATT's development rhetoric, the increasing negative discrimination against the trade of developing countries had not been yet redressed. As Gibbs notes, there were several measures that contributed to the deterioration of the economic position of developing economies:

> a) Voluntary export restraints and other 'grey area' measures directed against their most competitive exports, b) bilateral pressures by major importing

[93] Harvey argues that in contradiction with neo-classical theory, according to which the investor takes responsibility for the 'bad' investments, the IMF strategy aimed at bailing out the investors. Harvey (n 2) 29.

[94] Rodrik (n 88) 49.

[95] See Michalopoulos, *Developing Countries* (n 31) 32.

> countries aimed at obtaining trade concessions through the threat of trade sanctions, rather than the offer of reciprocal benefits, c) the extension of free-trade agreements and customs unions among developed countries, d) higher MFN tariffs on products of export interest to developing countries compared to those of interest to developed countries, e) the proliferation of restraints on textiles and clothing exports under the Multi-Fibre Agreements, f) the diminishing effectiveness of any GATT disciplines governing trade in agricultural products, and g) increased harassment from anti-dumping and countervailing duties.[96]

In addition, the GSP was being applied in a conditional and discriminatory fashion.[97] Furthermore, as Gibbs points out,

> the Tokyo Round codes appeared to represent a major step towards the 'GATT plus' approach advocated in developed countries circles in the early 1970s, according to which those countries would create an inner system of rights and obligations encompassing areas of mutual interest among themselves and leading to active consideration of the resurrection of the so-called conditional MFN clause.[98]

This would place the developing countries at a serious disadvantage. During UNCTAD VI, the coalition of 77 developing countries was still in place. However, as a result of the further discrimination threatened by the so-called GATT-plus approach, the thrust of their initiatives, until then informed by the principle of SDT, started to change. Developing countries began to appreciate the argument in favour of unconditional MFN and asserted the need for a strengthened multilateral trade system.[99]

C The Pressure Tactic: Unilateralism/Bilateralism/Multilateralism

In light of these developments, the legal arguments in favour of reciprocity started to gain ground. In addition to the economic crisis, the transformation of their trade regimes and the many obstacles GATT posed to the growth of their export sectors, developing countries had to face the new trade policy of the United States. The opposition to a broadened GATT mandate by developing countries at the beginning of the 1980s was to be tested by the bilateral and unilateral trade policy inaugurated by President Reagan. The underlying argument was that if developing countries did not go along with the multilateral response to the new requirements posed by

[96] M Gibbs, 'Special and Differential Treatment in the Context of Globalisation'. Note Presented to the G15 Symposium on Special and Differential Treatment in the WTO Agreements (New Delhi, 10 December 1998) 3.

[97] Michalopoulos, 'The Role of Special and Differential Treatment' (n 82) 9–10.

[98] See Gibbs (n 96).

[99] UNCTAD, Resolution 159 (VI) Belgrade (adopted 2 July 1983).

the trade-service-investment driven market integration, they would be left out of a changing trading system and the opportunities it was supposed to generate. A series of bilateral agreements signed by the United States in the 1980s reinforced this perception. Reagan signed the Caribbean Basin one way free-trade agreement in 1983[100] and a bilateral free-trade agreement with Israel in 1985.[101] In 1984, the US initiated talks for a free-trade agreement with Canada and Mexico. In 1985, Reagan asked and received authority for unilateral actions in order to eliminate unfair trade practices abroad. This included trade sanctions under section 301 of the 1974 Trade Act. It was at this point, between 1985 and 1986, that developing countries' cohesion started to vacillate. As Preeg recalls:

> An informal group of industrialised countries, the 'Dirty Dozen', held a series of private meetings and produced the first comprehensive ministerial declaration. For tactical reasons, the three large members—the United States, the EC and Japan—temporarily withdrew from the group while the smaller industrialised countries joined with about twenty moderate (ie, non-hard-line) developing countries to further develop and circulate the draft. Other developing countries joined, the big three re-joined and the now forty-eight participants formally constituted themselves as the G-48.[102]

The G-48 Draft Declaration carefully traded the liberalisation of the sectors of interest to developing countries for the inclusion of the 'three new issues' in the international trading system. The negotiating mandate was to include an agreement on safeguards, progressive liberalisation of textiles and clothing, liberalisation of agricultural and tropical products and a strengthened dispute settlement system. These issues had been outstanding since Committee III in 1963 had emphasised that many developed countries' restrictions to the trade of developing countries were GATT inconsistent.[103] The Dillon, Kennedy and Tokyo Rounds focused on the principle of non-reciprocity according to which developing countries were not expected to engage in full reciprocal concessions.[104] However, they did not contain any legally binding commitment on the part of developed countries to reduce tariff barriers as requested by Committee III. As for the safeguards issue,[105] developing countries had unsuccessfully

[100] Federal Research Division, 'Appendix B–Dominican Republic and Haiti: Caribbean Basin Initiative' (The Library of Congress, Federal Research Division, 1983) www.country-data.com/frd/cs/haiti/ht_appnb.html.

[101] Jewish Virtual Library, 'Reagan on Signing the Free Trade Area Implementation Act' (Jewish Virtual Library, A Division of the American-Israeli Cooperative Enterprise, 1985) www.jewishvirtuallibrary.org/jsource/US-Israel/RR6_11_85.html.

[102] Preeg (n 45) 58.

[103] See ch 2, II B.

[104] Respectively, the fifth, sixth and seventh rounds of GATT negotiations.

[105] GATT Art XIX provided for temporary imports restrictions when a surge of imports causes or threatens to cause 'serious injury to domestic producers'. The conditions for

requested during the Tokyo Round a solution to the problem posed by selective import restrictions. Therefore, the draft declaration offered a commitment by industrialised countries to negotiate these issues in exchange for developing countries' commitment to negotiate on the liberalisation of services and investments and the protection of intellectual property rights. The legal arguments in favour of reciprocal commitments, according to which developing countries would benefit from abandoning their insistence on unilateral actions from developed countries, had finally prevailed.

Within the evolving reciprocal system of multilateral negotiations, the fate of the principle of SDT was less clear. In the Punta del Este Declaration, the Contracting Parties agreed that 'the principle of differential and more favourable treatment embodied in Part IV... and in the Decision of the Contracting Parties of 28 November 1979 on Differential and More Favourable Treatment, Reciprocity and Fuller Participation of Developing Countries, applies to the negotiations'.[106] The scope of this provision, however, was contradicted by the underlying rationale of reciprocal commitments. If the principle were to be incorporated within the final agreements, the trade with developing countries, especially with respect to the new issues, would have been affected. The ambiguity between the language of the declaration including SDT and the implied reciprocity in the negotiations was left to the final stage of the Uruguay Round.

CONCLUSIONS

By the end of the Punta del Este Ministerial Meeting, the historic coalition of developing countries that in the past three decades had challenged the universal rules of trade drafted by the United States and United Kingdom had collapsed. Despite the confusion in the language regarding SDT, the majority of developing countries decided to pursue the objectives of the 1982 Work Programme through the acceptance of commitments in the new areas of services, investment and intellectual property rights. This represented a significant shift in the development rationale that had prevailed until then. The principle of reciprocity that was to emerge soon implied a

applying such restrictions included formal consultation within GATT to prove the existence of a serious injury, a non-discriminatory application of the said restrictions and compensation by way of import liberalisation on other products. As Preeg notes, however, this procedure was hardly ever observed and developed countries imposed, outside GATT, bilateral import quotas against developing countries' exports. The G-48 Draft therefore included a revision of the safeguard clause within the negotiating objectives, although the issue of selectivity versus non-discrimination was not mentioned. See Preeg (n 45) 24.

[106] GATT, Punta del Este Ministerial Declaration (n 72).

view of the bargaining process in the international trade arena as an exchange conducted by agents seen as rational utility-maximisers that stand on an equal footing with one another. As Preeg concludes, 'the decision by most developing countries to embark on negotiation of reciprocal commitments reflected a revised assessment of their economic self-interests'.[107]

The interpretation of the breakdown of the developing countries' coalition in terms of a rational choice for the most efficient trade policy is also congruent with the neo-liberal transformation of development thinking. Most of the economic and legal arguments concerning the shift place the so-called failure of developing countries to develop their trade 'as rapidly as that of the developed countries'[108] on their past economic policies and legal strategies, whereas the importance of external factors is at best downplayed if not overlooked. As a consequence, the shift in the development rationale is presented as the outcome of an inevitable and desirable historic process.

Contrary to these interpretations, the neo-liberal turn was the outcome of the events that in the 1970s and 1980s called for urgent action and the political decisions made in response. From the world recession to the monetarist responses of the industrialised countries, in particular the US decision to abandon the gold system and deregulate private finance; from the oil and debt crisis to the radical transformation of developing countries' economic structures imposed by the SAPs; from the negative discrimination suffered by developing countries under the GATT to the political and economic pressure exercised by the industrialised countries to bring in the 'new issues'; these responses were each time political rather than rational and neutral choices. In other words, this shift was the outcome of the interaction and mutual reinforcement of neo-liberal theories and the practices employed to advance the political and economic interests of the European Union and the United States in particular. Chapter four will further substantiate this claim by examining in detail the pressure exerted on developing countries from 1986 to 1994 in order to obtain their adherence to the US and EU agenda.

However, from a perspective that looks at the role of the 'science of development' within the international trading regime, its neo-liberal transformation and effects were made possible thanks to the framework established at the end of the colonial era: the need for developing countries to develop their trade as fast as that of the developed countries remained the premise for its transformation and continuous hegemony.[109] In the

[107] Preeg (n 45) 59.

[108] This, as discussed in ch 2, II B, was the GATT development norm produced by the Contracting Parties with the commissioning of the Haberler Report.

[109] *Ibid*.

immediate postwar period, the so-called failure of development was imputed to the dual economic structures of the ex-colonies so that their capitalist transformation through an interventionist state would deliver the promise of development. In the 1980s, the persistence of this failure is made to rest on the adoption of erroneous economic policies and legal claims by developing countries so that market forces become the appropriate development means. Both the legal and the economic arguments explaining this shift in terms of a 'rational choice' share the neo-liberal assumptions about the market mechanism and rational economic behaviour and, more fundamentally, the implicit assumptions of the 'science of development'.

4

The Uruguay Round and the Construction of the New Consensus

THE NEO-LIBERAL revolution of development thinking was received within the international trading system at the end of the Punta del Este Ministerial Meeting. Developing countries had opposed the inclusion of services, intellectual property rights and investment within the new round of negotiations. However, by 1986 the so-called hard liners, led by India and Brazil, had been isolated and they agreed on the launch of the new round. Eight years later, the Uruguay Round (UR) was completed and the World Trade Organisation (WTO) came into existence. By the end of the UR, ideas concerning the structural inequalities of the international trading system had disappeared as analytical concepts and the market was presented as an equal playing field where actors could engage in reciprocal and mutually beneficial negotiations. The failure of developing countries to develop their trade as rapidly as that of the developed countries was identified exactly with the result of those GATT provisions allowing for flexibility, especially non-reciprocity.[1]

The qualitative change brought about by the UR consisted of the reconceptualisation of the so-called Special and Differential Treatment. Although time-limited derogations allowing developing countries to comply with the WTO agreements were provided, the underlying rationale was that their interests would be best served by reciprocal and binding obligations. In addition, neo-liberal assumptions about the beneficial role of the market extended well beyond trade in goods. Whereas GATT rules had been limited to states' tariff policy, the WTO agreements reached

[1] As a result of the findings of the Haberler Report, GATT members agreed that the developing countries would be entitled to negotiate on a non-reciprocal basis (the so-called Enabling Clause) and established Part IV of the GATT, which authorised preferential tariff arrangements in favour of developing countries. See ch 2, II.

deeper into more areas of policy making. Moreover, unlike the GATT, the WTO was to be endowed with an effective dispute settlement system, which would be 'a world economic court in all but name'.[2]

However, the adoption of the UR agreements and the extent to which their rules would impact on the domestic regulatory policy of WTO members was not predetermined at Punta del Este, notwithstanding the importance of this event for the breaking down of developing countries' coalition. Despite the fact that an agreement to negotiate on the so-called new issues was in place, the exact scope of the mandate was interpreted differently by developed and developing countries. With regard to intellectual property (IP), the latter were only prepared to negotiate on counterfeit goods. As to services, India and Brazil had made sure that negotiations would be carried out on a separate track, so that GATT rules would not automatically apply to the regulation of services.[3] Finally, the negotiations on investment were supposed to clarify those trade-related investment measures deemed incompatible with GATT rules.

This chapter explores the process through which, between 1986 and 1994, the consensus around the developed countries' interpretation of the mandate was built. In particular, it challenges the literature that has presented the conclusion of the UR as the success of the US administration in resisting the pressure to abandon the multilateral system and also as the developing countries' decision to make the rational choice.[4] Indeed, the economic position of the United States at the end of the 1980s prompted a protectionist response by the US Congress. Confronted with an increasing deficit of its current account, unilateral and bilateral strategies were invoked in order to open markets abroad.[5] The successful conclusion of the UR seemed therefore to be threatened by the US retreat from the multilateral regime. However, regardless of whether the US would have really abandoned the multilateral trading system, this threat worked exactly to fulfil the US multilateral agenda, especially with respect to the new issues where its comparative advantage was greater.

[2] JHH Weiler, 'The Rule of Lawyers and the Ethos of Diplomats: Reflections on the Internal and External Legitimacy of WTO Dispute Settlement' (Harvard Law School, Jean Monnet Working Paper 2000) 21.

[3] TN Srinivasan, *Developing Countries and the Multilateral Trading System: From the GATT to the Uruguay Round and the Future* (Oxford, Westview Press, 1997) 32.

[4] See eg EH Preeg, *Traders in a Brave New World: The Uruguay Round and the Future of the International Trading System* (Chicago, University of Chicago Press, 1995) 165; M Kahler, *International Institutions and the Political Economy of Integration* (Washington DC, Brookings Institution Press, 1995) 33; S Edwards, 'Comments' in S Haggard (ed), *Developing Nations and the Politics of Global Integration* (Washington DC, Brookings Institution Press, 1995) 44.

[5] See P Gowan, *The Global Gamble: Washington's Faustian Bid for World Dominance* (London, Verso, 1999) 60–90.

On the other hand, the decision of developing countries to embrace the US agenda on the new issues has to be seen in light of their position within the changing international political and economic circumstances of the 1980s. As examined in chapter three, the oil and debt crisis that affected Latin American and African countries, and the Structural Adjustment Policies (SAPs) that followed, made their economies dependent on the export sectors.[6] Elimination of the discrimination against their trade was therefore more important than it had previously been. As argued in this chapter, although east and southeast Asian countries were in a different position, the unilateral and bilateral pressure from the US also threatened their export sectors and, more fundamentally, targeted the industrial policies on which they had relied. Thus, the intensification of pressures represented an incentive for developing countries and new emerging economies to support a rules-based multilateral system. As a result, the WTO agreements entered into force in 1995.

However, as observed with respect to the economic and legal arguments that positively qualify the breaking down of developing countries' coalition at Punta del Este,[7] the final agreements of the WTO are not the outcome of a rational choice. Rather, the triumph of economic liberalism within the WTO agreements owes much to the interplay of powerful economic and political forces that originated in the 1970s and intensified between 1986 and 1994 to culminate in the establishment of the WTO.

I OLD AND NEW ISSUES ON THE NEGOTIATING TABLE, CORPORATE ACTIVISM AND THE SINGLE UNDERTAKING APPROACH

The reasons for the protracted duration of the eighth round of GATT negotiations are many. First, the negotiating package launched at Punta del Este had been presented as the trade off between developing countries' interests in the elimination of the obstacles to their trade and the developed countries' intention to include the new issues within the negotiating mandate. Thus, unlike previous GATT rounds, where the focus had mainly been on tariff reductions on trade in goods, the ambitious agenda of the UR meant that for the first time in trading history, states had to agree on disparate subjects ranging from anti-dumping, textiles, agriculture, subsidies and dispute settlement to services, IP and investment. However, whereas the former issues had a long history within GATT, the link between the three new issues and international trade rose to centre stage only in the 1970s due to the new alliance between governments and the corporate sector in the north.

[6] See ch 3, III A.
[7] See ch 3, III.

Corporate activism had been a US feature since the Trade Act 1974, when the Advisory Committee on Trade Negotiations was first established. Chaired by Pratt, the CEO of the pharmaceutical company Pfizer, the committee was to inform the United States Trade Representative (USTR) of the industry's concerns in the Tokyo Round of GATT negotiations.[8] In 1986, Pratt was to launch the Intellectual Property Committee, whose members included Bristol-Myers, Du Pont, FMC Corporation, General Electric, General Motors, Hewlett-Packard, IBM, Johnson & Johnson, Merck, Monsanto, Pfizer, Rockwell International and Warner Communications, in order to focus on a comprehensive agreement on IP within GATT.[9] The Trade Act 1988 reactivated this advisory mechanism. Renamed the Advisory Committee on Trade Policy and Negotiations (ACTPN), this group was to play an active role in shaping the US agenda on services, investment and IP. As Ostry writes:

> [I]n cooperation with other US business groups, it has launched international initiatives in these areas, with Americans taking the lead in securing the cooperation and support of European and Japanese corporations. In point of fact, in these instances, where careful and detailed analysis and proposals from the private sector were fed into the Geneva process, we have the only examples of meaningful and effective involvement by the business community in Europe and Japan, as an international private sector 'spillover' of US business activism.[10]

Thus, the unprecedented involvement of the corporate sector in the UR of GATT negotiations signalled the entry of a new actor in the international trade arena. Although negotiations were officially carried out among states, the support of the private sector in the US, Europe and Japan was indispensable for achieving the final deal on the new issues.

Secondly, the difficulty of negotiating on such different grounds has to be seen in the context of the negotiating strategy advanced by the US. The adoption of the Single Undertaking Approach (SUA) meant that nothing would be agreed on until everything on the negotiating table was ultimately accepted. Implicitly, this meant that as a condition for addressing the long-outstanding issues hindering developing countries' trade, an agreement on the new issues was also to be reached. However, although

[8] MP Ryan, *Knowledge Diplomacy: Global Competition and the Politics of Intellectual Property* (Washington DC, Brookings Institution Press, 1998) 107.

[9] For a detailed account of the strategy employed by Pfizers's chairman Pratt and IBM's chairman Opel within the ACTPN and the Intellectual Property Committee during the Uruguay Round, in particular their role in getting Europe and Japan to support the launch of the new round of negotiations, see P Drahos and J Braithwaite, *Information Feudalism: Who Owns the Knowledge Economy* (London, Earthscan, 2002) chs 4, 6 and 7.

[10] S Ostry, *Governments and Corporations in a Shrinking World: Trade and Innovations Policies in the United States, Europe and Japan* (New York; London, Council of Foreign Relations, 1990) 22–23.

the Punta del Este Declaration provided the mandate to negotiate the inclusion of services, investment and IP rights within the international trading system, the content of the rules that were to discipline these areas was far from defined. The mandate on services provided that GATT rules would not be indiscriminately applied to trade in services so that negotiations would be undertaken on a separate track. This was the procedural compromise that the US achieved with India and Brazil and which seemed to imply that the SUA would not apply to services.[11]

Despite the fact that the negotiating mandate on intellectual property contained a tenuous reference to other areas of IP, the predominant focus was on counterfeit goods. Thus, the extension of IP regulation to patents, copyrights, trademarks, trade secrets, industrial layout and geographical indications was not a fait accompli in 1986, at least as far as developing countries were concerned. With regard to the negotiations on investment, the mandate was limited to those investment-related measures that contradicted the GATT principle of National Treatment (NT)[12] and the prohibition of quantitative restrictions.[13] Thus, despite the fact that the GATT mandate had been historically broadened to deal with areas previously exempted from international trade regulation, the extent to which the rules would impinge on the regulatory domestic policy of members was not determined in 1986.

Furthermore, Punta del Este reaffirmed by reference the provisions of Part IV and the Enabling Clause and, with respect to reciprocity, the principle that developing countries would not be required to make concessions that were inconsistent with their financial, developmental and trade needs.[14] However, the extent to which the underpinnings of the so-called special and differential treatment were compatible with the reciprocity required to satisfy the corporate drive behind the new issues, namely liberalisation of services and investments and protection and enforcement of IP rights, remained to be seen. Finally, and more importantly, all these issues were to be debated in a climate which differed from the one in which the UR had been launched. By the end of the 1980s, the US position started to shift from one of enthusiastic support for the UR to a more aggressive policy which privileged unilateral measures and bilateral agreements as the effective means for achieving market openness abroad.

[11] J Croome, *Reshaping the World Trading System: A History of the Uruguay Round* (The Hague; London, Kluwer Law International, 1999) 17.

[12] GATT Art III.

[13] GATT Art XI.

[14] See GATT, Punta del Este Ministerial Declaration (adopted 20 September, 1986) BISD 33S/19, pts I.B(iv) and I.B(v).

II THE RISE OF US PROTECTIONISM AND THE CONSOLIDATION OF THE PRESSURE TACTIC

The inclusion of the new issues had been the objective of the United States since 1982. However, by the end of the 1980s and the beginning of the 1990s, the US commitment to the multilateral trading system was weakening. The US was experiencing a growth of its Balance of Payments deficit. As Gowan points out, while a deficit existed in the 1960s and 1970s, this could be imputed to non-structural reasons, such as capital flows to Western Europe to assist with reconstruction and military expenses, especially in the context of the Vietnam War.[15] However, by the end of the 1980s there were structural reasons for the deficit of the current account in terms of both trade deficit and a rising international debt position. The trade deficit, which increased from US$138 billion in 1980 to US$170 billion in 1987 meant that the US was losing competitiveness in its productive sectors, in particular manufacturing.[16] The international debt, amounting to 70 per cent of GNP by the beginning of the 1990s meant that the US was highly dependent on foreign capital to finance its trade deficit.[17] A particular source of US concerns was Japan.[18] Not only was the US dependent on Japanese capital going into its Treasury bonds, Japan was also threatening to join forces with the new growth centres of east and southeast Asia, whose trade surplus with the United States had been constantly increasing.[19]

Despite the fact that the neo-liberal literature of the 1980s attributed the economic success of the Asian and east Asian economies to their pro-liberalisation, export-oriented attitude the reasons for their growth are more complex.[20] The SAPs of the International Monetary Fund (IMF) had managed to convert a large majority of developing countries in Latin America and Africa to the liberalisation of their tariff regimes. However, Asian countries had not borrowed from the IMF and had therefore escaped the debt trap. Furthermore, they relied on interventionist states balancing industrial policies through import substitution with promotion of export manufacturing.[21] Thus, their success was less a matter of pro-liberalisation programmes than the result of a careful balance between industrial policy and promotion of exports. Indeed, the former strategies became the target

[15] Gowan (n 5) 69.

[16] Drahos and Braithwaite (n 9) 85.

[17] Gowan (n 5) 69.

[18] Ostry, *Governments and Corporations* (n 10) 9.

[19] Gowan (n 5) 69–74.

[20] See eg B Balassa, *New Directions in the World Economy* (Basingstoke, The Macmillan Press, 1989) 95–96.

[21] S Ostry, *The Post-Cold War Trading System: Who's on First?* (Chicago, University of Chicago Press, 1997) 185.

of US policies by the end of the 1980s. As Ostry writes with regard to the US-Japanese trade relationship in this period:

> Early in 1989 the ACTPN report on US-Japan trade suggested that the United States should identify sectors where its companies are competitive but unable to gain access to the Japanese market, and negotiate 'appropriate' import levels into Japan under threat of retaliation if necessary. The ECAT [Emergency Committee for American Trade] had made a similar recommendation about Japan and urged the Bush Administration to 'vigorously' utilise the market access provisions of the 1988 Omnibus Trade Act, specifically section 301, as a further means of increasing access to the Japanese market for US producers.[22]

Thus, the new wave of protectionism in the United States was to give rise to a three-track approach to international trade that exerted a great influence on the UR negotiating process. The thrust of the approach was that the United States would participate at the multilateral level in order to promote, on the one hand, market openness in the areas of services and investments, and on the other, international protection and enforcement of IP rights. However, if no substantial market access and strengthened IP rights' protection were achieved within GATT, the United States would have pursued the bilateral route and threatened unilateral trade retaliation. As seen in chapter three, President Reagan had both promoted bilateral free-trade agreements and made use of the 1974 Act to pressure countries into accepting the new issues on the negotiating table.[23] Rather than weakening after the Punta del Este Declaration, however, this strategy was reinforced. The 1988 Omnibus Trade and Competitiveness Act gave the President the power to negotiate under fast-track authority in the UR and simultaneously conclude regional free-trade agreements. In addition, the President received congressional mandate to pursue an aggressive policy to protect US interests at home and abroad.[24] There were several methods used in order to redress the so-called unfair trade relationship with competitive countries.

First, the procedures dealing with anti-dumping were strengthened by targeting 'circumvention', namely the practice of exporting components of products to be assembled in the US in order to escape the imposition of anti-dumping duties.[25] Secondly, the threat of retaliation was used in order to set deadlines for achieving market access in the telecommunication sector.[26] Thirdly, the scope of section 301 was expanded to 'take actions to

[22] Ostry, *Governments and Corporations* (n 10) 29.
[23] See ch 3, III C.
[24] See Drahos and Braithwaite (n 9) 88–90.
[25] Preeg (n 4) 79.
[26] *Ibid*.

improve access for US companies in foreign markets'.[27] Thus, the definition of unfair trade practices abroad was expanded to include 'denial of opportunities for the establishment of an enterprise, denial of IP protection, export targeting, denial of workers' rights, and foreign government tolerance of anticompetitive activities'.[28] Furthermore, the link between section 301 and IP was strengthened. Section 301 authorised the USTR to list and, within 30 days, investigate those countries whose IP practices resulted in unfair access for US firms. The USTR began to prepare 'priority watch lists' of countries, which included Korea, Brazil, India, Mexico, China, Saudi Arabia, Taiwan and Thailand.[29] Despite the fact that between 1985 and 1994 only 11 of the original 95 actions under section 301 were initiated by the USTR, with the US imposing trade sanctions only on Brazil and China,[30] the importance of section 301 is best described by Drahos and Braithwaite in the following words:

> The aim of the 301 process was to push and prod developing countries into accepting intellectual property rules that would allow their economies to be integrated into a global knowledge economy being led by the US entrepreneurs. For this purpose it was more important to give countries the feeling that their behavior on intellectual property was the subject of constant surveillance ... Once under surveillance a country found itself drawn into an atmosphere of threat, with the possibility of a 301 action lurking in the background. Rather than risk a full-blown dispute with the USTR, countries would attempt to do something on IP to appease the USTR and avoid a really bad 301 assessment.[31]

The countries targeted under section 301 were carefully chosen. Korea, as an emerging economic power in southeast Asia, had a strategic relevance with respect to the multilateral negotiations under the UR. Brazil was particularly important in South America and threatened to join India in opposing the broadening mandate on IP. Given the fact that Korea's and Brazil's trade with the United States in 1985 amounted to 35.6 per cent[32] and 25 per cent[33] respectively, the threat of trade sanctions under section 301 weighed heavily on their export sectors. Therefore, making sure these countries changed their IP laws would not only bring them closer to the IP levels of protection sought by the US, but the US success would act as a warning for other southeast Asian and South American countries in the context of the UR. As a result of the actions initiated under section 301, Korea reached an agreement with the US on IP.[34] Following the imposition

[27] *Ibid.*
[28] *Ibid.*
[29] See Ryan (n 8) 78.
[30] Drahos and Braithwaite (n 9) 99.
[31] *Ibid* 100.
[32] *Ibid* 102.
[33] *Ibid* 105.
[34] *Ibid* 89.

of US$39 million of tariff increase on Brazilian exports, Brazil also amended its copyright law in 1987 and its patent law in 1988.[35] This sent a clear signal to other South American countries declining to protect US IP rights. The outcome was that the US 'targeted its Section 301 actions on forms of conduct that it was seeking to control through the UR, such as disrespect for US intellectual property laws and restrictions on US foreign investments'.[36]

At the multilateral level, the United States required a comprehensive change in the dual treatment that GATT had reserved for developed and developing countries. McPherson had condemned the concept of special and differential treatment, especially the principle of non-reciprocity and the use of Article XVIII for Balance of Payment reasons.[37] However, faced with the opposition by developing countries to the abandonment of their 'special and differential' status, the scope and extent of the inclusion of Part IV within the new agreements was left for the final stage of the UR, when the rules in the new areas had been defined. In the meantime, however, the United States pressed for the graduation of the new emerging markets and, in 1989, withdrew its tariff preferences from Taiwan, Hong Kong and Singapore.[38] Thus, the US three-track approach sent a plain message: if negotiations at the multilateral level did not accommodate the US concepts of market access and fair trade, which embraced both the liberalisation of services and investments and the protection of its companies' IP rights, it would deploy its arsenal of unilateral and bilateral instruments in a fully-fledged trade war. Carla Hills, the US trade representative, made this clear:

> Our strategic goal is to open markets ... we must prefer to use multilateral negotiations to achieve this end, but we will engage in bilateral and plurilateral efforts and take selective unilateral action when such action can be effective in opening foreign markets and establishing equitable and enforceable rules.[39]

At the regional level, the US talks with Canada concerning the creation of a free-trade area between the two states also gained political momentum. Another significant regional development was the creation of the European Union (EU), which intensified fears of a trading 'fortress', not only on the part of the United States, but also in Japan.[40] Japan and the southeast Asian countries became increasingly concerned with the regional economic blocs in Europe and North America and this gave them a particularly

[35] *Ibid* 104.

[36] J Braithwaite and P Drahos, *Global Business Regulation* (Cambridge, Cambridge University Press, 2000) 180.

[37] See ch 3, II D.

[38] See Drahos and Braithwaite (n 9) 89.

[39] C Hills at her Senate confirmation hearing; quoted in Preeg (n 4) 89.

[40] See Preeg (n 4) 82.

strong interest in a strengthened multilateral framework for open trade. A few years after the launch of the comprehensive round of negotiations at Punta del Este, the multilateral momentum seemed to have lost ground. Having played a fundamental role in the initiation of the new round, the United States and the European Community (EC) appeared to have reversed their trade strategy. However, the result was not the abandonment of the multilateral fora. Rather, these developments contributed to the spread of a sense of great urgency and responsibility among GATT members. Faced with the threat of a trade war that would have impacted not only countries affected by the 1980s debt crisis, but those that had avoided its trap, developing countries were subjected to enormous pressure to conclude the UR. Furthermore, under the new protectionist threats from the US and the EC, developing countries' positions on the various issues could be easily dismissed. As shown below, their scope for negotiating within the parameters of the Punta del Este Declaration was further limited.

III THE MONTREAL/GENEVA MID-TERM REVIEW: WEAKENING THE OPPOSITION TO A BROADER MANDATE

The Punta del Este Ministerial Declaration was divided into two sections. Due to the compromise between the hard-line developing countries and the United States, services would be a subject of negotiations separate from the GATT legal regime.[41] The second section included, in addition to IP and investment, the issues of long-standing importance for developing countries, namely, anti-dumping, safeguards, subsidies and countervailing duties, textiles, agriculture, tropical products and dispute settlement.[42] Negotiations would start immediately and, after a mid-term assessment in Montreal in 1988, they were supposed to be concluded in 1990. As the Montreal meeting of 1988 approached, the agricultural issue emerged as the major subject of disagreement between the United States and the Europeans. The US position was that all trade distorting measures in agriculture were to be abolished within ten years, whereas the EC was prepared to concede only short-term measures.[43]

Although the US had been responsible for the exemption of agriculture from GATT rules since the 1950s,[44] its interests had shifted in the 1980s.

[41] See Srinivasan (n 3) 32.

[42] GATT, Punta del Este Declaration (n 14).

[43] See MJ Trebilcock and R Howse, *The Regulation of International Trade* (London; New York, Routledge, 2005) 334.

[44] The US had requested and obtained in 1955 a GATT waiver to impose quantitative restrictions on agricultural goods. See JH Jackson, *The World Trading System: Law and Policy of International Economic Relations* (Cambridge, MA, The MIT Press, 1997) 58.

During the Kennedy and Tokyo Rounds, European export subsidies had concentrated on dairy products, which did not threaten US exporters. At the beginning of the 1980s, however, the EC started to heavily subsidise the export of grains, thereby directly competing with US exporters.[45] Agriculture had therefore become a US fair trade issue to be pursued during the UR. Indeed, the agricultural controversy between the US and EC was to become the major impasse in the UR.

Agricultural liberalisation had played a crucial role in developing countries' acceptance of the round. Nevertheless, their concerns would be marginalised and the discussion conducted by the two major players. The agricultural issue within the round blatantly exposed the reality of negotiations. As with the process that led to the drafting of GATT rules, negotiations were formally conducted on multilateral terms yet the fundamental decisions were made by the US and EC. Certainly the coalition of agricultural exporting countries, the so-called CAIRNS group, played a role in supporting the US demands for liberalisation.[46] However, the bargaining strength of this group owes much to the fact that agriculture liberalisation was a fundamental US objective.

The compromise language adopted in the Montreal/Geneva mid-term package called for a restraint on increasing current support and a long-term goal of providing 'substantial progressive reduction in agricultural support and protection'.[47] This language contained no precise legal obligations and the content of the commitments necessary to remove the obstacles to agricultural trade was left to future negotiations. In a similar vein, the agreement on the reduction of tariffs in non-agricultural trade provided for an overall reduction of one third. However, it did not specify how the cuts were to be made. Although many countries had argued for a given percentage across the board, the US resisted it in order to avoid significant reductions in sensitive areas such as textiles and proposed instead a request and offer approach on each item.[48] On textiles as a whole, the package merely referred to the need to provide modalities on the integration of the sector within GATT rules. In addition, no progress was made on safeguards, anti-dumping, subsidies and countervailing duties, so further work was needed in these areas.[49]

However, substantial progress was made in the areas of services and IP. The Quad members, namely the US, the EC, Japan and Canada, had resolved their differences over IP and presented a common position

[45] See Preeg (n 4) 96.
[46] See Jackson (n 44) 314.
[47] See Preeg (n 4) 92.
[48] *Ibid* 90.
[49] *Ibid* 91.

according to which negotiations would have to focus on all IP rights.[50] This meant not only counterfeit goods, but patents, copyrights, industrial designs, geographical indications and trade secrets. Despite the fact that India and Brazil were still resisting the broadening of the mandate, they could not rely on the support of other developing countries, especially Korea and the ASEAN (Association of South East Asian Nations) countries.[51] The pressure tactic was indeed working. The US tariff penalties against Brazil came two months before the mid-term review, thereby weakening Brazilian opposition to the inclusion of substantive standards on the negotiating table.[52] The India-Brazil axis, which firmly opposed the extension of the mandate beyond counterfeit goods, was vacillating. As a result, the Ministerial Declaration provided that the basic rules of GATT would apply to the negotiations in IP and that adequate standards of protection, their effective enforcement within the national legal systems and multilateral dispute settlement would pertain to areas beyond counterfeit goods.[53]

The group on services had worked throughout 1987 and 1988 on a separate track. Despite the fact that several developing countries led by Brazil complained they had been rushed into negotiating issues whose significance and impact they could not assess at such an early stage,[54] their arguments were simply dismissed. The discussion centred on the US refusal to concede the gains of liberalisation to those countries which did not undertake reciprocal commitments. As the terms of the debate were already set, the position of the developing countries with respect to the negotiations on services changed during the Montreal meeting and they started to support the inclusion of the movement of persons, using the language of comparative advantage, within the modes of supply.[55] The mid-term package provided that a multilateral framework on trade in services would come into force by the end of the UR and that it was to be informed by the principles of transparency, Most Favoured Nation (MFN), NT, market access, specific safeguards and progressive liberalisation.[56]

[50] See SK Sell, 'Multilateral Corporations as Agents of Change: The Globalisation of Intellectual Property Rights' in AC Cutler, V Haufler and T Porters (eds), *Private Authority and International Affairs* (Albany, SUNY Press, 1999) 185–86.

[51] See Croome (n 11) 114.

[52] See Drahos and Braithwaite (n 9) 135–36.

[53] *Ibid.*

[54] See Croome (n 11) 105–06.

[55] See A Oxley, *The Challenge of Free Trade* (London, Harvester Wheatsheaf, 1990) 108–09.

[56] See Preeg (n 4) 90.

IV BRUSSELS MINISTERIAL MEETING: REINTRODUCING RECIPROCITY

Despite the fact that the agricultural issue was still at an impasse, the negotiating groups continued to work in preparation for the Brussels meeting of 1990 which was supposed to conclude the UR. The consensus around the Montreal/Geneva platform was increasing due to the unilateral pressures the United States was exerting through section 301 on Brazil, India, China, Mexico, Taiwan and Thailand.[57] The Brussels meeting witnessed the final shift in the area of IP rights from the developing countries' earlier opposition to the broadening of the mandate towards the more modest aim of achieving some provisions that would take into account their developmental needs, in addition to the trade offs they aimed to obtain in agriculture, dumping, subsidies and countervailing duties and dispute settlement.

Within the negotiating group on IP, the United States, the EC, Japan and Canada presented a text which would form the basis for the comprehensive agreement on IP rights. This included all IP subject matter, standards of protection and enforcement, although there was still no consensus on the protection of life forms and the conferral of time-limited derogations to developing countries. The text drew heavily from the report issued in 1988 by the Intellectual Property Committee, entitled the *Basic Framework of GATT Provisions on Intellectual Property: Statements of Views of the European, Japanese and United States Business Communities* and drafted over the period of two years by the business community of the United States, Japan and the Europeans.[58] The response of the developing countries to the text was varied. Although some countries led by India continued to support The World Intellectual Property Organisation as the appropriate venue for discussing IP matters, Brazil, Korea and Peru were prepared to accept it, provided that rules on IP balanced the rights of IP holders with their obligations to transfer technology.[59]

A group of Latin American and African countries expanded on the Brazilian position and proposed the inclusion of interpretative rules that took into consideration the transfer and dissemination of technology and the need for states to adopt measures to protect public health and maintain sovereign control of anti-competitive practices.[60] Other proposals led to concessions in the areas of compulsory licensing[61] and a prolonged time

[57] See Ryan (n 8).

[58] See Drahos and Braithwaite (n 9) 123.

[59] See J Watal, *Intellectual Property Rights in the WTO and Developing Countries* (The Hague; London, Kluwer Law International, 2001) 28–29.

[60] *Ibid* 32. These proposals would provide the basis for Arts 7, 8 and 40 of the WTO Agreement on Trade Related Aspects of Intellectual Property Rights (TRIPs).

[61] Thus, TRIPs Art 31 would provide for the right of states to allow the use of the subject matter of a patent without the authorisation of the patent holder. This right, however, was to

for complying with the rules envisaged in the Quad proposal.[62] By 1990, the majority of developing countries had therefore abandoned their refusal to deal with the massive intrusion into their IP domestic policy and aimed instead at carving out, from the Quad proposal, a space where their right to a special treatment by virtue of their developmental needs would be recognised. The reciprocity the US had aimed for was finally taking place. The text that would require all developing countries to radically transform their domestic legal systems in order to give effective protection to foreign IP holders was therefore ready for minor amendments in order to be finally approved.

The negotiating group on services relied on the Montreal/Geneva platform to inform discussions between 1989 and 1990. An understanding already existed with regard to the basic principles that would apply to services, namely transparency, market access and NT. However, two major issues were still unresolved. First, with respect to sectoral coverage, the US was determined to obtain an agreement whose rules would apply to all service sectors, except for the ones explicitly exempted by members.[63] Secondly, with regard to the MFN principle, the US refused to accord access to its market in the absence of reciprocal commitments.[64]

Developing countries resisted both arguments, in particular with regard to the so-called top-down approach to sectoral coverage.[65] Eventually the US accepted the compromise offered by Switzerland, according to which service sectors had to be specifically committed. However, once a sector had been listed, the specific commitments of NT and MFN would apply unless otherwise stated.[66] Presenting this as a concession reluctantly made, the US made clear that no further talks would take place unless progress was made on the subject of interest to them, notably the achievement of a substantial degree of reciprocal commitments.[67] The concern expressed by Brazil and other developing countries, namely that they were not in a position to make commitments limiting their sovereign rights without assessing their full impact, was therefore silenced. In addition, even as developing countries framed their request for the inclusion of movement of

be qualified by several conditions. First, the user must have unsuccessfully attempted to obtain authorisation from the patent holder on 'reasonable commercial terms'. Secondly, the licensing needs not to be exclusive; in other words, anyone who applies must be given a licence on the same terms and conditions. Thirdly, the use of the licence must be primarily intended for the internal market and, finally, the patent holder is entitled to 'adequate remuneration'.

[62] See Croome (n 11) 216–17.
[63] See Trebilcock and Howse (n 43) 357.
[64] *Ibid* 358.
[65] See Preeg (n 4) 104–05.
[66] *Ibid.*
[67] See Croome (n 11) 214.

natural persons within the mandate in terms of comparative advantage, the response of the US was that further negotiation would not take place unless its request for meaningful liberalisation commitments was accepted.[68]

With substantial progress made in the negotiating groups on services and IP, the attention shifted towards the issues of interest to developing countries. Agriculture, textiles, safeguards, anti-dumping and strengthened GATT rules were of crucial importance for the elimination of the obstacles to developing countries' trade. At Brussels, however, the US and Europeans did not seem prepared to remove such discrimination straightforwardly. In addition to the trade offs in the new issues, developing countries were required to accept a certain degree of reciprocity as a condition for liberalisation in the sectors of export interest to them. With regard to the safeguards issue, the negotiating group started discussion on the basis that 250 'voluntary restraints' were to be disciplined within a new agreement on safeguards.[69]

Most of these measures related to the textile sector, which was protected under the Multi-fibre Agreement (MFA), and developing countries argued for their phasing out within six years.[70] As the Punta del Este Ministerial Declaration provided,

> negotiations in the area of textiles and clothing shall aim to formulate modalities that would permit the eventual integration of this sector into GATT on the basis of strengthened GATT rules and disciplines, thereby also contributing to the objective of further liberalization of trade.[71]

However, the United States opposed the six-years' proposal with a final compromise providing for ten years. Furthermore, supported by the EC, Japan and Canada, the United States argued that liberalisation in the textile sector could be achieved only if export-competitive developing countries also committed to phasing out their restrictions.[72] Thus, the liberalisation of textiles and the Safeguards Agreement were linked to the need for developing countries to accept reciprocal obligations.

The anti-dumping issue also related to the use of import restrictions that constrained the trade of developing countries. These measures had been increasing in the 1980s, and the United States and Europe accounted for the majority of the anti-dumping duties imposed.[73] The abuses were

[68] *Ibid.*

[69] See Preeg (n 4) 101.

[70] *Ibid.*

[71] GATT, Punta del Este Ministerial Declaration (n 14), pt I(D).

[72] Developing countries were also asked to accept restrictions on their ability to use Balance of Payment measures as provided in GATT Art XVIII. This was the basis of the so-called graduation requests from the developed countries. See Preeg (n 4) 102.

[73] See Trebilcock and Howse (n 43) 235.

concentrated mainly in the methods used for determining the price at which products were deemed to be dumped and the criteria for assessing injury to the domestic industry. Developing countries therefore supported an agreement which would discipline these practices in a transparent manner. However, the United States and Europe resisted the formulation of such an agreement until the issue of circumvention, that is, the practice of exporting units of products which would be assembled in the importing country in order to avoid anti-dumping duties, was adequately addressed.[74] No compromise was therefore achieved at Brussels with respect to anti-dumping rules.

As to the strengthening of the GATT rules, developing countries had insisted on a stronger multilateral framework with an effective dispute settlement system in order to put an end to the bilateral pressures and unilateral threats they were facing. However, the US insisted that the issues to be resolved prior to discussing the institutional reform of the GATT were the commitments embodied in the agreements.[75] Thus, the Canadian proposal envisaging the creation of a World Trade Organisation was to be left for the final stage of the round. What seemed certain from the US point of view was that membership of the new institutional framework would be conditional on acceptance of all UR agreements.[76] This was another dimension of the reciprocity advocated by the US and Europeans: making GATT rules 'fairer' was conditional on the successful formulation of the rules on the issues of interest to them. However, the most contentious issue remained agriculture. As happened during the Montreal meeting, negotiations on this issue were carried out exclusively between the US and the EC. The former had shifted its position from requiring a complete elimination of farm support to demanding a 75 per cent reduction of domestic support and a 90 per cent reduction of export subsidies over ten years.[77] However, the EC was prepared to concede only a 30 per cent reduction on its internal support. Furthermore, the reduction was to be based on the level of domestic support provided in 1986, which meant only 15 per cent reduction on the basis of the support given in 1990.[78] As a result of the US and EC failure to reach an agreement, the meeting was suspended.

[74] See Preeg (n 4) 102.
[75] *Ibid* 125.
[76] *Ibid*.
[77] *Ibid* 118.
[78] *Ibid*.

V FROM BRUSSELS TO MARRAKESH: CLINTON'S AGGRESSIVE APPROACH TO MARKET OPENNESS

Compared with the initial opposition from the group of the ten developing countries, substantial progress had therefore been made with regard to the issues advocated by the United States at Punta del Este. Although developing countries had interpreted the language of the declaration as covering only counterfeit goods, by the early 1990s India and Brazil had accepted a comprehensive agreement covering all IP. With regard to services, despite the unresolved issues, an agreement providing for progressive liberalisation in all service sectors was solidly in place. The reasons for the shift in the position of developing countries have already been examined: the world recession, the oil and debt crisis, the end of the Cold War, the influence of neo-liberal thinking, the aggressive US trade policy and the persistent discrimination against their trade interests were some of the factors explaining the change in direction of the developing countries.[79] Thus, one important outcome developing countries expected to achieve through the acceptance of the northern agenda was the elimination of such discrimination and the guarantee of a rule-based multilateral system. However, at Brussels, confronted with the commitment to fulfil their side of the bargain, the US and EC hesitated. The successful conclusion of the negotiations seemed to be threatened by their intransigence over the agricultural issue. In fact, the achievement of the objectives of the two powers was never threatened. The US threat of withdrawal from the multilateral stage worked exactly in its interest. Despite the extended duration of the round, in 1994 the US achieved its initial aim of bringing within the international trade system the new issues, diluting the meaning and effect of the special and differential treatment for developing countries, and providing a powerful mechanism for ensuring compliance with the agreements.

The US pressure on developing countries continued in the 1990s through the combined use of section 301 in the area of IP and demands for graduation as a quid pro quo for concluding the textiles and the safeguards agreements. In 1990, Brazil announced it would renounce the use of Article XVIII for Balance of Payments purposes, thereby accepting the US request for graduation.[80] This was followed by a series of liberalisation reforms in both Brazil and India in mid-1991 that reduced the barriers to foreign direct investment.[81] Notwithstanding the success already achieved in these areas, the newly elected Clinton Administration intensified the pressure for market access abroad. The intellectual climate in which the

79 See ch 3, III.

80 See Preeg (n 4) 134.

81 See Srinivasan (n 3) 35.

administration operated was expressed in works such as Laura Tyson's *Who's Bashing Whom?* which explicitly declared multilateral institutions as irrelevant and recommended 'aggressive unilateralism'.[82] Tyson would soon become Clinton's chairperson of his Council of Economic Advisers. The newly appointed US Trade Representative, Mickey Kantor, made clear that 'the days of the Cold War, when we sometimes looked the other way when our trading partners failed to live up to their obligations, are over. National security and our national economic security cannot be separated'.[83]

Indeed, the Clinton Administration took national economic security seriously and established a National Economic Council in the White House to operate together with the National Security Council.[84] During the period leading to the conclusion of the UR, it used both unilateral threats and bilateral and regional instruments to advance its agenda at the multilateral level. The unilateral strategy focused on the so-called Big Emerging Countries, six of which, India, China, Indonesia, Korea, Thailand and Malaysia, were east and southeast Asian countries.[85] In 1993, President Clinton made clear that the objective was

> the establishment of a new commercial strategy focusing on the overseas markets that hold the most promise for US exports and investments over the long term. [The US] selected ten economies, designated as the Big Emerging Markets (BEMs), and designed a strategy aimed at encouraging commercial cooperation with the BEMs and helping US firms seize the opportunities the markets offer.[86]

His commercial strategy was aimed directly at those economies considered to be the new productive centres of dynamic capital accumulation which directly threatened US economic interests. As Gowan writes:

> The key word was to bring about economic and political 'convergence' between the United States and the targeted states: in other words transforming the domestic economics and politics of these states to achieve a kind of Gleichschaltung between them and US capitalism … The Clinton administration openly called for a partnership with US business to break into these markets and Commerce Secretary Ron Brown directly urged US companies to seek political help from the administration on *particular contracts*. In addition the Ex-Im

[82] LD Tyson, *Who's Bashing Whom: Trade Conflicts in High-Technology Industry* (Washington DC, Institute for International Economics, 1992). In Preeg (n 4) 154.

[83] M Kantor, quoted in Gowan (n 5) 78.

[84] See HR Nau, *Trade and Security: US Policies at Cross-Purposes* (Washington DC, American Enterprise Institute, 1995) 1–15.

[85] The other four countries were Mexico, Argentina, Poland and Brazil.

[86] Letter from President Clinton in US Department of Commerce, 1995; quoted in Srinivasan (n 3) 88.

> Bank, OPIC and the Trade Development Agency were geared up for providing prior assistance to US companies seeking entry and domination in markets in the BEMs.[87]

On the regional front, Clinton fully supported the conclusion of the North American Free Trade Agreement in 1993, threatening Europe over the agricultural issue with the launch of a trade war from the North American bloc.[88] He then pressed for the Open Door Policy with east Asia bilaterally and through APEC regionally to create a community of Asia Pacific Economies.[89] Unilateral, bilateral and regional tactics were therefore deployed in the final years of the UR negotiations. Certainly, the aggressive US trade policy pointed to the fact that, had it failed to reach a comprehensive agreement, the US would have resorted to more bilateral and unilateral pressures. In fact, however, this tactic reinforced the direction in which developing countries had already embarked and contributed to their support for the successful conclusion of the round. The stage for the final years of the negotiations was therefore set.

VI THE FINAL AGREEMENT: TOWARDS AN EQUAL PLAYING FIELD?

A The New Issues …

The negotiations on IP could rely on the platform of the Brussels meeting and were concluded as early as 1991.[90] The final compromise for achieving an agreement on IP was made with the United States accepting that developing countries would be entitled to phase in their commitments within five years and least-developed countries were allowed ten years.[91] The other concession developing countries obtained in 1993 was that certain violation complaints would not be brought under the dispute

[87] Gowan (n 5) 79.

[88] *Ibid* 87.

[89] See CF Bergsten, 'APEC and World Trade' (1994) 73 *Foreign Affairs* 1.

[90] See Croome (n 11) 276.

[91] See M Matsushita, TJ Schoenbaum and PC Mavrodis, *The World Trade Organisation: Law, Practice, and Policy* (Oxford, Oxford University Press, 2003) 407. Within the WTO, there was to be no definition of developing countries. 'Members announce for themselves whether they are "developed" or "developing" countries. However, other members can challenge the decision of a member to make use of provisions available to developing countries'. www.wto.org/englih/tratop_e/devel_e/d1who_e.htm. However, the case of Viet Nam's accession to the WTO is significant: although it entered the WTO in 2007 as a 'developing country', its accession has been made conditional upon the relinquishment of several flexibilities provided for developing countries in the WTO agreements. See WTO, 'Accession of Viet Nam: Report of the Working Party' (27 October 2006) WTO Doc. WT/ACC/VNM/48, paras 286–88; 329–32. As for Least Developed Countries (LDCs), the WTO was to refer to the criteria adopted by UNCTAD which describes LDCs as a 'category of States that are deemed highly disadvantaged in their development process (many of them for geographical reasons), and facing more than other countries the risk of failing to come out

settlement system for five years.[92] In addition, developed countries committed to provide incentives for the transfer of technology to least-developed countries and technical assistance for enabling developing countries to implement the agreement.[93] The provisions on Special and Differential Treatment were therefore spelled out. Developing countries would be allowed to benefit from time-limited derogations and a commitment from developed countries to provide technical assistance and incentives to their companies to promote transfer of technology.[94]

The neo-liberal transformation of the developing countries' legal regimes in relation to IP had therefore been accomplished. Eight years after the launch of the UR at Punta del Este, the US had achieved its three initial aims. First, the Agreement on Trade Related Aspects of Intellectual Property Rights (TRIPs) would ensure that IP protection abroad was as extensive as that prevailing within the US domestic system. Thus, WTO members were required to afford protection not only to counterfeit goods, but to patents, copyrights, industrial designs, layouts, geographical indications and trade secrets. Secondly, the US managed to establish a link between the TRIPs Agreement and the WTO dispute settlement thereby ensuring the effective enforcement of IP rights abroad.[95] Finally, the extension of patent protection to micro-organisms and micro-biological processes fulfilled the third objective on the US agenda, namely the international protection and effective enforcement of biological innovations.[96]

As to the negotiations on services, the US was still refusing to accord MFN status in the telecommunications and financial sectors.[97] Due to the pressure from its industries, especially those in the financial sector, it was unwilling to concede liberalisation to countries that did not reciprocate. According to the Clinton Administration's Open Door Policy, access to these markets was crucial in order to ensure the position of its capital abroad. To accommodate the US refusal to grant unconditional MFN, a transitional period of six months was provided to allow further negotiations to take place. Had the outcome not satisfied US expectations, the

of poverty'. www.unctad.org/Templates/Page.asp?intItemID=3618&lang=1. The list adopted by UNCTAD currently comprises of 50 LDCs www.unctad.org/Templates/Page.asp?intItemID=3641&lang=1.

[92] See Croome (n 11) 275.

[93] See Watal (n 59) 32.

[94] The general commitments to the transfer of technology and technical assistance would be included in TRIPs Arts 66 and 67. Arts 7 and 8 (Objectives and Principles) would also contain a reference to the transfer and dissemination of technology. Their binding force, however, was to be assessed in the years following the conclusion of the Uruguay Round. Ch 5 will examine the legal enforceability of these provisions.

[95] TRIPs Art 64.

[96] TRIPs Art 27.3.

[97] See Croome (n 11) 271–72.

Americans would have been allowed to take a MFN exception and continue negotiations bilaterally. Negotiations were therefore carried out after the conclusion of the UR and an agreement was reached in 1997.[98] The Decision on Basic Telecommunications also provided for further negotiations aiming at the progressive liberalisation of trade in telecommunications transport networks and services with 'no basic telecommunications excluded a priori'.[99] The last controversial issue between the US and EC regarded audio visuals. Clinton had promised his Hollywood lobby he would obtain liberalisation of the European quotas on foreign films and television programmes, but the French stood firm and the issue was also postponed after the conclusion of the UR.[100] Although this discussion was carried out exclusively on US-EU terms, India supported the US position while Brazil stood by the EC.[101]

This was symptomatic of the political shift of the coalition that had previously opposed the liberalisation of services. As seen in the previous section, developing countries' approach to services soon after Punta del Este emphasised the fact they were not prepared to accept a comprehensive set of rules on services which directly touched on their domestic regulatory structures and whose impact they could not assess. However, by the end of the 1980s, this position was replaced by a more accommodating approach that relied on the doctrine of comparative advantage to argue for the inclusion of the movement of natural persons among the modes of supply to be disciplined by the final agreement. However, the history of the UR negotiations on services points to an interpretation of this shift in terms other than the so-called rational choice imputed to developing countries. The aggressive US market-access approach, the refusal of the Quad to deal with developing countries' concerns, the overall stakes the latter had in other negotiating sectors of the UR and the literature that emphasised the gains developing countries could make by liberalising their competitive service sectors contributed to this shift.[102] The neo-liberal agenda on services was therefore completed. Although countries were expected to continue to liberalise their service sectors after the conclusion of the round, the beneficial impact of such a process had ultimately been accepted. The final compromise in order to get developing countries fully on board was

[98] See Trebilcock and Howse (n 43) 380.

[99] Decision on Negotiations on Basic Telecommunications, Art 1 (15 April 1994) LT/UR/D-5/4.

[100] See Preeg (n 4) 146, 172.

[101] See JP Singh, 'Wiggle Rooms: New Issues and North–South Negotiations during the Uruguay Round', Paper prepared at the Conference on Developing Countries and the Trade Negotiation Process (Geneva, UNCTAD, 6–7 November 2003) 25 www.ruig-gian.org/ressources/dupont-Singh.pdf.

[102] See eg JN Bhagwati, 'Splintering and Disembodiment of Service and Developing Nations' (1984) 7 *The World Economy* 133; see also B Balassa 'Interest of Developing Countries in the Uruguay Round' (1988) 11 *The World Economy* 39.

made by including the movement of natural persons within the scope of services liberalisation.[103] Equally important for developing countries was the 'flexible' language of the modalities for future negotiations. First, the so-called bottom-up approach would allow countries to choose the sectors they wished to liberalise and the extent of the commitments they were prepared to make in these sectors.[104] Secondly, future negotiations aiming at the progressive liberalisation of services were to take into account 'national policy objectives and the level of development of individual members both overall and in individual sectors'.[105] The General Agreement on Trade in Services (GATS) was therefore finally packaged.

The agreement on investment did not result in the kind of liberalisation the US had envisaged when it sought its inclusion based on free access to foreign markets and NT for foreign investors. The US position was that all performance requirements, namely the conditions a state can attach to foreign entities wishing to invest in its territory, were trade distorting and therefore needed to be prohibited.[106] The Agreement on Trade Related Investment Measures (TRIMs) achieved a more modest result. It defined and prohibited those trade-related investment measures which are deemed to be inconsistent with GATT Article III (National Treatment) and GATT Article XI (Prohibition of Quantitative Restrictions).[107] Countries are therefore not allowed to impose local content, import and export restrictions, some trade balancing and foreign exchange balancing requirements as conditions for approving investments or providing advantages and incentives.[108] Developing countries and least-developed countries were provided with five years and seven years respectively to comply with the Agreement.[109] Although these provisions seem to reiterate existing GATT rules, the

> text leaves open for GATT panels to find that measures not on the list violate the GATT, and in addition the fact that no list of 'green light' or explicitly non-GATTable measures is provided means that no further protection is extended to Contracting Parties against unilateral retaliatory action by the United States on the basis of its market access approach. Indeed, additional legitimacy could well be conferred on the US approach in that The Final Act

[103] The General Agreement on Trade in Services (GATS), Art I.2(d).

[104] This was achieved through the distinction between general rules that apply to all countries (Transparency and MFN) and National Treatment and Market Access rules that apply only to countries scheduling specific commitments. The next chapter will discuss in greater detail these provisions and the extent to which they provide WTO members with such flexibility.

[105] GATS Art XIX.

[106] See Trebilcock and Howse (n 43) 455.

[107] TRIMs Art 2(1).

[108] Jackson (n 44) 317.

[109] TRIMs Art 5.

provides for a five years review of the provisions of TRIMs, possibly with a view to including new provisions on 'investment policy and competition policy' (Article 9).[110]

The scope of the TRIMs Agreement may therefore seem modest. However, as will be argued in chapter five, the fact that developing countries have signed an agreement that links trade with investment measures, provides for future negotiations and is subject to an effective dispute settlement system is of historic and political relevance. Furthermore, the success of the US market-access approach to investment has to be evaluated within the general framework provided by the GATS and the TRIPs Agreement. One particular mode of supply covered by the GATS, 'commercial presence', refers to the right of establishment of foreign investors abroad. Given the fact that at the end of the 1980s US comparative advantage was shifting from the manufacturing industry to the services sector, the extent of commitments made by states under 'commercial presence' is of crucial importance to the market access strategy adopted by the US and EU.

B ... and the Same Old Ones

With the three new issues fully negotiated, developing countries turned their attention to the trade offs they expected to make in the sectors of interest to them. The agricultural impasse between the United States and the EC threatened the outcome of the round until the very final stage in December 1993. The final deal covered export subsidies, market access for imports and domestic support. With regard to domestic support, the final text provided for a 20 per cent reduction from the 1986–88 base period,[111] with the exception of programmes that were supposed to have only minimal trade-distorting effects, the so-called green-box and blue-box subsidies.[112] As Preeg noted, 'the reduction of internal support measures will likely have limited impact on restraining surplus production in Europe and the United States since such reductions had already been undertaken to a large extent by the time the agreement was concluded'.[113] Market access for imports would be achieved through a process of 'tariffication', according to which all non-tariff measures, such as quotas, voluntary export restraints and import bans would be converted into tariffs.[114]

[110] Trebilcock and Howse (n 43) 456.

[111] The Agreement on Agriculture, Art 1. Developing countries bound their reduction to 13.3 per cent over a ten-year period and least-developed countries were exempted from reductions (Art 15.2).

[112] *Ibid* Art 6 and Annex 2.

[113] Preeg (n 4) 192.

[114] The Agreement on Agriculture, Art 4. Developed countries agreed to reduce their tariffs by 36 per cent and developing countries by 24 per cent.

This meant that for the first time agriculture would be brought back within the GATT framework. However, as Jackson wrote soon after the conclusion of the round 'some non-tariff barriers for certain products were "tariffied" to yield a tariff of 800 or even 1000 percent! It is not likely that much trade will flow with those kind of borders protection'.[115] As for export subsidies, the reduction would amount to 21 per cent by value and 36 per cent by volume over six years on the 1991–92 base-period and subsequent liberalisation would take place after the conclusion of the round 'with a view to phasing out' export subsidies. As part of the Special and Differential Treatment mandated by the Punta del Este Declaration, developing countries would be required to reduce their export subsidies on an average of 24 per cent by value and 14 per cent by volume.[116] Thus, the Agreement on Agriculture (AoA) did not achieve full liberalisation. It had been drafted between the United States and the EC and was the result of the careful balance between their competing interests.

As to the Agreement on Textiles and Clothing (ATC), the US, supported by the EC, had insisted on reciprocal liberalisation from competitive textile exporting countries, particularly the Asian economies. The compromise language that allowed the agreement to come into force provided for a commitment of textile competitive countries to 'achieve improved access'.[117] Thus, the text provided that quotas would be eliminated over a ten-year period and in four stages. However, the Agreement allowed for 49 per cent of quotas to be eliminated only at the end of the transitional period. As with the AoA, the ATC brought this previously exempted discipline within the international trade system. However, full liberalisation was postponed until the end of the ten-year period. Moreover, reductions applied only to restrictions imposed under the MFA and the bilateral agreements outside GATT. The result would be that

> in the case of many products in question, the bound MFN tariff rates remain quite high, and are in themselves unaffected by these liberalisation commitments. Tariff reductions achieved in the UR, while substantial, will nevertheless leave in place tariffs on many textile and apparel items that are much higher than the average for industrial products generally.[118]

Anti-dumping rules were supposed to end the protectionist abuses that had characterised the two previous decades. The final Agreement provided for an obligation on the investigative authorities to give a written explanation for their actions.[119] In addition, there was to be greater transparency as to what constituted 'negligible imports' (less than 3 per cent of total imports)

[115] Jackson (n 44) 315.
[116] The Agreement on Agriculture, Art 1(e).
[117] Preeg (n 4) 169.
[118] Trebilcock and Howse (n 43) 494.
[119] The Anti-dumping Agreement, Art 6.

and 'de minimis margins' (2 per cent of export prices) which required authorities to terminate their investigation.[120] However, the US managed to maintain the practice on anti-circumvention as the Agreement did not clarify its legal status.[121] The US could therefore continue to impose, without scrutiny, anti-dumping duties when the investigating authorities believed that the assembling of products from imported parts or components had occurred in order to avoid anti-dumping actions. Moreover, under the standard of review provision, the Agreement left intact the GATT practice of not allowing a challenge to the standards applied by the importing countries. Thus, the US obtained its original objective demanded by the private sector and congressional leaders to maintain the current situation despite the opposition of developing countries.[122]

The Agreement on Subsidies and Countervailing Measures disciplined three categories of subsidies. Permissible subsidies were exempted from countervailing duties (green-light subsidies),[123] actionable subsidies were to be subject to countervailing duties only if they caused adverse effects (amber subsidies)[124] and export subsidies and those made conditional on local content requirements were prohibited (red-light subsidies).[125] Thus, the US administration obtained the right to subsidise promising technology through the green-light boxes which allowed for 75 per cent of the costs of 'industrial research' and 50 per cent of 'pre-competitive development activity' to be covered.[126] On the other hand, national industry subsidies used by developing economies were prohibited or actionable.[127] With regard to the Special and Differential provisions, developing countries were given eight years to comply with the Agreement, and least-developed countries were not required to phase out prohibited subsidies.[128]

Finally, the Agreement on Safeguards provided for more transparency in the use of GATT Article XIX. Injury determination was defined more specifically.[129] Furthermore, safeguard measures could not exceed eight years and were subject to review by the Safeguards Committee. Existing voluntary restraints also had to be phased out within four years. In order

[120] *Ibid* Art 5.8.

[121] See Preeg (n 4) 170.

[122] *Ibid.*

[123] The Agreement on Subsidies and Countervailing Duties, Art 10.

[124] *Ibid* art. 8.

[125] *Ibid* Art 3.

[126] Government assistance for regional development would be exempted from countervailing duties, provided it did not target a specific industry. In addition, assistance for meeting environmental targets was allowed as long as it did not cover more than 20 per cent of the costs encountered by an industry adapting to new requirements and could be made only once. However, these subsidies were to become actionable in 2000.

[127] See UNDP, *Making Global Rules Work for People* (New York, Earthscan Publications Ltd, 2003) 195–200.

[128] The Agreement on Subsidies and Countervailing Duties, Art 27.4.

[129] The Agreement on Safeguards, Art 4.

to achieve greater transparency in the application of safeguard measures and control by the Safeguards Committee, developing countries compromised on the issue of selectivity they had pursued since the Tokyo Round. Although the Agreement provided that safeguard measures would be applied to a product imported irrespective of its source,[130] it then allowed members to depart from the MFN approach in specific cases after consulting the Safeguards Committee.[131] The selectivity issue was therefore not definitively resolved with the UR. With the rules fully in place, the US was ready to support the creation of the World Trade Organisation.[132] The WTO would be endowed with an effective dispute settlement system for ensuring compliance with the WTO agreements.

CONCLUSIONS

After eight years of long and difficult negotiations, the World Trade Organisation came into existence. One hundred and twenty-eight countries accepted the Final Act establishing the WTO and its agreements. In the words of Peter Sutherland, who had acted as Director General of GATT in the final stage of the negotiations:

> On 15 December 1993 the world changed. Maybe not as dramatically as the moment when the Berlin Wall fell, but then unlike that very demolition job, the success of the Uruguay Round was a work of *construction* ... It will be seen as a defining moment in modern history. Put simply, governments came to the conclusion that the notion of a *new world order* was not merely attractive but absolutely vital; that the *reality of the global market* ... required a level of *multilateral cooperation never attempted before*[133] (emphasis added).

The successful conclusion of the Uruguay Round was therefore presented as the triumph of reason on both the developed and developing countries' part. Both had accepted the inevitability of a 'new world order' shaped by the 'reality of the global market'. The United States and the Europeans had resisted mounting protectionist pressures, whereas the developing countries had abandoned their initial opposition to the expansive scope of the international trade regime and recognised they could gain from the comparative advantage they had in the new sectors.

[130] *Ibid* Art 2.

[131] *Ibid* Art 5.

[132] The other important agreements which formed an integral part of the Final Act establishing the WTO cover sanitary and phyto-sanitary measures, technical barriers to trade, government procurement, rules of origin, import licensing procedures, customs valuation and pre-shipment inspection.

[133] P Sutherland, 'Global Trade: The Next Challenge' in GATT, *News of the Uruguay Round*, (NUR082) (Geneva, 28 January 1994).

Without doubt, the deficit of the US current account generated a protectionist impetus to pursue market openness abroad by means of unilateral and bilateral actions. The latter, however, were not independent of the multilateral agenda advanced at Punta del Este. They were instrumental to the US's primary objective, that of creating a trade-service-investment driven market integration at the multilateral level.[134] As a consequence of this concerted strategy, their respective economic positions and the increasing influence of neo-liberal literature, developing countries started to support a multilateral rule-based system. However, rather than being the outcome of a logical and inevitable historical process, the neo-liberal revolution of the international trade regime was a political construction of the Quad led by the United States.

[134] See ch 3, II.

5

The World Trade Organisation: The Power of Transnational Capital and the Reduction of Domestic Regulatory Space

THE BRETTON WOODS Conference had shaped the international economic regime along the lines of the capitalist requirements of the United States and the United Kingdom. Trade in goods was one of its fundamental pillars as it provided them with access to the ex-colonies' markets, where they could extract the economic resources necessary for production at home and place the consequent output.[1] The development framework of the postwar period supported this enterprise by positing capital accumulation, rapid economic growth and industrialisation as the desirable ends of development to be achieved through the help and expertise of the advanced members of the international community and the international economic institutions.[2] The GATT participated in the imperial enterprise of the postwar period in two important respects. First, it posited liberal trade as a crucial means of development and consequently required the ex-colonies to develop their trade in goods 'as rapidly as that of the industrialised nations'.[3] Secondly, contrary to its free trade and development rhetoric, it actively hindered the trade of developing countries by promoting selective liberalisation.

The crisis of the 1970s, however, challenged the economic rationality of the postwar period. The experiments within and across the three industrial poles with trade-service-investment driven market integration pointed to the gains northern capital could derive from extending this model at the

[1] See ch 1, II and ch 2, I.

[2] The role of states in promoting these objectives, however, remained crucial in both the developing and the developed countries.

[3] This, it has been argued, is the development norm that the GATT established with the Haberler Report in the 1950s. See ch 2, II A–B.

international level. Neo-liberal development thinking provided the theoretical premise for this shift by positing the need for a less active role of the state and a more vigorous reliance on market forces. The international trading regime embodied in the World Trade Organisation (WTO) reflected this new paradigm. Its competence could no longer be limited to trade in goods but needed to be extended to previously exempted areas of international regulation, namely services, investment and intellectual property (IP) rights. Contrary to the view according to which the neo-liberal transformation of the international trading regime is the outcome of an inevitable historical process, this shift was the result of the political and economic strategy of the capitalist powers, in particular the US and EC.

The reformulation of the development norm, however, remained central to the success of this concerted strategy. Predicated on a different failure on the developing countries' part, the neo-liberal development norm the WTO embodied required the abandonment of ideas concerning the structural inequalities of the international trading regime that had underlined the GATT practices of non-reciprocity and Special and Differential Treatment (SDT). As examined in chapter three, legal and economic arguments against the GATT's so-called flexible approach to development contributed to reinforcing the view that the interests of developing countries would be best served by a multilateral rules-based system founded on reciprocal and binding obligations for all members. Emphasising the gains developing countries could expect to make by specialising on the export sectors in which they had comparative advantage, the economic arguments repudiated import substitution policies and pointed to the beneficial role of trade liberalisation.[4] By stressing the ineffectiveness of unilateral commitments by developed countries within GATT, the legal arguments discarded non-reciprocity and differential treatment in favour of legally binding obligations under a multilateral rules-based system.[5]

This chapter therefore addresses the neo-liberal development rationale embodied in the WTO agreements. In particular, it assesses whether the shift from the GATT to the WTO has entailed the outcomes that the arguments in support of reciprocal liberalisation have posited. The first part asks whether, by accepting the WTO agreements, developing countries have managed to put an end to the developed countries' practice of discrimination against their trade. This entails an examination of the

[4] See eg M Matsushita, TJ Schoenbaum, PC Mavrodis, *The World Trade Organisation: Law, Practice, and Policy* (Oxford, Oxford University Press, 2003) 378–81. See also, C Michalopoulos, *Developing Countries in the WTO* (Basingstoke, Palgrave, 2001) 30–32.

[5] See BM Hoekman and MM Kostecki, *The Political Economy of the World Trading System: From GATT to WTO* (Oxford, Oxford University Press, 1995) 239–40; TN Srinivasan, 'Trade and Development: Developing Countries in the World Trading System, 1947–1999' (Yale University, Department of Economics, 1999) 5–8 www2.cid.harvard.edu/cidtrade/Issues/srinivastad.pdf.

effects of the anti-dumping and safeguards agreements, which purported to introduce legal clarity in these areas, and the agreements on agriculture and textiles which are supposed to liberate the comparative advantage of developing countries. The aim is to ascertain the extent to which WTO legal norms and practice regarding developing countries' competitive exports differ from the GATT's.

The second part focuses on the effects of the WTO legal disciplines on investment, services, and IP rights that developing countries have accepted as a compromise for the former agreements. In particular, it analyses the qualitative shift from the GATT to the WTO with respect to the regulatory autonomy of its members. The objective is to compare the gains developing countries have made in the areas of interest to them with those that Multinational Enterprises (MNEs) can be expected to derive from the extension of WTO legal competence into the new areas. This will serve to contextualise the claim, developed further in chapter six, that the WTO's legal edifice and its development approach represent the successful attempt of the major capitalist powers to reorganise the post-1970s world economic system in the interest of their transnational capital.

I ASSESSING THE 'TRADE OFF': THE MARKET ACCESS ISSUES

Since the GATT's Haberler Report of 1955, developing countries have complained about the discriminatory practice of developed countries against their trade. In particular, they have emphasised the obstacles to their agricultural and textile exports posed by high tariffs, quantitative restrictions and export subsidies. In addition, they have pointed to the increasing tariff escalation in non-agricultural goods and the abuse of anti-dumping by developed countries.[6] The Uruguay Round (UR) agreements were therefore supposed to redress the long-outstanding imbalances that had characterised much of GATT practice. An assessment of the post-UR achievements in these areas is therefore necessary in order to ascertain whether the WTO legal norms have resulted in the elimination of the historical obstacles to developing countries' trade. Reasoning from within the neo-liberal development framework, liberalisation of agriculture and textiles and the regulation of dumping, countervailing duties and safeguard measures are crucial to developing countries' success in the multilateral trading system. This is especially the case since, as a result of the neo-liberal policies of the 1980s, their domestic economies have become increasingly dependent on the export sectors.[7]

[6] See ch 3, III B.

[7] See ch 3, III A.

A Agriculture

Agriculture is the sector in which developing countries were expected to make the greatest gains due to their comparative advantage. As seen in chapter four, the WTO Agreement on Agriculture did not achieve substantial liberalisation. Due to the US-EU compromise, domestic support and export subsidies were reduced but not eliminated and non-tariff barriers were converted into tariffs but not immediately removed.[8] The Agreement was based on the understanding that liberalisation would have gone further after the conclusion of the round. However, the progress made since with respect to the reduction of subsidies has been very modest. As Stiglitz and Charlton aptly note:

> [T]he overall level of OECD farm protection was not noticeably reduced. In 1986–8 farm subsidies were equivalent to 51 per cent of all OECD farm production, and fourteen years later, after the implementation of the Uruguay Round commitments, at more than US$300 billion, they still accounted for 48 per cent of all farm production.[9]

The process of 'tariffication', according to which non-tariff measures had to be converted into tariffs in order to be subsequently reduced, has not produced tangible results either. Indeed, developed countries converted their non-tariff measures into very high tariffs.[10] Furthermore, given the fact that they had committed to reduce their tariffs by an average of 36 per cent by 2000, the overall level of bound tariffs after the reduction is higher than that existing in the pre-UR phase.[11] Another important issue is the so-called tariff escalation, notably the sustained practice through which the developed countries have increased their tariff rates on products from the developing countries according to their stage of processing. As previously seen, the Haberler Report had, as early as the 1950s, denounced this discriminatory practice and pointed to the fact that, contrary to the spirit of the GATT, developed countries were hindering the industrialisation process of developing countries. This situation has not been remedied post-UR. Rather, recent studies point to a substantial increase in tariffs.[12]

[8] See ch 4, VI B.

[9] JE Stiglitz and A Charlton, *Fair Trade For All: How Trade Can Promote Development* (Oxford, Oxford University Press, 2005) 50.

[10] For instance, the US bound its tariffs on sugar at 244 per cent and on peanuts at 174 per cent; the EU bound its tariffs at 213 per cent on beef and 168 per cent on wheat; Japan applies a 353 per cent tariff on wheat and Canada a 360 per cent tariff on butter and a 236 per cent tariff on eggs. See M Khor, 'Globalisation and the South: Some Critical Issues' (UNCTAD Working Paper No 147, 2000) 17 www.unctad.org/en/docs/dp_147.en.pdf.

[11] TW Hertel and W Martin, 'Liberalising Agriculture and Manufactures in a Millennium Round: Implications for Developing Countries' (2000) 23 *The World Economy* 455, 457.

[12] For instance, the EU has raised its tariff from 15 per cent at the first stage of processing to 24 per cent at the complete stage of processing in food manufacturing; Canada from 3 per

B Textiles and Clothing

The Agreement on Textiles and Clothing (ATC) was also supposed to redress the past imbalances in the sector. Industrialised countries had specifically targeted the exports of developing countries through the Multi-Fibre Agreement (MFA), which permitted exporters of textiles and apparel to negotiate bilateral quotas with the importer on each item listed in the Agreement.[13] Thus, the major achievement of the UR was the elimination of the so-called 'voluntary export restraints' and their conversion into tariffs. The ATC, however, back-loaded these commitments until the end of the ten-year phase-out period. As a consequence, developed countries were allowed to maintain as much as 49 per cent of the value of imports under quotas until the end of 2004. In addition, although the developed countries have satisfied the quantitative requirements of tariff conversion included in the ten-year plan, they have chosen to liberalise products included in the list but previously not restricted through quotas, thereby diminishing the actual liberalisation benefits expected in the first three phases of the plan.[14]

Moreover, even after the phase-out period, tariff barriers were expected to remain high, approximately in the range of 15–35 per cent.[15] Thus, not only was the complete removal of quotas postponed until the end of 2004, the actual liberalisation benefits expected after the completion of the phase-out period were to be measured against the subsequent increase in tariff rates.[16] Thus, as Stiglitz and Charlton note, the actual market access for developing countries has not confirmed the estimates that the OECD, World Bank and GATT Secretariat published soon after the conclusion of the UR, where it was held that a substantial share of welfare gains would accrue to developing countries.[17] For instance, despite the fact that many of the tariff rates applied by developed countries amount to 5 per cent on average, Hoekman writes that

cent to 42 per cent and Japan from 36 per cent to 65 per cent. See N McCulloch, LA Winters and X Cirera, *Trade Liberalisation and Poverty: A Handbook* (London, Centre for Economic Policy Research, 2001) 178.

[13] For an analysis of the impact of the MFA on the trade of developing countries, see KO Kufuor, *World Trade Governance and Developing Countries: The GATT/WTO Code Committee System* (London, Blackwell Publishing, 2004) 20–24.

[14] See Khor (n 10).

[15] See MJ Trebilcock and R Howse, *The Regulation of International Trade* (London; New York, Routledge, 2005) 183.

[16] For instance, 'in 2001 clothes and shoes accounted for only 6.5 percent of US imports in value terms but they brought in nearly half of the US$20 bn of US tariff revenue. More tariff revenue was collected by the US government on the import of shoes than on the import of automobiles, even though the value of shoe imports is around one tenth of the value of automobiles'. Stiglitz and Charlton (n 9) 125.

[17] Stiglitz and Charlton (n 9) 46 fn7, 125. The authors point out that one OECD study estimated the gains for DCs at US$90 bn, or one third of the total gains from the UR.

tariffs for some commodities are over 100 per cent. Such tariff peaks rates above 15 per cent are often concentrated in products that are of interest to developing countries. In 1999, in the US alone, imports originating in least developed countries (LDCs) generated tariff revenue of $487 million, equal to 11.6 per cent of the value of their exports to the US, and 15.7 per cent of dutiable imports.[18]

Hertel and Martin have made a similar assessment in the context of non-agricultural trade, where the average tariff rate applied by developed countries to the manufactured exports from developing countries amounts to 3.4 per cent compared with only 0.8 per cent of the tariff rate applied to other developed countries' exports of manufacturing.[19] In addition, in order to qualify the degree of market openness that developing countries have obtained as a result of the UR, one has to assess the level of non-tariff barriers that constrain their trade, notably anti-dumping and safeguard measures. Rather than diminishing as a result of the agreements introduced to discipline their use, these actions have increased since the conclusion of the UR.

C Safeguards and Anti-Dumping

Since safeguards measures are in principle non-discriminatory, can be applied only temporarily and provide for the right of exporters to be compensated, the favourite trade remedy has become anti-dumping, which, in contrast, allows discrimination against specific exporters and provides for a longer period of application. Between 1999 and 2000, more than 1000 dumping cases were initiated. Indeed, developing countries have increasingly made use of anti-dumping actions.[20] However, the US and the EU remain the largest initiators, accounting for 490 of them.[21] Although the anti-dumping agreement has introduced greater transparency with regard to what constitutes dumping, the fact that the US managed to retain its standards of review has provided the domestic authorities with a considerable degree of flexibility during the investigation phase. As a result,

> the accused must respond in a short period of time to a long demand for information (in English), and when the accused is unable to do so, the US government acts on the basis of "best information available" (BIA), usually the information which has been provided by the American Company trying to keep

[18] B Hoekman, 'Strengthening the Global Trade Architecture for Development: The Post Doha Agenda' (2002) 1 *World Trade Review* 23, 25.

[19] Hertel and Martin (n 11).

[20] See JM Finger, F Ng and S Wangchuk, *Antidumping as Safeguard Policy* (Washington DC, World Bank, 2001) econ.worldbank.org/files/3172_wps2730.pdf.

[21] TN Srinivasan, 'Developing Countries and the Multilateral Trading System after Doha' (Economic Growth Centre, Discussion Paper No 842, 2002) www.econ.yale.edu/~egcenter/.

> out its rivals. High initial duties are imposed, which regularly get revised downward when better information becomes available. But meanwhile, long-term damage has been done.[22]

Thus, the nature of anti-dumping practice has not substantially changed since the conclusion of the UR.[23] Although anti-dumping has become the principal trade remedy used by the developed countries, safeguard measures are also on the increase.[24] Hence, the UR has brought back within the international trading system the areas of interest to developing countries. After more than 40 years, the WTO agreements on agriculture, textiles and clothing, safeguards and anti-dumping were supposed to end the discrimination against developing countries' trade. However, the practice following the conclusion of the UR seems to contradict the spirit of the said agreements. The complete elimination of textile quotas had to wait another decade, and there were no substantial commitments for the reduction of the high tariff rates. In agriculture 'there is no obligation past what is reflected in existing schedule'.[25] The increasing misuse of anti-dumping and safeguard measures also belies the commitments of the developed countries to put an end to the discrimination against the trade of developing countries. Thus, the market access so forcefully pursued by the US and the Europeans since Punta del Este with respect to the so-called new issues has not materialised as far as developing countries' comparative advantage is concerned. Despite the fact that the provisions of the agreements signal a shift from the GATT legal regime, the practice of WTO developed members does not seem to differ substantially from that under the GATT.

D Implementation Costs

As soon as developing countries started to comply with the WTO agreements, the implementation costs involved became apparent. The Single Undertaking Approach (SUA) required developing countries to implement all the agreements which were part of the Final Act.[26] The Agreement on Customs Valuation, the Agreement on the Application of Sanitary and Phytosanitary Measures and the Agreement on Technical Barriers to Trade are three instances of WTO agreements whose implementation costs have

[22] Stiglitz and Charlton (n 9) 127.

[23] See Finger, Ng and Wangchuk (n 20).

[24] See Stiglitz and Charlton (n 9) 128.

[25] JM Finger, 'The Grand Bargain: Will the WTO get over it?' in DLM Kennedy and JD Southwick (eds), *The Political Economy of International Trade Law: Essays in Honour of Robert Hudec* (Cambridge, Cambridge University Press, 2002) 302.

[26] Excluding the plurilateral agreements on civil aircraft, government procurement, dairy and bovine meat which did not form part of the Single Undertaking Approach.

begun to be assessed. The Agreement on Customs Valuation provides for methods national authorities need to follow in order to determine the transaction value of the shipment in question. As Finger and Schuler note, the 'agreement on customs valuation is one that complements the practice of developed countries'.[27] This means that while developed countries' regimes are predominantly in accordance with the norms of the agreement, developing countries need to undergo intensive restructuring of their customs regimes in order to comply with the same requirements. The authors note that implementing the agreement involves both physical and administrative dimensions with costs totalling US$ 10 million per country.[28]

The Agreement on the Application of Sanitary and Phytosanitary Measures (SPS) and the Agreement on Technical Barriers to Trade encourage countries to abide by various procedures, methods and standards laid down in international conventions in order to apply sanitary, phytosanitary and technical measures at their borders.[29] Since the international conventions the agreements refer to were drafted by developed countries, these provisions place a larger compliance onus on developing countries wishing to apply these measures on imports. Also, exporters from developing countries are required to meet the high standards of developed countries' measures if they wish to gain access to northern markets. Although Finger and Schuler focus only on the SPS Agreement, they estimate that the costs necessary to meet its requirements in the surveyed developing countries ranged from US$ 3.3 million in Turkey to US$ 108 million in Brazil.[30] If the costs to comply with the Agreement on Trade Related Aspects of Intellectual Property Rights (TRIPs) are also taken into account, the authors conclude that

> the figures for just three of the six Uruguay Round agreements that involve restructuring of domestic regulations come to $150 million. One hundred and fifty million dollars is more than the annual development budget for eight of the twelve least developed countries for which we could find a figure for that part of the budget.[31]

[27] JM Finger and P Schuler, 'Implementation of Uruguay Round Commitments: The Development Challenge' (2000) 23 *The World Economy* 511, 514.

[28] *Ibid* 515.

[29] As to the SPS Agreement, countries can rely on standards other than those conforming to the international conventions. However, they have to comply with the provisions of the agreement, and, in case of measures imposing more stringent standards than those provided for by the conventions, they need to undergo a risk assessment process. For a discussion of the complexities involved in complying with the agreement, see F Macmillan, *The WTO and the Environment* (London, Sweet and Maxwell, 2001) 148–53.

[30] Finger and Schuler (n 27) 519.

[31] *Ibid* 525.

II LIBERALISATION RHETORIC AND PRACTICE: OPENING MARKETS, PROTECTING CAPITAL

Hence, the discrimination against developing countries' most competitive exports has not been eliminated, despite the increased discipline introduced by the UR agreements. Immediately after the conclusion of the UR, it became apparent that developed countries were not living up to their commitments. It is worth emphasising that these commitments underlie the theoretical case for liberalisation which developed countries have argued for since Punta del Este. Thus, taking the neo-liberal framework of the WTO at its face value, namely accepting that liberalisation based on international specialisation and comparative advantage leads to greater export earnings, economic growth and ultimately development, the practice of the WTO's developed members violates the very spirit of these agreements. In addition, while the liberalisation gains for developing countries are far from being realised, they are expected to fulfil the obligations under the WTO agreements and bear the costs of implementation.

If the issue of developing countries' market access can be assessed in light of its long history within the international trading system, the impact of the novel agreements on services, investment and IP is much more difficult to evaluate. The legal provisions of the agreements emphasise the beneficial role of liberalisation in services and investments on the one hand, and the benefits deriving from the enhanced protection of IP on the other. However, they do not mandate indiscriminate liberalisation and unlimited protection of IP rights. Rather, the provisions seem to aim at balancing these objectives with the regulatory autonomy members need in order to pursue domestic policy objectives. Notwithstanding the letter of the agreements, it will be shown that the most important aspect of their combined effects has been the reduction of domestic regulatory powers and policy space of WTO members and a corresponding intensification of the power of transnational capital.

In order to demonstrate that these agreements are capable of conferring unprecedented rights on transnational corporations, it is necessary to put the extension of investors' rights that the WTO provisions entail in a historical context. Whereas the remainder of this chapter is concerned with the legal analysis of the provisions of the agreements, chapter six will substantiate the claim that the WTO aims to promote the unhindered movement of capital by examining the practices that the developed members, especially, the US and EU, have followed since the conclusion of the UR. These two aspects of the WTO architecture, however, deserve equal attention since it is the legal framework of the agreements that provides the premise for the developed countries' negotiating practice.

A Investors' Rights in Historical Context

The rights of investors vis-à-vis the right of states to regulate the economic activity in their territories became a prominent international issue once the ex-colonies achieved independence. Indeed, as soon as the newly independent states claimed their sovereign rights to control the economic activities of foreign investors within their territories, a new branch of international law, the so-called international law on foreign investments, emerged to respond to the ex-colonies' claims. As Sornarajah points out, prior to decolonisation, there was no need for an international law on foreign investments since the protection of investors' assets and operations was secured through the incorporation of the colony's regime within the legal order of the colonial power.[32] Political and economic sovereignty, however, involved the right of the ex-colonies to expropriate foreign property, exclude the foreign investors from their territory and impose conditions on the investments accepted.

As seen in chapter one, the first controversy concerning the international protection of foreign investments dates back to the Havana Charter of the 1940s. During the negotiations which were supposed to give birth to the third leg of the Bretton Woods system,[33] the so-called less developed countries opposed the United States' proposal for granting National Treatment (NT) and Most Favoured Nation (MFN) to foreign investors. The disagreement also concerned expropriation, with the United States requiring legal commitments from capital-importing countries not to expropriate or, in the event of expropriation, to pay full compensation.[34]

Due to the opposition of the so-called less developed countries, the final text of the investment chapter recognised the international legality of expropriation. Concurrently, it required capital-importing countries to grant 'adequate security' to existing and future investments.[35] As Brown points out, 'adequate security' included the fact that expropriation had to occur on 'just' terms. Although no definition of the term 'just' was agreed, the inclusion meant that the United States could resort to the so-called nullification and impairment procedure under trade rules in case of unjust

[32] M Sornarajah, *The International Law on Foreign Investments* (Cambridge, Cambridge University Press, 1994) 8–12.

[33] The other two components of the postwar international regime were the International Monetary Fund (IMF) and the IBRD (now the World Bank).

[34] See WA Brown, *The United States and the Restoration of World Trade* (Washington DC, Brookings Institution Press, 1950) 99–102.

[35] United Nations Conference on Trade and Employment, 'Havana Charter for an International Trade Organization, Final Act and Related Documents '(New York, Lake Success, April 1948) Art 12.

expropriation.[36] However, the Charter also provided for the right of each state to 'determine whether and to what extent and upon what terms it will allow future foreign investments'.[37] This provision meant that states were not under an obligation to grant NT and MFN as the US proposal had envisaged. This, as Dattu notes,

> sparked opposition to the Havana Charter from the very US-based multinational enterprises that had initially spearheaded the initiative to include investment provisions in an international economic agreement … It was partly as a result of this disagreement that the Havana Charter was eventually abandoned.[38]

As soon as the rest of the colonies acquired independence, the struggle between developed and developing countries over the protection of foreign investments intensified.[39] There were conflicting views as to what the so-called international law on foreign investments would entail. Since there was no multilateral treaty on investments that could be considered *lex generalis* capable of universal application, the controversy focused on customary law. The developed countries relied on the customary principle of 'state responsibility for injuries to aliens' to extend the protection each state owed to foreign nationals to investors as well.[40] According to Sornarajah, the 'developed states have maintained that aliens must be treated according to an international minimum standard, which could be a higher standard than that accorded by a host state to its own nationals'.[41] Newly independent countries, on the other hand, rejected this principle, asserting their right to apply national laws to foreign investors' activities and, in addition, to discriminate in favour of domestic investors.[42]

The objective of the developed countries was therefore to elevate the treatment of foreign investors above that provided for by the national legal regimes of the host states with respect to their own nationals. Since no consensus existed as to the scope and content of customary international

[36] Brown (n 34) 153. The 'nullification and impairment' procedure authorised countries to suspend their trade concessions, scheduled during negotiations, in relation to countries that had not fulfilled their obligations under the GATT.

[37] United Nations Conference on Trade and Employment, 'Havana Charter' (n 35) Art 12.

[38] R Dattu, 'A Journal from Havana to Paris: The Fifty-years Quest for the Elusive Multilateral Agreement on Investments' (2000–01) 24 *FORDHAM International Law Journal* 275, 288.

[39] Expropriation was eventually accepted as a legitimate practice, provided it was meant to pursue a public purpose, did not discriminate on racial grounds and entailed due process. However, the issue of compensation continues to be the subject of conflict between developed and developing countries as to whether it entails 'prompt, immediate and effective' compensation, as argued by the US, or 'adequate' compensation, as argued by the developing countries. See Dattu, *ibid* 281.

[40] See Sornarajah (n 32) 122–23.

[41] *Ibid.*

[42] See G Roy, 'Is the Law of State Responsibility Part of Customary International Law?' (1959) 55 *American Journal of International Law* 552.

law, other mechanisms were employed in order to further this objective, most of which derived from the activity of international commercial arbitrators. For instance, the so-called theory of internationalisation of state contracts, which goes back to the first arbitral awards of the 1950s, aimed to remove the contract between the host state and the foreign investor from the ambit of the host state's national law and subject it to international law.[43] In other words, the state contract would be considered akin to an international treaty and not subject to the domestic legal system of the host state.

In a similar vein, commercial arbitrators have argued that state contracts are subject to a system of rules known as *lex mercatoria*. As Sornarajah writes, 'the claim is that as a result of the accumulation of arbitral awards and the consistency with which arbitrators have adopted certain doctrines, a system of law applicable to transnational business disputes has now been created'.[44] Furthermore, according to the so-called theory of economic development agreements, contracts between developing countries and foreign investors would be considered akin to international treaties, and therefore outside the domestic legal regime of the host state. The underlying reason was that the activity of the foreign investor contributed to the economic development of the host state, thereby deserving international protection.[45] Thus, although capital exporting countries did not participate in the formulation of these doctrines directly, they nonetheless supported them. As Sornarajah observes, this

> may evidence a rare instance of an attempt of private power being used to create public international law. The sources which were used to create the rules of protection were the teachings of highly qualified publicists and arbitral awards. They were weak sources which could be utilised by private power; the capital-importing states, against whose interests the system was created, did not have recourse to any means countering the creation of these laws.[46]

[43] See AFM Maniruzzaman, International Development Law As Applicable Law to Economic Development Agreements: A Prognostic View' (2001) 20 *Wisconsin International Law Journal* 1; see also, AW Mewett, 'The Theory of Government Contracts' (1959) 5 *McGill Law* Journal 222. For a critique of early arbitral awards adopting the theory, see A Anghie, *Imperialism, Sovereignty and the Making of International Law* (Cambridge, Cambridge University Press, 2005) 223–45.

[44] Sornarajah (n 32) 354.

[45] It is worth emphasising that the theory applied to developing countries only: a contract between a developed country and a foreign investor would remain subject to the domestic legal system of the host state. For an early exposition of the theory, see JN Hyde, 'Economic Development Agreements' (1962) 105 *Hague Recueil* 271.

[46] Sornarajah (n 32) 324–25.

B The Changing Investment Climate of the 1980s and 1990s: Securing Protection Abroad

Despite the fact that the theories formulated by commercial arbitrators and publicists were used in several arbitral awards,[47] developing countries rejected the view that the principles they embodied constituted customary international law. Hence, with no multilateral binding treaty or definite customary international law on the protection of foreign investments, between the 1960s and 1970s developing countries enjoyed a considerable degree of autonomy in accepting and disciplining foreign investments within their territory. Host states could therefore establish screening procedures to evaluate the beneficial impact of a given investment on the basis of which they would decide whether to allow the foreign economic activity within their territory. States could also impose conditions on the operations of the foreign investors. The so-called performance requirements included the obligation of the foreign investor to employ local workers, purchase local imports, establish joint ventures with a local enterprise, transfer technology, bring a certain percentage of capital from abroad and export a certain amount of output.[48] Thus, screening procedures and performance requirements were the means through which many developed and developing countries used foreign investments as a means of industrial policy.

During the 1980s, however, the international environment became more favourable to the unrestricted flows of foreign investments. As seen in chapter three, the gains for northern transnational corporations deriving from vertical integration were considerable. Furthermore, as a consequence of the debt crisis and the Structural Adjustment Policies, developing countries started to rely more heavily on foreign investments. As Khor points out, during the 1980s and 1990s, developing countries liberalised their foreign investment policies in order to attract Foreign Direct Investments (FDI),[49] even though much of the flows targeted only a few developing countries and least-developed countries in particular have received a very small proportion despite having liberalised their policies.[50] The liberalisation impetus concerned not only FDI, but extended to portfolio investments as well.[51] As Picciotto writes:

[47] *Ibid* 42, fn 39.

[48] *Ibid* 100–14.

[49] Foreign Direct Investments (FDI) refers to the activity of economic entities that involve the transfer of capital to the host state for the purpose of carrying out an economic activity under the total or partial control of the foreign investor.

[50] See Khor (n 10) 4.

[51] Portfolio Investments, as opposed to FDI, do not require the direct involvement (through management or control) of the investor in the economic activity carried out in the host state.

> Foreign portfolio capital flows to developing countries (commercial bank lending, debt issue, and portfolio equity investment) have been estimated at $6–8bn p.a. in 1982–9, but jumped to over $32bn in 1992, and nearly $80bn in 1993, exceeding FDI and official lending, and far larger than the peak of commercial bank lending in 1982.[52]

Two consequences followed from the new investment climate. First, the number of Bilateral Investment Treaties (BITs) increased exponentially.[53] A bilateral investment treaty, contrary to state contracts, is an international agreement with legally binding obligations on the parties to the treaty.[54] Despite their differences, BITs usually define the type of investments covered by the agreement, the standard of treatment that each party affords to the foreign investor of the other party and the rules applicable in the event of expropriation or any other dispute concerning the agreement.[55] Thus, as Sornarajah observes, due to the uncertainty that existed as to the content and scope of the 'international law on foreign investment', bilateral investment treaties became the best way for capital-exporting countries to secure high levels of protection for their foreign investors.[56] However, as BITs remained *lex specialis* between the parties to the agreement, the developed countries did not abandon the objective of achieving a multilateral code on investments.

Secondly, and consequently, the US and EC tried to obtain a multilateral agreement on investment within the UR negotiations. Developing countries, however, were well prepared to counteract the free market access approach to foreign investments the US had launched.[57] In light of historical experience, they were aware of the consequences of accepting NT and MFN as part of a comprehensive multilateral agreement on investments. The capital-exporting countries therefore reverted to the OECD, whose 'membership consisted of "like-minded countries" to negotiate the Multilateral Agreement on Investments (MAI)'.[58] The far-reaching provisions of the draft agreement are worth mentioning as they show the implications of the US free market access approach for the domestic

[52] S Picciotto, 'Linkages in International Investment Regulation: The Antinomies of the Draft Multilateral Agreement on Investments' (1998) 19 *University of Pennsylvania Journal of International Economic Law* 731, 746.

[53] More than 2000 BITs had been signed by the year 2000, most of them between developed and developing countries. See M Sornarajah, *The International Law on Foreign Investments* 2nd edn (Cambridge, Cambridge University Press, 2004) 204.

[54] However, for a criticism of the view that BITs can be compared to international treaties between countries with equal power, see JW Salacuse, 'BIT by BIT: The Growth of Bilateral Investment Treaties and their Impact on Foreign Investments in Developing Countries' (1990) 24 *International Lawyer* 654, 655.

[55] Sornarajah (n 32) 237–60.

[56] *Ibid* 275.

[57] Trebilcock and Howse (n 15) 455.

[58] Dattu (n 38) 275–76.

regulatory autonomy of states. The draft treaty provided for the right of establishment of foreign investors abroad, the state's obligation to treat foreign investors at least as favourably as domestic investors, the obligation not to discriminate among foreign investors,[59] the possibility of investor-state dispute resolution,[60] and the effective removal of the so-called performance requirements, specifically export requirements, local content and domestic sourcing requirements, and technology transfer.[61]

The implications for the regulatory autonomy of the signatories were enormous. First, countries would no longer be allowed to place restrictions on the entry of foreign investors (so-called pre-entry NT). Secondly, once established, foreign investors could not be discriminated against in favour of domestic investors (so-called post-entry NT) or investors from other parties to the agreement (MFN). Thus, important instruments of industrial policy such as joint venturing, ownership limits and transfer of technology, in addition to the above mentioned performance requirements, would be prohibited.[62] Thirdly, 'since the MAI envisaged direct access to international arbitration by investors, it would make these arbitrators the judges of the validity of any national laws which might be considered contrary to the MAI's principles'.[63] Although disagreement existed among the OECD countries with regard to the scope of the expropriation provisions[64] and the dispute settlement mechanism, the draft treaty represented the most ambitious project ever attempted for the unhindered movement of capital across the borders. As Picciotto writes, the project was to 'extend the IMF's aims and jurisdiction to liberalization of capital flows, which, combined with the MAI and the liberalization of financial services under the WTO, would have created a single global capital market under the aegis of the IMF'.[65] No provisions, however, contained any obligation on the part of MNEs.

The treaty was negotiated in secrecy among the trade ministers of the OECD countries. The intent was to reach an agreement among the major

[59] OECD, The MAI Negotiating Text (Paris, OECD, 22 April 1998) DAFFE/MAI(98)7REV1, 13 www.oecd.org/dataoecd/46/40/1895712.pdf.

[60] *Ibid* 70.

[61] *Ibid* 18–20.

[62] *Ibid* 21.

[63] S Picciotto, 'What Rules for the World Economy' in S Picciotto and R Mayne (eds), *Regulating International Business: Beyond Liberalisation* (Basingstoke, Macmillan, 1999) 13.

[64] These provisions were based on Chapter 11 of the North American Free Trade Agreement (NAFTA). The most alarming NAFTA provisions on expropriation the US tried to replicate in MAI include compensation for takings in the public interest and government actions deemed to be 'tantamount' to expropriation. NAFTA tribunals have pointed out that in order for government action, which also includes environmental measures, to be considered expropriation, the measure needs to produce a serious impact on the investor's property. Whether this can be left to trade tribunals is therefore a serious matter. See Trebilcock and Howse (n 15) 463–64.

[65] Picciotto, 'What Rules' (n 63) 9.

capital-exporting countries and then open it for accession to the developing countries. The latter being mainly capital-importing countries and in need of attracting FDI, they would have been unable to reject it.[66] As Picciotto and Mayne note, the MAI failed for several reasons. There was disagreement among the OECD countries themselves as Europe resisted the far reaching US proposals with regard to the scope of the expropriation provisions and the investor-state dispute resolution.[67] Also, the secrecy with which the negotiations were conducted by trade ministers without parliamentary debate and the outrage of public opinion contributed to the failure of the agreement. Thus, compared with the broad scope of the MAI, the reach of the Agreement on Trade Related Investment Measures (TRIMs) may seem very modest. Nonetheless, the assertion that the United States' aggressive market-access strategy was not fulfilled within the WTO needs further exploration. Only by investigating the combined effects of the three agreements it is possible to evaluate the success of the US market-access strategy.

C The 'Modest' TRIMs Agreement

Unlike the MAI, which was to provide for pre-entry and post-entry NT in addition to the ban on performance requirements,[68] the TRIMs Agreement has, to date, achieved a much more modest outcome. Only trade-related investment measures, notably those deemed to distort trade, are prohibited. These are investment measures in that they relate to the activity economic entities carry out in the host countries and are trade related because they directly affect the flows of trade. Host states may employ them in order to achieve several aims. For instance, the host state may require the foreign investor to export a share of its production so as to ensure that some of the MNEs' gains, in the form of foreign exchange, will accrue to it (the so-called export-performance requirements). It may also require that foreign investors limit their imports to a share of their exports to ensure that MNEs' activity does not lead to a deficit of its balance of payments (the so-called trade-balancing requirements). Finally, it may want to limit the share of MNEs' imports (so-called import-performance requirements) or require MNEs to purchase part of the inputs necessary for production from domestic producers (the so-called local-content requirements) so as to stimulate domestic production.

[66] Trebilcock and Howse (n 15) 470.
[67] Picciotto, 'What Rules' (n 63).
[68] See Matsushita, Schoenbaum, Mavrodis (n 4) 537.

Thus, the TRIMs Agreement explicitly prohibits local content, some trade-balancing (those which violate NT) and import and export requirements (those which violate the prohibition of quantitative restrictions).[69] Trade scholars have pointed out that the agreement is in actual fact a reiteration of the pre-Uruguay Round ban on measures that are inconsistent with the GATT principle of NT and the prohibition of quantitative restrictions on imports and exports.[70] It does not extend to other performance requirements, such as transfer of technology and joint venture requirements which states are still free to adopt. Moreover, it does not affect the right of host states to deny entry to MNEs and does not provide for investor-state dispute resolution. In this respect, the TRIMs Agreement is nothing like the kind of multilateral framework based on pre-entry and post-entry NT the US had envisaged.[71] In addition, the agreement's SDT provisions allowed developing countries five years and least-developed countries seven years to comply with the obligations of the agreement.

However, there are several other aspects that need to be taken into consideration when assessing the present and future impact of the TRIMs Agreement. First, whereas states are prevented from using trade-distorting investment measures, the same trade-distortion rationale does not apply when the activity of MNEs is at issue. The agreement ignores, by not acknowledging, the so-called Restrictive Business Practices (RBPs) in which MNEs may engage and which have far-reaching effects at the domestic and global level. As Morrissey notes:

> Commonly cited examples include transfer pricing, price fixing and market allocation agreements (which imply that the volumes and values of imports and exports desired by the MNE are not those desired by the host), and tied selling, whereby the parent limits with whom the subsidiary can deal. A more general point is that, even in the absence of demonstrable RBPs, the close relationship between the parent and the subsidiary may distort the trade flows of the subsidiary. Although internalisation may not be essential, it increases the ability of MNEs to restrict the behaviour of subsidiaries.[72]

The result is that the TRIMs Agreement is solely concerned with restrictions on government actions: it does not pose corresponding obligations on MNEs. Secondly, although the measures it prohibits are equally concerned

[69] TRIMs Arts 1–2.

[70] See eg, P Low and A Subramanian, 'Beyond TRIMs: A Case for Multilateral Action on Investment Rules and Competition Policy?' in W Martin and LA Winters (eds), *The Uruguay Round and the Developing Countries* (Cambridge, Cambridge University Press, 1996) 380–408; see also JH Jackson, *The World Trading System: Law and Policy of International Economic Relations* (Cambridge, MA, The MIT Press, 1997) 316–17; Matsushita, Schoenbaum, Mavrodis (n 4) 524.

[71] Srinivasan, 'Trade and Development' (n 5) 53.

[72] O Morrissey, 'Investments and Competition Policy in the WTO: Issues for Developing Countries' (2002) 20 *Development Policy Review* 63, 66.

with foreign and domestic investors, the important point is that performance requirements are instruments of industrial policy that countries have used extensively in the past to make sure that investments were of substantial benefit to their economy.[73] Even if GATT provided for such prohibitions, no case indeed arose that directly challenged investment measures except for the FIRA case,[74] where the panel found local content requirements to be in violation of Article III:4 (NT). However, with regard to export manufacturing requirements it went on to assert that 'there is no provision in the General Agreement which forbids requirements to sell goods in foreign markets in preference to domestic markets'.[75] Thus, in more than four decades, only one case was brought before the GATT, and the panel's cautious interpretation in relation to export-performance requirements points to the lenient approach to industrial policy GATT Contracting Parties tacitly shared.

By spelling out the prohibitions on government actions, the TRIMs Agreement has extended, although modestly, the analysis of the FIRA panel to a more defined and broader set of industrial policy instruments. As Morrissey observes:

> [T]he principle of national treatment as applied to the TRIMs Agreement implies the prohibition of performance requirements as an instrument of industrial policy. Presumably, this relates to performance requirements that are trade-related, although in practice it can apply to almost any measures.[76]

Hence, the significance of the agreement is not limited to the restrictions on the host states' industrial policy instruments and the absence of corresponding obligations on MNEs. Investment measures are for the first time within the scope of WTO negotiations. Trebilcock and Howse also note that the list of prohibited measures is not exhaustive. Panels may in future find that performance requirements, other than those included in the illustrative list, are trade distorting. As they point out

> in the Indonesian Autos case (not appealed), the panel held the TRIMs Agreement has an 'autonomous legal existence' from the GATT (para 14.62). It also held that the Agreement could apply to performance requirements that were a condition for receipt of subsidies, even if the subsidy measures themselves might be covered by the Agreement on Subsidies and Countervailing Measures.[77]

[73] G Dunkley, *The Free Trade Adventure: The WTO, The Uruguay Round and Globalism: A Critique* (London, Zed Books, 2000) 68.

[74] *Canada: Administration of the Foreign Investments Review Act*, Report of the Panel (adopted 7 February 1984) BISD 30S/140. Hereafter, the FIRA case.

[75] *Ibid* para 5.18.

[76] Morrissey (n 72) 69.

[77] Trebilcock and Howse (n 15) 456.

As a result, the TRIMs Agreement leaves the door open for WTO panels to expand the list of prohibited measures. Thus, it has not, from a strict legal point of view, fundamentally altered GATT provisions. However, it represents a successful attempt to expand WTO competence in the area of foreign investments, and there is no reason to doubt that future negotiations will not be limited to trade-related investment measures. Indeed, the agreement provides for future negotiations to be carried out in relation to investment and competition policy.[78] During the first WTO Ministerial Conference held in Singapore, the US and the EC sought to launch a new round of negotiations on investments, competition policy, trade facilitation and government procurement.[79] Under the investment rubric, the main objective was to achieve a comprehensive agreement regulating investment measures regardless of whether they distort trade flows and to extend regulation at the pre-establishment phase.[80] Rules on competition were to address government actions that give 'unfair' advantage to domestic firms. However, no action concerning MNEs' monopolisation and anti-competitive practices was envisaged.[81] An agreement on government procurement would have to introduce transparency with regard to government purchases of goods and services in the first stage and NT and due process for foreign firms at a later stage.[82] Finally, trade facilitation rules were meant to establish obligations on members to simplify and reduce the costs associated with trade in goods and services.[83] Thus, the cumulative effect of the so-called Singapore issues was to further restrict the ability of host states to adopt industrial policy instruments.

The US and EU approach to investment liberalisation and the Singapore issues is entirely consistent with the neo-liberal rationale that discards earlier policies aimed at redressing the structural imbalances of the international trading regime and views all players as positioned on an equal footing with one another. Thus, the United States did not achieve in the UR the degree of market openness it had wished for its foreign investors. However, it is necessary to evaluate the significance of the agreement from an historical, economic and political perspective. Developing countries have long opposed a multilateral agreement on investments that would constrain their industrial policy and enhance the economic and political influence of MNEs on their territory. This opposition has been somewhat weakened by the acceptance of the WTO competence on investments and the future negotiations this entails. Furthermore, to fully

[78] TRIMs Art 9.

[79] These have been referred to as the 'Singapore issues'.

[80] See Trebilcock and Howse (n 15) 470.

[81] See Stiglitz and Charlton (n 9) 53, 269.

[82] *Ibid* 273–74.

[83] *Ibid.*

appreciate the historical, political and economic relevance of the shift in the investor-state power relationship, the actual and potential impact of TRIMs Agreement provisions must be seen within the larger framework that the GATS and the TRIPs Agreement entail.

D The 'Flexible' General Agreement on Trade in Services (GATS)

The General Agreement on Trade in Services (GATS) was ratified and implemented by WTO members as part of the Single Undertaking Approach (SUA). As previously noted, the final compromise achieved at the end of the UR between the United States and the hard line developing countries was based on the so-called bottom-up approach to liberalisation.[84] Rather than adopting uniform rules applying indiscriminately to all service areas, countries would decide which sectors to liberalise and to what extent. The GATS has therefore been presented as a flexible agreement which allows WTO members to retain their right to regulate, exclude public services from liberalisation, withdraw previously made commitments and decide the appropriate pace of liberalisation.[85]

Despite the fact that the GATS has been recognised to apply to 'all relevant areas of domestic regulation' and extend its reach 'into areas never before recognised as trade policy',[86] its flexibility is simultaneously held to be one of the greatest achievements of the WTO as it allows a fair balance between the rights and obligations of its members. However, the post-UR assessment of the legal provisions of the GATS has made it possible to appreciate the scope of such flexibility. This section is therefore concerned with the legal analysis of GATS provisions. In particular, it seeks to analyse the extent to which the GATS legal rules can be effectively relied on by WTO members to preserve their public policy space and, conversely, by foreign investors seeking protection of their rights in the markets of WTO members.

i The GATS Scope and Exceptions

The GATS differs from the GATT in that its core liberalisation rules, notably NT and Market Access, apply only to measures and sectors to which governments have agreed to commit in their schedules. It is therefore

[84] See ch 4, VI A.

[85] See WTO, 'GATS-Facts and Fiction Booklet' (WTO, Services, 2001) 7–11 www.abcdoha.org/services/pdfs/WTO_Paper_GATS.pf. Hereafter WTO booklet.

[86] R Ruggiero, 'Towards GATS 2000—A European Strategy'. Address given by Renato Ruggiero, former WTO Director-General, to the Conference on Trade in Services, organised by the European Commission in Brussels (WTO News-Speeches, 2 June 1998) www.wto.org/english/news_e/sprr_e/bruss1_e.htm.

the specific commitments that states have made which represent the degree of liberalisation undertaken under the WTO. Before analysing the specific features of the bottom-up approach, it is necessary to point to those provisions that apply to all members, irrespective of whether or not they have made specific commitments. The GATS applies to all government measures affecting 'trade in services'. This means that laws, regulations, and administrative decisions of central, regional or local governments and authorities, including 'non–governmental bodies in the exercise of powers delegated' are subject to its rules.[87]

Although the agreement does not define services, it lists the means (so-called modes of supply) through which services are provided internationally. In addition to cross-border services (supplied from the territory of one member into the territory of another party),[88] consumption abroad (supplied in the territory of one member to a service consumer of another member)[89] and movement of natural persons (supplied by natural persons of one party in the territory of another party),[90] the GATS importantly covers commercial presence (the presence of service-providing entities of one party into the territory of another party).[91] The latter mode of supply thus refers to foreign direct investment, which, as the WTO Secretariat notes, 'is the most important mode of supply of services, at least in terms of future development, and also raises the most difficult issues for host governments and for GATS negotiations'.[92] The examination of this mode of supply is therefore crucial in order to appreciate the power investors have had conferred on them by the GATS provisions. Although limited to the services sector, GATS disciplines foreign direct investments at the multilateral level, thereby providing for the first time a comprehensive set of rules on the rights of foreign-service providers.

The agreement applies to all government measures affecting 'trade in services' with no sector excluded a priori. This gives the GATS an unprecedented broadness of scope. Unlike barriers to trade in goods, which mainly refer to tariffs and quantitative restrictions, barriers to trade in services include professional qualification requirements, state monopolies, foreign investment regulations and exchange and capital movement controls.[93] The heterogeneous nature of barriers to trade in services marks a

[87] GATS Art I.3.
[88] GATS Art I.2(a).
[89] GATS Art I.2(b).
[90] GATS Art I.2(d).
[91] GATS Art I.2(c).
[92] WTO, 'An Introduction to the GATS' (October 1999) 3; quoted in S Sinclair and JG Grieshaber-Otto, *Facing the Facts: A Guide to the GATS Debate* (Ottawa, Canadian Centre for Policy Alternatives, 2002) 15.
[93] Matsushita, Schoenbaum, Mavrodis (n 4) 229.

fundamental departure from the international trade regime as envisaged in the GATT. The GATS effectively touches on

> fundamental domestic regulatory choices (such as between regulated monopoly or competition in a particular sector) or quality regulation, for instance requirements for the training and certification of professionals that allow for limited recognition of foreign credentials but do not directly discriminate on the basis of the nationality of the provider as opposed to the source of her training.[94]

The scope of the GATS is therefore immense, applying to a diverse range of barriers in more than one hundred specific service sectors,[95] including transport, tourism, environmental, recreational and cultural services, educational, health and social services and business and financial services. Only three exceptions are provided for in the agreement. The first, and most important is that the GATS does not apply to services provided in the exercise of government authority.[96] The WTO has stressed the importance of this provision, emphasising the fact that public services are exempted from the application of GATS rules.[97] However, the extent to which this is accurate requires further examination. Services are excluded if provided neither on commercial terms nor in competition with one or more service suppliers.[98] Assessing when this is the case is not straightforward as the terms 'commercial basis' and 'in competition with' are not clearly defined in the agreement. In many countries, public services are provided by governments along with private provision of like services. Trebilcock and Howse, for instance, note that

> these criteria would not apply to most public services that are provided in mixed economies, where there is usually some combination of public and private provisions (for example healthcare in almost all developed countries, with Canada still being an exception), and some competition between providers in some segments of the market (government post-offices vs. private delivery firms).[99]

Macmillan, however, adopts a more nuanced approach. Analysing the provisions with respect to environmental services, she argues that a reasonable interpretation of the term 'commercial basis', which Article I.3 distinguishes from 'competitive basis', would point to those services

> supplied at arm's length in the market place, that is, at the full commercial cost. If this is so, it may not always be easy, at first blush, to tell whether

[94] Trebilcock and Howse (n 15) 352.

[95] See GATT, 'Services Sectoral Classification List' (10 July 1991) Uruguay Round Document MTN.GNS/W/120.

[96] GATS Art I.3(b).

[97] See WTO Booklet (n 85) 2.

[98] GATS Art I.3(c).

[99] Trebilcock and Howse (n 15) 374.

> environmental services have been supplied to consumers on this basis. This is because a 'commercial price' would have to factor in an amount that amortised all costs to the supplier, including the costs of supply and maintenance of infrastructure.[100]

Ascertaining whether consumers are charged a commercial price is therefore a difficult task. Moreover, as Macmillan observes, there are two reasons for states to become the principal suppliers of (environmental) services. First, because of the public goods nature of the services, there may be fewer economic incentives for private firms to invest in them. In this case, it might be suggested that the service at issue will not be supplied on a commercial basis. Secondly, the state may wish to avoid the creation of a private monopoly. Should this be the reason for the state involvement, Macmillan argues that 'it seems reasonable to assume they may be, nevertheless, being supplied on a commercial basis'.[101] This would suffice, according to Article I.3(c), to exclude the service from the governmental exception as one of the two conditions is not satisfied. Thus, although the co-existence of public and private providers does not necessarily imply that the former are supplied on commercial terms or are in competition with the latter, the question arises as to what exactly the governmental authority exclusion might entail, and the WTO Secretariat has not yet provided a concrete example. This discussion may be considered of speculative import since no regulation has yet been challenged. However, the consequences of leaving such an interpretation to the WTO bodies are enormous for the regulatory space of members.

The second general exception concerns GATS-inconsistent measures necessary to protect public morals, public order, human, animal or plant life or health and measures necessary to prevent deceptive or fraudulent practices and the privacy of individuals.[102] The third exception concerns the right of states to adopt GATS-inconsistent measures necessary for the protection of their essential security interests.[103] Whereas Article XIV *bis* allows states to take unilateral leave from GATS disciplines when national security interests are at issue, according to Article XIV they have to demonstrate that GATS-inconsistent measures neither entail arbitrary or unjustifiable discrimination nor a disguised restriction on trade in services. In addition, they will have to demonstrate that no less discriminatory or trade-restrictive measure can achieve the same result (the so-called necessity test). The drafting of this Article recalls the language of GATT Article XX. However, as Macmillan points out with respect to the environmental exceptions, unlike GATT Article XX, GATS Article XIV does not apply to

[100] Macmillan (n 29) 203.
[101] *Ibid.*
[102] GATS Art XIV.
[103] GATS Art XIV bis.

measures relating to 'exhaustible natural resources', thereby further limiting the scope of the exception.[104] Thus, whereas the scope for GATS disciplines is very broad, the extent to which countries can successfully rely on the exceptions is somewhat less precise than the WTO's Facts and Fictions asserts.[105] Members can invoke with no further hurdle the 'national security exception'. However, they have to undergo the 'necessity test' to rely on Article XIV. As to the government authority exclusion, the scope of this exception is still not clear and the ultimate decision will derive from the interpretation of WTO panels and Appellate Body.[106] On the other hand, the extent to which states are bound by the GATS disciplines is determined by its general rules and specific commitments.

ii The Most Favoured Nation

The most important rule applying to all members irrespective of their specific commitments is the Most Favoured Nation principle, according to which members cannot discriminate between like foreign services or foreign-service providers. It is evident that MFN does not mandate any specific degree of market openness; it simply extends the GATT principles of non-discrimination to trade in services. However, there is a qualitative difference with regard to the way in which MFN operates within the two agreements. Whereas in the GATT MFN requires states not to discriminate between like foreign goods, in the GATS the rule applies to both foreign services and foreign-service providers. This means that MFN 'can be better understood as a most-favoured-foreign company rule' according to which 'any regulatory or funding advantage gained by a single foreign commercial provider must be extended, immediately and unconditionally, to all'.[107] The result is that states that have not made specific commitments in the sector at issue and wish to prevent new service providers from taking advantage of a favourable treatment previously conferred on a service provider, will face opposition by all MNEs operating in the sector. Hence, despite the fact that MFN does not create a legally binding obligation for members to undertake specific liberalisation commitments, it has the practical effect of making any reversal of benefits previously conferred very

[104] Macmillan (n 29) 39.

[105] WTO Booklet (n 85) 7.

[106] Panels, the Appellate Body and the Dispute Settlement Body are the three institutions that administer the WTO dispute settlement system.

[107] Sinclair and Grieshaber-Otto (n 92) 46. For instance, they point to the negotiations concerning China's accession to the WTO and note that China expressed the intention to limit foreign ownership of life insurers at 50 per cent. However, one US company (AIG) had been previously allowed 100 per cent ownership. The EU consequently sought MFN during China's accession process. Although China refused to do so, the authors point out that 'because of MFN, European insurers are satisfied that, whichever way the US–China dispute is settled, they will be entitled the best treatment given AIG'. *Ibid* fn115.

difficult. In other words, it can be used as an effective means to 'consolidate commercialisation whenever it occurs'.[108]

iii National Treatment and Market Access

Articles XVI and XVII are the heart of GATS bottom-up approach. In order to apply, NT and market access need to be explicitly listed in the GATS schedules of each member. Moreover, states are allowed to include limitations to the operation of both principles. The WTO Secretariat has therefore emphasised the flexibility that the agreement entails and stressed that the list of commitments is a matter of sovereign choice for each member.[109] As a consequence, members are permitted to select the pace of liberalisation according to their specific needs. Both principles, however, require careful scrutiny. Borrowed from GATT, NT requires members to treat foreign services and foreign-service providers at least as favourably as domestic services and service providers. The underlying rationale is therefore that of non-discrimination.

However, the de facto non-discrimination test the GATS adopts is very strict. Article XVII provides that states can grant 'either formally identical treatment or formally different treatment to that it accords to its own like services and service suppliers'. It then specifies that formally identical or formally different treatment 'shall be considered to be less favourable if it modifies the conditions of competition in favour of services or service suppliers of the Member compared to like services or service suppliers of any other Member'. This provision has been interpreted by a WTO panel to mean that a non-discriminatory measure with no actual effects on 'trade in services' can still be found GATS-inconsistent if it is merely capable of distorting trade.[110] As Trebilcock and Howse note, 'this approach to National Treatment, which goes beyond a ban on intentionally discriminatory measures, reflects the view that equal treatment implies adjustment of domestic regulatory regimes so that foreign suppliers have *substantively* equal competitive opportunities'.[111] It is worth reiterating that, while foreign investors are recognised as having substantively equal opportunity, the barriers GATS NT aims at redressing are matters of domestic regulatory policies in areas as sensitive as health, education and water distribution.

[108] *Ibid* 46.
[109] WTO Booklet (n 85) 2.
[110] In the Canadian Autos case, the WTO panel agreed that the National Treatment provision 'protects competitive opportunities, no actual trade flows'. WTO, *Canada: Certain Measures Affecting the Automobile Industry*, Report of the Panel (adopted 11 February 2000) WT/DS139/R para 10.303.
[111] Trebilcock and Howse (n 15) 366.

In addition to NT, countries that fully commit their services sector have to comply with the Market Access provisions. Whereas NT allows each member to choose any policy, provided it does not discriminate de jure or de facto, market access provisions prohibit certain policy instruments regardless of whether they are discriminatory. If a state has made full commitments under Market Access, Article XVI bans it from imposing limits or restrictions on the number of services suppliers, total value of service transactions, number of services operation or number of natural persons employed in a particular service sector, types of legal entity through which a service is supplied and foreign capital participation.[112] Thus, market access, unlike NT, will apply to government measures whether they discriminate or not. In addition, a footnote to this Article provides that when a state has fully committed a sector and where 'cross-border movement of capital is an essential part of the service itself', the state is also committed to the liberalisation of capital movements.[113] Full commitments under Market Access therefore amount to the free-market access approach the US intended to pursue within the TRIMs Agreement. Performance requirements such as limitation of foreign ownership and joint venturing, together with restrictions on the number of foreign investors, can no longer be used by states.

iv The Right to Regulate

The far-reaching effects of full NT and market access are purported to be balanced with the GATS provisions that allow states to decide about the scope of their sector-by-sector commitments.[114] The WTO emphasises that the agreement 'allows governments to determine the level of obligations they will assume'.[115] There are, however, several points this official statement leaves out. First, countries are allowed to list country-specific exceptions to their commitments only at the initial stage. Thus, if a government realises the adverse effects of its specific liberalisation commitments under the GATS, it cannot add limitations for non-conforming measures at a later stage. Without doubt, Article XXI allows countries to modify and withdraw a specific commitment after three years of the scheduling.[116] However, the country at issue is under the obligation to compensate the affected party, usually by replacing existing commitments with others in the same area.[117] It is worth noting that if a negotiated

112 GATS Art XVI.2.
113 GATS Art.XVI.1 fn 8.
114 GATS Arts XVI.2 and XVII.1.
115 WTO Booklet (n 85) 6.
116 GATS Art XXI.1(a).
117 GATS Arts XXI.2 and XXI.3.

settlement is not achieved, Article XXI may allow for cross-retaliation in other WTO areas.[118] Thus, WTO members, especially developing countries, wishing to reverse previous commitments might face retaliation in their key export sectors. From this angle, GATS has the effect of locking in liberalisation by making it difficult to reverse the liberalisation process. As the WTO itself acknowledges, 'because unbinding is difficult, the commitments are virtually guaranteed conditions for foreign exporters and importers of services and investors in the sector to do business'.[119]

In addition to the purported freedom to list exceptions to the specific commitments, the Preamble of the GATS fully recognises the 'right of Members to regulate, and to introduce new regulations, on the supply of services within their territories in order to meet national policy objectives'. Although the Preamble does not create legally enforceable rights or obligations, it is certainly meant to influence the panels' and Appellate Body's interpretation of the GATS provisions, especially when sensitive matters of domestic policy are at issue. However, it is equally important to emphasise that this

> preambular reference cannot be construed as excusing government regulation from conforming to the GATS. Regulations are clearly listed among the wide range of government measures restricted by the GATS. Regulatory measures, whatever their form or purpose, must conform with the GATS provisions in the main text and a member's specific commitments.[120]

In other words, members are free to regulate as long as the regulation is consistent with the general rules of the GATS and the country's specific commitments. To interpret the Preamble otherwise would make the legal obligations of the GATS non-enforceable, thereby defeating the whole purpose of the agreement. Hence, the arguments advanced by the WTO with respect to members' right to regulate and devise the desirable level and pace of liberalisation need to be treated most cautiously. A strictly legal investigation of the GATS suggests that its provisions have the potential to substantially restrict fundamental instruments of industrial and public policy as no international treaty has done before. Indeed, in order to do so states must fully commit under NT and Market Access. A neo-liberal interpretation of the WTO bargaining process, according to which members negotiate under a rules-based system on an equal footing with one another, would view the liberalisation commitments as the result of the exercise of members' freedom of choice. It has been demonstrated that this rules-based system has the potential for intruding into the regulatory space

[118] See Sinclair and Grieshaber-Otto (n 92) 33.

[119] WTO, 'GATS: Rules for Growth and Investments' (WTO, Understanding the WTO, the Agreements) www.wto.org/english/thewto_e/whatis_e/tif_e/agrm6_e.htm.

[120] Sinclair and Grieshaber-Otto (n 92) 42.

of WTO members while enhancing the power of foreign investors. However, in order to show how these potential effects materialise, the legal analysis carried out so far needs to be complemented with an examination of the GATS negotiating practice. As it will be argued in the next chapter, nowhere is the stark contrast between the GATS legal disciplines and its negotiating practice more evident than with regard to the negotiations between developed and developing countries. The progressive liberalisation process mandated in Article XIX and commenced in 2000 defeats the whole neo-liberal view of the WTO rules-based system as a level playing field where parties exercise their 'freedom of choice'.

E The 'Balanced' TRIPs Agreement

Although the TRIPs Agreement does not directly regulate foreign investments, its provisions encourage the liberalisation of investment flows through the protection of the investor's technology. Since high technology is one of the most valuable assets in the capital structure of MNEs, the protection of patents, trademarks, trade secrets and trade names becomes a crucial source of gains for subsidiaries investing abroad. As Burt writes, 'This is an important protection of FDI because nearly all FDI undertakings involve technology transfer from the MNE to a subsidiary in the host country'.[121] However, the gains from the agreement are purported to benefit capital-importing countries as well as the investors. As Burt goes on to argue, 'Protection of this technology will provide additional incentives for such a transfer'.[122] This argument is reiterated by Dattu, who claims that 'the protection of such technology removes another source of insecurity for foreign investors and promotes the transfer of technology between countries, in particular between developed and developing countries'.[123]

Thus, the argument in support of the inclusion of IP rights with regard to technology within the international trading system is twofold: the increased security of the IP investors will stimulate investment flows which, in turn, will benefit capital-importing countries in terms of both increased capital availability and transfer of technology. This section therefore examines the TRIPs Agreement legal provisions from a specific perspective, that of the IP investors' rights vis-à-vis the host state. It investigates whether the extension of foreign investors' rights through the effective protection of their technology assets and the consequent obligations on

[121] EM Burt, 'Developing Countries and the Framework for Negotiations on Foreign Direct Investments in the World Trade Organisation' (1997) 12 *American University International Law Review* 1015, 1039.

[122] *Ibid.*

[123] Dattu (n 38) 294–95.

states to conform to the TRIPs Agreement legal rules is complemented with equally binding obligations on their part to transfer technology.

i Minimum Standards, NT and MFN: The Protection Triad

Of the three WTO agreements examined so far, the TRIPs Agreement is the one that most openly targets the legal systems of developing countries in order to provide effective protection to the IP rights of foreign investors. Although all members are under the TRIPs Agreement obligations, it is the legal systems of developing countries that need to be reformed accordingly as the standards the agreement embodies are those prevailing in the developed countries. Since the beginning of the negotiations that led to the adoption of the TRIPs Agreement, the collaboration between developed countries' governments and corporate power has never been so evident.[124] On behalf of the corporate industries, TRIPs Agreement embodies the US three-goals strategy towards developing countries.

First, it requires all WTO members to adopt standards of IP protection as extensive as those prevailing in the territory of the developed countries. Thus, the agreement provides substantive norms for the protection of the various forms of IP rights, namely, copyrights, trademarks, patents, geographical indications, integrated circuits and trade secrets. This means that each state is under the obligation to establish a legal system that grants minimum standards of protection for each of the above-mentioned IP categories.[125] These standards are then extended internationally through the operation of NT. Hence, each member is obliged to accord to the nationals of other WTO members 'treatment no less favourable than that it accords to its own nationals with regard to the protection of intellectual property'.[126] In addition, in accordance with the principle of MFN, any advantage, favour, privilege and immunity one member grants to the nationals of another member concerning the protection of IP must be extended 'immediately and unconditionally' to the nationals of all other WTO members.[127]

Secondly, the TRIPs Agreement ensures the effective enforcement of IP rights within each legal system. All WTO members are therefore required

[124] See ch 4, I.

[125] For copyrights, TRIPs Art 12 provides a minimum term of protection of 50 years either from the initial date of authorised protection or the making of the work. As to trademarks, Art 18 provides for a term of protection of no less than 7 years since registration, with the latter renewable indefinitely. Art 33 provides for a minimum term of patent protection of 20 years from the filing date. Art 26.3 confers industrial designs a term of protection of 10 years, which also applies to layout designs of integrated circuits under Art 38. Finally, unlimited protection is conferred upon undisclosed information (trade secrets) under Art 39.

[126] TRIPs Art 3.

[127] TRIPs Art 4.

to provide IP holders with an effective enforcement mechanism. In particular, enforcement procedures must not be 'unnecessarily complicated and costly, or entail unreasonable time-limits or unwarranted delays'.[128] In addition, the TRIPs Agreement requires states to 'make available to right holders civil judicial procedures concerning the enforcement of any intellectual property right'.[129] Judicial authorities need to have conferred on them the power to issue injunctions,[130] including interim injunctions 'where the delay is likely to cause irreparable harm to the right holder',[131] and award damages.[132] Finally, the TRIPs Agreement brings IP within the scope of the multilateral dispute settlement mechanism provided by the WTO.[133]

Therefore, the TRIPs Agreement provisions ensure that all WTO members provide a level of protection of IP rights as extensive and effective as that prevailing in the developed countries. One consequence of this is that the costs of implementation in order to bring the domestic legal systems into compliance with the agreement are, in substantially larger part, borne by developing countries. Although it is certainly important to point to the soaring costs that implementation entails,[134] the significance of the TRIPs Agreement extends well beyond economic calculations.

First, the degree of control that the TRIPs Agreement exercises over domestic civil and administrative procedures is unprecedented.[135] Despite the fact that the WTO agreements are binding only on states, the TRIPs Agreement provides IP holders with effective means for protecting their rights within the domestic legal systems of all WTO members. In addition, it secures the right of states to bring before the WTO dispute settlement bodies non-compliance complaints against other members on behalf of their IP holders. Furthermore, members are under the obligation to notify their domestic laws and regulations concerning the protection of IP to the TRIPs Council,[136] which is also responsible for monitoring the domestic compliance with the agreement. Therefore, the TRIPs Agreement effectively operates as a system of surveillance and control at different levels: domestic institutions are made responsible for adopting and enforcing TRIPs-compliant policies; the TRIPs Council monitors implementation and enforcement of IP rights; IP holders have access to the administrative and civil procedures of WTO members to enforce their rights; states can follow

[128] TRIPs Art 41.2.
[129] TRIPs Art 42.
[130] TRIPs Art 44.1.
[131] TRIPs Art 50.3.
[132] TRIPs Art 45.
[133] TRIPs Art 64.
[134] See Finger and Schuler (n 27) 514.
[135] See Trebilcock and Howse (n 15) 415.
[136] TRIPs Art 63.2.

their corporate sector's claims of non-compliance and bring actions before the WTO dispute settlement bodies; and finally, the latter may allow cross-sectoral retaliations for failures to comply with its IP standards.[137]

Secondly, the core provisions of the TRIPs Agreement, namely NT and MFN, apply to legal persons rather than goods. By treating foreign and domestic legal entities even-handedly, non-discrimination has the effect of restricting the power of states to favour domestic IP holders in order to pursue national economic and social priorities. In the past, developed countries have intensively made use of foreign technology without affording IP protection in order to build their domestic technological capacity.[138] In other words, the unhindered use of foreign technology and creations was considered to be a legitimate means of industrial policy. Developing countries, however, are now denied the same right as a result of the TRIPs Agreement. The focus of the arguments is on the diffusion of technology and innovation, which is presumed to follow from the increased security gained by IP holders. Thus, in the neo-liberal inversion of logic, it is the role of the foreign investor carrying the technology, rather than that of the state, which acquires central relevance in the pursuit of domestic policy objectives. This becomes apparent if one looks at the TRIPs Agreement as a platform for the endless increase of IP holders' rights at the international level. As will be discussed in chapter six, the combination of minimum standards of protection, NT and MFN within the TRIPs Agreement and the bilateral activity of capital-exporting countries with capital-importing countries points to a precise strategy devised by the former to pressure the latter into affording greater protection to their IP holders.[139]

Thirdly, NT and MFN are more than the simple extension of the logic of non-discrimination to IP rights. By requiring states not to discriminate between domestic and foreign IP holders, and to extend immediately and unconditionally any advantage given to one national to all WTO nationals, the agreement views all forms of IP as 'international commodities'. In effect, these principles and their indiscriminate application to all forms of IP, from cultural to technological production, signal the homogenisation of IP rights 'to a single, one dimensional property phenomenon, that is, a capitalist commodity, and then proclaim the essential equality of all

[137] See J Braithwaite and P Drahos, *Global Business Regulation* (Cambridge, Cambridge University Press, 2000) 87.

[138] See R Wade, 'What Strategies are Viable for Developing Countries Today? The World Trade Organization and the Shrinking of "Development Space"' (2003) 10 *Review of International Political Economy* 621, 626.

[139] See P Drahos, 'BITs and BIPs: Bilateralism in Intellectual Property' (2001) 4 *The Journal of World Intellectual Property* 791.

commodities in the global marketplace'.[140] Hence, the neo-liberal assumption about the international trading regime as an 'equal playing field' is extended to knowledge, culture and technology.

ii Transfer of Technology, Flexibilities and Exceptions

Despite the fact that the World Bank's official figures estimate the net gains the United States is expected to make from the full application of the TRIPs Agreement at around US$19 billion a year,[141] developing countries are also believed to benefit, in the long term, from the enhanced protection of IP. The argument is that as foreign investors' security is enhanced, they will more likely invest through their subsidiaries abroad and consequently transfer the technology to the host states in which they operate.[142] In order to achieve this objective, the TRIPs Agreement complements NT and MFN with provisions aimed at balancing the rights of IP holders with obligations to transfer technology. Thus, Article 7 provides that

> [t]he protection and enforcement of intellectual property rights should contribute to the promotion of technological innovation and to the transfer and dissemination of technology, to the mutual advantage of producers and users of technological knowledge and in a manner conducive to social and economic welfare, and to a balance of rights and obligations.

Moreover, according to Article 8,

> [a]ppropriate measures, provided that they are consistent with the provisions of this Agreement, may be needed to prevent the abuse of intellectual property rights by right holders or the resort to practices which unreasonably restrain trade or adversely affect the international transfer of technology.[143]

Since these Articles are an integral part of the 'objectives and principles' of the TRIPs Agreement, they are supposed to guide its implementation and the interpretation of its provisions. However, a closer reading of both Articles 7 and 8 does not suggest a straightforward assessment of their legal scope. IP 'should' contribute to the transfer and diffusion of knowledge. States 'may' need to adopt measures in order to prevent anti-competitive abuses by IP holders as long as they conform with the agreement. The vagueness of these provisions bears the question of the extent to which they can be legally enforced. As to the provisions

[140] A Story, C Darch and D Halbert, *The Copy/South Dossier: Issues in the Economics, Politics and Ideology of Copyrights in the Global South* (Canterbury, The Copy/Couth Research Group, 2006) 49.

[141] See Wade (n 138) 624.

[142] Dattu (n 38) 294–95; Burt (n 121) 1039.

[143] TRIPs Art 40 provides illustrative examples of anti-competitive practices in contractual licensing, practices and conditions, namely exclusive grantback conditions, conditions preventing challenges to licences' validity and coercive package licensing.

concerning 'Least-Developed Country Members', TRIPs Article 66 seems to adopt a more mandatory language in stating that 'Developed country Members shall provide incentives to enterprises and institutions in their territories for the purpose of promoting and encouraging technology transfer to least-developed country Members in order to enable them to create a sound and viable technological base'.[144]

However, as with Articles 7 and 8, the question arises as to whether these provisions allow states to deny TRIPs Agreement protection to IP holders who have not complied with measures aimed at facilitating the transfer of technology or preventing anti-competitive abuses.[145] The fact that these provisions have not yet been relied on points to the indeterminateness of their legal scope, and consequently their effectiveness as instruments of technology transfer is doubted.[146] The only enforceable legal provisions by developing countries are those concerning the time-limited derogations from the TRIPs Agreement legal norms. Thus, developing countries were given five years to implement the agreement, whereas least-developed countries were entitled to ten years; however, NT and MFN were to apply immediately. Thus, whereas effective protection and enforcement of IP rights has been achieved through the TRIPs Agreement legal provisions, the corresponding obligations on IP holders supposed to balance its immediate adverse effects for developing countries seem to have been much less effective.[147]

[144] Similarly, TRIPs Art 67 provides that 'developed country Members shall provide, on request and on mutually agreed terms and conditions, technical and financial cooperation in favour of developing and least-developed country Members. Such cooperation shall include assistance in the preparation of laws and regulations on the protection and enforcement of intellectual property rights as well as on the prevention of their abuse, and shall include support regarding the establishment or reinforcement of domestic offices and agencies relevant to these matters, including the training of personnel.'

[145] See Trebilcock and Howse (n 15) 411.

[146] The only WTO Member to invoke one of these provisions has been, oddly enough, the US, which has submitted that, according to Art 7, 'the provisions of the Agreement are designed to result in mutual advantages to producers and users, and contribute to a balance of rights and obligations'. However, the panel refused to take Art 7 into consideration in its report. See United States—Section 110(5) of US Copyright Act, WTO Doc WT/DS160/R (first written submission of the US, para 22). As will be examined in the next chapter, the indeterminateness of these provisions also informs the current debate concerning the conflict between the TRIPs provisions on patentability and the requirements of technology transfer and benefit sharing under the 1992 UN Convention on Biological Diversity (5 June 1992) 31 ILM 818.

[147] Furthermore, the TRIPs Agreement was negotiated and adopted by developing countries under the impression, if not the assurance, that the unilateral threats they had been subject to in the past would be replaced with a rules-based multilateral system. As will be argued in the next chapter, this has not been the case and the proliferation of bilateral pressures has complemented unilateral threats.

CONCLUSIONS

The TRIPs Agreement represents the first successful attempt at universalising IP standards. In apparent contradiction with the other WTO agreements promoting the liberalisation of goods, services and, to a certain extent, investments, the TRIPs Agreement protects IP from competition by giving IP owners a temporary monopoly power. As previously argued, however, the inclusion of IP rights within the international trading regime has to be seen in the context of the restructuring of the global economy along the lines of a trade-service-investment driven market integration.[148] So-called vertical integration between high wage industrialised countries and low wage developing countries meant that greater economic gains for MNEs could flow from liberalising services and investments and, simultaneously, universalising and enforcing the protection of IP rights. This explains the apparent contradiction between the free-market assumptions underlying the agreements on goods, services and investments and the protectionist content of the TRIPs Agreement. The three agreements were carefully drafted to serve the interests of MNEs and their home countries, whereas the main targets are the markets and legal systems of developing and newly industrialised countries.[149]

This chapter has focused on the two arguments underlying the WTO neo-liberal development framework, namely that trade liberalisation and reciprocity generate a beneficial outcome for all WTO members. Thus, by assessing the framework on its own terms, it has shown how the practice of the WTO developed members continues to discriminate against the trade of developing countries. Furthermore, the GATS, TRIPs and TRIMs Agreements provide the first international legal provisions for the effective protection and enforcement of foreign investors' rights and have the potential of greatly impinging upon the regulatory autonomy of WTO members. The next chapter will corroborate this claim by scrutinising the latest efforts developed countries have made in order to enhance the power of their transnational capital. These efforts have taken place in the middle of a negotiating round that was supposed to correct past imbalances that had hindered the trade of developing countries.

[148] See ch 3, II B.

[149] Free trade economists have argued that the TRIPs Agreement is misplaced within the WTO. Bhagwati for instance, has asserted that 'intellectual property protection is a matter of collecting royalties, and including them in a trade institution such as the WTO seriously distorted what that organisation should accomplish.' See J Bhagwati. 'Don't Cry for Cancun' (2004) 83 *Foreign Affairs* 52, 57. However, Bhagwati's argument presupposes that the WTO is a free-trade organisation, which is exactly the assumption that this chapter has challenged by assessing the legal framework of the three agreements and its potential to confer unprecedented rights upon foreign investors.

6

Of Failures and Promises: The Many Lives of the Doha Development Round

IN THE YEARS following the Uruguay Round (UR), it has become apparent that, although the World Trade Organisation (WTO) has brought back agriculture and textiles within its legal regime and introduced disciplines on safeguard measures and anti-dumping duties, the negative discrimination against developing countries' trade has not been eliminated. Hence, in order to redress the imbalances of the UR, trade ministers from WTO members met at Doha in 2001 to launch a comprehensive round of multilateral trade negotiations with a 'new historic mandate'.[1] In the words of US Trade Representative Robert Zoellick:

> Doha lays the groundwork for a trade liberalisation agenda that will be a starting point for greater development, growth, opportunity and openness around the world ... On a range of issues, such as agricultural liberalisation and the reduction of tariffs on non-agricultural goods, we have shown how our interests can converge with the developing world. I believe that we in the United States have an enhanced appreciation for the interests of developing nations in trade.[2]

Great emphasis has therefore been placed on the significance of this 'historic' event for development. However, the central theme of this book is that development has always occupied a central position within the international trading system. Since the Mandate System under the League of Nations, the scientific authority of development thinking has been constructed and deployed to further the trade interests of the major capitalist powers. This chapter therefore examines whether the Doha

[1] JE Stiglitz and A Charlton, *Fair Trade For All: How Trade Can Promote Development* (Oxford, Oxford University Press, 2005) 1.

[2] R Zoellick (Office of the US Trade Representative, 14 November 2001); quoted in Stiglitz and Charlton (n 1) 57.

Development Round marks a shift in the modality through which the science of development has operated within the international trade regime since the end of the colonial period.

It first asks whether the principles and objectives embodied in the Doha Declaration signal a departure from the neo-liberal development rationale that views the international trade arena as a level playing field where actors achieve, through reciprocally binding obligations, 'mutually advantageous arrangements'.[3] The declaration seems to point to a softening of the WTO neo-liberal assumptions by calling into question the principle of reciprocity and placing emphasis on the inequalities generated by international trade rules. However, a closer look at the declaration shows that the neo-liberal hold over development persists in that the universal beneficial role of trade liberalisation and deeper integration remains the premise for achieving development. In other words, the objectives of the Doha Development Round are confined to the correction of the imbalances that have prevented developing countries from enjoying the benefits purported by neo-liberalism.

Within the confines of the WTO neo-liberal framework, the chapter then moves on to examine whether the UR imbalances have finally been addressed. The analysis of the negotiations between 2001 and 2009 shows that, rather than delivering 'development, growth, opportunity and openness around the world',[4] the Doha Development Round has been consistently used by the US and EU to enhance the market-access opportunities for their transnational capital, while they oppose attempts to eliminate the discrimination against the trade of developing countries. This reveals a fundamental contradiction in the WTO neo-liberal rhetoric about free trade and multilateralism. At a more fundamental level, however, the outcome of the Doha Round exposes the continuity of the *modus operandi* of the 'science of development' within the international trading regime.

I THE ROAD TO DOHA: REFLECTING ON THE UR IMBALANCES

The legal framework of the WTO agreements on agriculture, textiles and clothing, anti-dumping duties and safeguard measures was supposed to address the negative discrimination against developing countries' trade that had characterised GATT history. However, since the agreements came into force, the gains in agriculture have been modest, since developed countries' export subsidies, domestic support and high tariff rates are still displacing

[3] See Preamble of Agreement Establishing the World Trade Organisation (15 April 1994) LT/UR/A/1. Hereafter WTO Preamble.

[4] See above, text to n 2.

developing countries' competitive exports.[5] Textiles liberalisation has been back-loaded, and high tariffs have resulted even after the phasing out of quantitative restrictions.[6] Anti-dumping duties and safeguard measures have also been on the increase.[7] In addition, the costs of implementing the WTO agreements have weighed heavily on developing countries' budgets.[8] The legal analysis of the Agreement on Trade Related Investment Measures (TRIMs), the Agreement on Trade Related Aspects of Intellectual Property Rights (TRIPs) and the General Agreement on Trade in Services (GATS), however, has suggested that unlike the GATT, the WTO is capable of reaching deeper into the domestic regulatory space of WTO members.[9] As Ostry remarks, the WTO system implies a

> degree of intrusiveness into domestic sovereignty [that] bears little resemblance to the shallow integration of the postwar years with its focus on border barriers. The WTO has shifted trade policy from the GATT model of negative regulation—what governments must not do—to positive regulation, or what governments must do.[10]

Moreover, the 'degree of intrusiveness' is not limited to the legal provisions of the above-mentioned agreements. The WTO's mandate provides for further negotiations in the areas of services,[11] investment and competition policy in order to achieve progressive liberalisation of international trade. Thus, during the first Ministerial Conference[12] held in Singapore in 1996, the EU advocated the launch of a new round of negotiations on investments, competition policy, trade facilitation and government procurement, the so-called Singapore issues.[13] As with the process leading to the launch of the UR, consensus was first achieved among the major trading partners, the EU, the US and Japan (the so-called TRIAD), in order to then present their common proposal to the rest of the WTO members.[14] However, the

[5] See ch 5, I A.
[6] See ch 5, I B.
[7] See ch 5, I C.
[8] See ch 5, I D.
[9] See ch 5, II C–E.
[10] S Ostry, 'The Changing Scenario in International Governance' (Ottawa, Royal Society of Canada, 20 November 1999). See also TN Srinivasan, 'Developing Countries and the Multilateral Trading System after Doha' (Economic Growth Centre: Discussion Paper No. 842, 2002) 5 www.econ.yale.edu/~egcenter.
[11] GATS Art XIX.
[12] Ministerial Conferences, which take place every two years, are the highest level of decision-making at the WTO. Their purpose is to enable ministers to make decisions on how to move forward on all matters under any of the multilateral trade agreements.
[13] In the previous chapter it was argued that the Singapore issues, as proposed by the EU, would have further restricted the ability of host states to regulate the activities of foreign investors. See ch 5 II C.
[14] The US initially opposed the inclusion of competition policy within the agenda, viewing anti-trust as a matter of domestic law enforcement. However, in 1999, after Japan announced it would back the EU proposal, the US joined the EU call for a new round of

developing countries' reaction to the TRIAD's proposal was immediate. During the third Ministerial Conference which was held in Seattle, India, Egypt, Pakistan, Zimbabwe and part of ASEAN opposed any negotiations that would further the investment agenda of the EU.[15] In particular, India argued that a new round of negotiations should concentrate on correcting the UR imbalances and flaws in the implementation of the existing agreements.[16] Eventually, the EU refusal to negotiate on the elimination of agricultural distortion unless the Singapore issues, especially investments, were incorporated in the negotiating agenda led to the collapse of the Seattle ministerial meeting.[17]

The developing countries' call for the elimination of the discrimination against their trade found increasing support in studies published by influential international organisations. For instance, prior to Seattle, the United Nations Conference on Trade and Development (UNCTAD) had pointed to the need to redress the imbalances of the UR by extending transition periods—in order to comply with the TRIPs, TRIMs and customs valuations provisions—increasing technical assistance, removing tariffs on exports from the least-developed countries and providing better access for textiles and clothing.[18] In addition, Rubens Ricupero, former Secretary General of UNCTAD, produced a report highlighting the obstacles developing and especially least-developed countries faced in accessing northern markets despite the preference schemes in their favour.[19] In a study for the World Bank, Finger and Schuler also pointed to the implementation costs that the WTO agreements involved and emphasised the foreseeable costs of introducing obligations in the new areas.[20] The common thread of these studies was that, in order for the benefits of trade liberalisation to materialise, the discrimination against developing countries' competitive exports had to be eliminated. In other words, these studies did not object to the development rationale embodied in the WTO

negotiations on the Singapore issues. See JS Odell, 'The Seattle Impasse and its Implications' in DLM Kennedy and JD Southwick (eds), The Political Economy of International Trade Law: Essays in Honour of Robert Hudec (Cambridge, Cambridge University Press, 2002) 403.

[15] *Ibid.*

[16] See Srinivasan (n 10) 19.

[17] See Odell (14) 417.

[18] See S Ostry, 'The Uruguay Round North-South Grand Bargain: Implications for Future Negotiations' in Kennedy and Southwick (n 14) 293.

[19] R Ricupero, 'Ministerial Round Table on Trade and Poverty in Least developed Countries' (UNCTAD, 19 March 2001) www.unctad.org/Templates/webflyer.asp?docid+2587&intItemID=2054&lang&equal.

[20] JM Finger and P Schuler, 'Implementation of the Uruguay Round Commitments: The Development Challenge' (2000) 23 *The World Economy* 511, 525. See also JM Finger, 'Comment: The Uruguay Round North-South Bargain: Will the WTO Get Over It?' in Kennedy and Southwick (n 14) 301–09.

agreements, according to which trade liberalisation leads to greater economic growth and development. They did, however, criticise the developed countries' negotiating agenda in that it privileged market access in the new areas rather than removing the obstacles that prevented developing countries from reaping the benefits of trade liberalisation.[21]

Confronted with the Seattle failure and mounting public criticism, the WTO responded with a reinvigorated focus on development. On 14 November 2001, ministers agreed to launch a new round of negotiations at Doha which, in the words of US Trade Representative Zoellick, aimed at delivering growth, development and prosperity to the world.[22] Negotiations under the Doha Round, therefore, were to redress the imbalances of the UR and finally deliver the development promise of the multilateral trading system.

II THE DOHA AGENDA

A Principles and Objectives: Multilateralism, Free Trade, Development

Before examining the negotiating mandate of the Doha Declaration, a brief analysis of its principles and objectives is necessary in order to evaluate whether it represents a substantial shift from the WTO neo-liberal development framework that posits trade liberalisation as universally beneficial and reciprocal and binding obligations as the means for achieving the said result. The Declaration contains a number of principles that concern the relationship between trade and development.[23] First, WTO members recognise the 'the multilateral trading system embodied in the World Trade Organization has contributed significantly to economic growth, development and employment throughout the past fifty years'.[24] As a consequence, they stress their commitment to the principle of trade liberalisation and their rejection of protectionism reaffirming 'the principles and objectives set out in the Marrakesh Agreement Establishing the World Trade Organization'.[25] This refers to the WTO objectives of

> raising standards of living, ensuring full employment and a large and steadily growing volume of real income and effective demand, and expanding the

[21] See World Bank, 'Trade, Development and Poverty Reduction'. Paper prepared jointly by the staff of the World Bank and the IMF for the consideration of the Development Committee (31 March 2000).

[22] See above, text to n 2.

[23] WTO, Doha Declaration (14 November 2001) WTO Doc WT/MIN(01)/DEC/1. Hereafter, Doha Declaration.

[24] *Ibid* para 1.

[25] *Ibid*.

> production of and trade in goods and services…to enhance the means for doing so in a manner consistent with their respective needs and concerns at different levels of economic development.[26]

Although the WTO emphasises the need to take into account the concerns of developing countries, this section of the WTO Preamble must be read in conjunction with a subsequent paragraph which points to 'mutually advantageous arrangements directed to the substantial reduction of tariffs and other barriers to trade and to the elimination of discriminatory treatment in international trade relations' as a means of 'contributing to these objectives'.[27] Thus, the Doha Declaration reiterates the WTO assumption according to which the elimination of discrimination in international trade is conducive to economic growth and development. Moreover, by referring to 'mutually advantageous arrangements' as the means to achieve the WTO's objectives, the Declaration also endorses the neo-liberal assumption of the multilateral trading regime as a level playing field where all state actors are in a position to negotiate on an equal footing with one another.

Secondly, there is a recognition that the benefits of trade liberalisation extend to developing countries. Recognising that international trade 'can play a major role in the promotion of economic development and the alleviation of poverty', WTO members commit to focusing the work programme on developing countries' needs and interests.[28] The assumption is therefore that 'the increased opportunities and welfare gains that the multilateral trading system generates'[29] will materialise for developing countries as they already have for developed country members. Finally, recognising that 'the challenges Members face in a rapidly changing international environment cannot be addressed through measures taken in the trade field alone', WTO members commit to continue to work with the Bretton Woods institutions for 'greater coherence in global economic policy-making'.[30] In other words, the Declaration embraces what Rodrik describes as the 'Enlightened Standard View' of the WTO, namely the 'recognition that there is more to integration than simply lowering tariffs and non-tariff barriers to trade … the WTO's focus on expanding market access and deepening integration through the harmonization of a wide range of "trade-related" practices is precisely what development requires'.[31]

Thus, the principles embodied in the Doha Declaration do not substantially depart from the neo-liberal assumptions leading to the adoption of

[26] WTO Preamble (n 3).
[27] *Ibid.*
[28] Doha Declaration (n 23) para 2.
[29] *Ibid.*
[30] *Ibid* para 5.
[31] D Rodrik, 'The Global Governance of Trade as if Development Really Mattered' (UNDP Working Paper, 2001) 2–3 www.servicesforall.org/html/Governance/Rodrik-Trade%20&%20Development.pdf.

the UR agreements. The belief in the multilateral system of trade negotiations and the beneficial impact of trade liberalisation has been upheld and further extended to the reduction of poverty and elimination of marginalisation of least-developed countries.[32] Trade liberalisation is still deemed to be the engine of development and the WTO multilateral rules-based system its means. Within this framework, the Declaration posits the need to remove the obstacles that have prevented developing and especially least-developed countries from enjoying 'recovery, growth and development'.[33] In other words, whereas the UR agreements failed to deliver substantial market access for developing countries' competitive exports, the Doha Round was supposed to remedy this situation.

B Work Programme: Towards a Softening of the WTO Neo-Liberal Agenda?

The negotiating objectives set under the Work Programme therefore aimed at addressing the specific concerns of developing and least-developed countries within the international trading regime. Their examination is thus necessary in order to appreciate the extent to which, if fulfilled, they would have redressed the UR imbalances and delivered the benefits supposed to derive from trade liberalisation based on comparative advantage. A related question is whether the measures necessary to address developing countries' so-called specific needs required a moderation of the WTO neo-liberal insistence on the principle of reciprocity.

i Agriculture

The gains developing countries were expected to make from general liberalisation, in particular the elimination of export subsidies and the reduction of domestic support,[34] had been the subject of several studies prior to the Doha Ministerial Conference.[35] At Doha, ministers agreed 'without prejudging the outcome of the negotiations' to commit themselves to achieve: 'substantial improvements in market access, reduction of, with a view of phasing-out, all

[32] Acknowledging 'the particular vulnerability of the least-developed countries and the special structural difficulties they face in the global economy', WTO members commit to 'addressing the marginalization of least-developed countries in international trade and to improving their effective participation in the multilateral trading system'. Doha Declaration (n 23) para 3.

[33] *Ibid* para 1.

[34] See MJ Trebilcock and R Howse, *The Regulation of International Trade* (London; New York, Routledge, 2005) 345.

[35] See AO Krueger, 'Developing Countries and the Next Round of Multilateral Trade Negotiations' (World Bank Policy Research, Working Paper No 2118, 1999); see also GE Schuh, 'Developing Countries Interests in WTO Agricultural Policy' in Kennedy and

forms of export subsidies; and substantial reductions in trade-distorting domestic support'.[36] Moreover, Special and Differential provisions would be an integral part of the negotiating process in order to allow developing countries to meet their development and food security needs.[37] Hence, the negotiating mandate on agriculture, together with the general objective of establishing 'a fair and market oriented trading system through a programme of fundamental reform encompassing strengthened rules and specific commitments ... to correct and prevent restrictions and distortions in world agricultural markets',[38] reiterates the WTO trade-liberalisation rationale that views international specialisation based on comparative advantage as conducive to economic growth and development. This, however, seems to be moderated by the provisions required to address the development and food security concerns of developing countries.

ii Textiles

No mention was made of the textiles issue. Despite the fact that developing countries had called for an acceleration of the pace of trade liberalisation, the developed countries argued they had been respecting the provisions of the Agreement on Textiles and Clothing (ATC) and were therefore not prepared to renegotiate them.[39] The issue of high tariff rates following the phasing out of quantitative restriction on textiles was therefore not addressed.

iii Market Access for Non-Agricultural Products

Studies had shown that developed countries' tariff rates remained high with respect to the manufactured exports from developing countries, despite the fact that the average rates in developed countries were low.[40] At Doha, ministers agreed 'to reduce or as appropriate, eliminate tariffs, including the reduction of tariff peaks, high tariffs and tariff escalation, as well as non-tariff barriers, in particular on products of export interest to developing countries'.[41] Ministers also agreed to take into account the specific needs of developing and least-developed countries in the course of

Southwick (n 14) 435–48; T Hertel and W Martin, 'Liberalising Agriculture and Manufactures in a Millennium Round: Implications for Developing Countries' (2000) 23 *The World Economy* 455, 455–69.

[36] Doha Declaration (n 23) para 13.
[37] *Ibid* para 14.
[38] *Ibid* para 13.
[39] See Srinivasan (n 10) 22.
[40] Manufacture exports from developing countries face an average tariff rate of 3.4 per cent, compared with only 0.8 per cent faced by developed countries' exports. See Stiglitz and Charlton (n 1) 50.
[41] Doha Declaration (n 23) para 16.

negotiations, including the provision of 'less than full reciprocity' in making commitments. As for the provisions concerning least-developed countries, the declaration expressed the members' commitment to the objective of duty-free and quota-free market access for least-developed countries' exports.[42] This seemed to redress the issue of tariff escalation and tariff peaks directed at developing countries' industrial exports. Whether the requirement of 'less than full reciprocity' and the commitments in favour of least-developed countries represented a substantial departure from the WTO requisite of reciprocal binding commitments would be tested in the course of negotiations.

iv Trade-Related Aspects of Intellectual Property (IP) Rights

The Declaration addressed three concerns regarding the TRIPs Agreement. First, it called on the Council for TRIPs to study the relationship between TRIPs and the Convention on Biological Diversity (CBD).[43] Secondly, it stressed that the TRIPs Agreement should be interpreted 'in a manner supportive of public health, by promoting both access to existing medicines and research and development into new medicines'.[44] A Declaration on the TRIPs Agreement and Public Health[45] was also adopted, emphasising that the agreement should not 'prevent members from taking measures to protect public health … the Agreement can and should be interpreted and implemented in a manner supportive of WTO's members right to protect public health, and in particular, to promote access to medicine for all'.[46]

Another concern the Declaration addressed regarded the difficulty for countries with insufficient or no manufacturing capacity to avail themselves of compulsory licences.[47] In this respect, the Declaration required that an expeditious solution be found by the Council.[48] Therefore, the Doha Declaration placed particular emphasis on the rights of states to protect public health and, by instructing members to study the relationship

[42] *Ibid* para 42.

[43] *Ibid* para 19. The main concern had to do with the fact that the TRIPs Agreement did not require, as a condition for granting patents, the fulfilment of the obligations deriving from the UN CBD. See UN Convention on Biological Diversity (5 June 1992) 31 ILM 818. In particular, it did not prevent the appropriation of biological resources, so-called traditional knowledge and folklore by foreign entities without the consent of the country or communities in which the 'resources' are located, or the obligation to share the benefits deriving from the said appropriation.

[44] Doha Declaration (n 23) para 17.

[45] WTO, Declaration on the TRIPs Agreement and Public Health (20 November 2001) WTO Doc WT/MIN(01)/DEC/2.

[46] *Ibid* para 4. See FM Abbott, 'WTO TRIPs Agreement and its Implications for Access to Medicines in Developing Countries' (UK Commission on Intellectual Property Rights, Study Paper 2a, 2002) www.iprcommision.org/text/documents.htm.

[47] See ch 4 (n 61).

[48] Doha Declaration (n 23) para 6.

between the TRIPs Agreement and the CBD, it seemed to address developing countries' concerns with respect to their biological resources. Besides this, the Doha Declaration merely reiterates the TRIPs Agreement objectives of balancing the exclusive rights of intellectual property (IP) holders with the public purpose of IP protection, namely the encouragement and diffusion of knowledge and technology.

v Services

The issue of imbalance in the level of UR service commitments had been raised by UNCTAD prior to the Doha Ministerial Meeting, pointing to the need for the new round of negotiations to focus on the sectors of interest to developing countries.[49] At Doha, ministers recognised that 'the negotiations on trade in services shall be conducted with a view to promoting the economic growth of all trading partners and the development of developing and least-developed countries'.[50] To this end, members 'noted' that movement of natural persons is an important mode of supply for developing countries. Also, by referring to General Agreement on Trade in Services (GATS) Articles IV and XIX, the Declaration confirmed that, during negotiations, developing and least-developed countries would be required to open 'fewer service sectors, liberalising fewer types of transactions and progressively extending market access in line with their development situation'.[51]

Thus, members reiterated the so-called GATS flexibility with regard to the level of commitments and the degree of liberalisation demanded of developing countries. In addition, they emphasised that the Development Round would be devoted to enhancing their participation in the multilateral system through commitments on the movement of natural persons. The Doha Declaration, therefore, reaffirms the beneficial role of liberalisation in services. Accordingly, it requires members to enhance the growth opportunities for developing countries by liberalising their competitive service sectors.

vi Singapore Issues

Developing countries had manifested their opposition to negotiations on the Singapore issues during the Seattle conference. However, as a result of the Single Undertaking Approach (SUA) that was to characterise the Doha Round, the attainment of the objectives set out with regard to agriculture, non-market access, TRIPs and services was conditional on the trade offs

49 See Srinivasan (n 10) 5; see also Stiglitz and Charlton (n 1) fn1.
50 Doha Declaration (n 23) para 15.
51 *Ibid* para 15. See also GATS Art XIX.

they were prepared to make in the areas of interest to developed countries, namely competition policy, transparency in government procurement, trade facilitation and investment. With regard to investment, ministers recognised 'the case for a multilateral framework to secure transparent, stable and predictable conditions for long-term cross-border investment, particularly foreign direct investment'.[52]

The negotiations would therefore aim at progressively extending market access for foreign investors, taking 'due account of the development policies and objectives of host governments as well as their right to regulate in the public interest of their development situation'.[53] Negotiations on competition policy, transparency in government procurement and trade facilitation would take place at the same time and on the same terms as set forth for negotiations on trade and investments.[54] Thus, the Doha Work Programme incorporated, notwithstanding the developing countries' opposition, the Singapore issues. However, the mandate for launching negotiations on these issues was to be given 'on the basis of a decision to be taken, by explicit consensus' at the fifth Ministerial Conference in Cancun.[55]

vii Special and Differential Treatment

As argued in chapter four, one of the substantial shifts in the development rationale of the WTO was the rejection of the GATT principle of non-reciprocity for developing countries. Although the WTO formally retained the principle of Special and Differential Treatment (SDT), this was reconceptualised to mean principally longer implementation periods and technical assistance by the developed countries. Although the UR agreements included 145 SDT provisions, most of them provided for longer compliance periods and 'best-endeavour' efforts by developed countries.[56] In 2001, some developing countries officially voiced their criticism of the SDT as articulated in the UR agreements.[57] They argued that SDT had been significantly eroded as a result of the assumptions that 'the level of

[52] Doha Declaration (n 23) para 20.

[53] *Ibid* para 22.

[54] *Ibid* paras 23–27.

[55] *Ibid* para 20. Developing countries interpreted this legal provision to mean that explicit consensus was to be reached not only on the modalities for the negotiations but, most importantly, on the question of whether to undertake negotiations in the first place. India in particular required the chairman of the Doha Ministerial Conference to clarify that the launch of the negotiations had to be agreed on by explicit consensus. See Srinivasan (n 10) 26.

[56] See WTO, 'Implementation of Special and Differential Provisions in WTO Agreements and Decisions' (WTO Committee on Trade and Development, 2000) WTO Doc WT/COMTD/W/77.

[57] See WTO, 'Preparations for the Fourth Session of the Ministerial Conference: Proposal for a Framework Agreement on Special and Differential Treatment'. Presented by Cuba, Dominican Republic, Honduras, India, Indonesia, Kenya, Malaysia, Pakistan, Sri Lanka, Tanzania, Uganda and Zimbabwe (2001) WTO Doc WT/GC/W/442.

development had no relationship with the level of rights and obligations under the multilateral system, [and] that the same policies could be universally applied provided that longer transition periods and technical assistance were available', and they complained that 'developing countries had not been given the choice to reject this conception due to the single undertaking approach'.[58]

The Doha Declaration 'notes' the concerns expressed in this framework and members agree that 'all special and differential treatment provisions shall be reviewed with a view to strengthening them and making them more precise, effective and operational'.[59] Thus, there was an understanding that a review of SDT provisions would be carried out in order to clarify which ones are mandatory and, more importantly, to devise strengthened provisions in order to address the concerns expressed by developing countries. Therefore, the Doha mandate with respect to SDT seemed to imply a rethinking of the reciprocity principle and, consequently, of the WTO neo-liberal interpretation of the international trading regime as a level playing field where equal actors make 'mutually advantageous arrangements'.[60] Whether it also signalled a departure from the GATT practice of making impressive statements without undertaking legally binding obligations would be tested in the course of negotiations.

Thus, the Doha Declaration gave WTO members the mandate for comprehensive negotiations in the areas of agriculture, non-agriculture market access (NAMA), SDT, TRIPs, services and the Singapore issues. At the heart of the Declaration was the recognition that since the majority of WTO members are developing and least-developed countries, the round was to promote their full participation in the multilateral trading system. Ministers therefore agreed 'to place their needs and interests at the heart of the Work Programme', and this was to be achieved by 'promoting enhanced market access, balanced rules, and well targeted, sustainably financed technical assistance and capacity building programmes'.[61] The spirit of the Doha Declaration, however, is entirely consistent with the WTO neo-liberal framework in that it identifies development with liberalisation, enhanced export opportunities and further integration in a 'wide range of trade-related practices'.[62]

Hence, taking the neo-liberal development framework of the Doha Declaration at its face value, the question arises as to whether the developed countries' practice of making impressive statements without undertaking

[58] *Ibid.*
[59] Doha Declaration (n 23) para 44.
[60] See WTO Preamble (n 3).
[61] Doha Declaration (n 23) para 2.
[62] Rodrik (n 31).

legally binding obligations has undergone any substantial change.[63] The fact that negotiations had to be carried out under the SUA already cautioned against such an assessment. Even though the declaration's emphasis on SDT seemed to point to a softening of the principle of reciprocity, the adoption of the SUA meant that developing countries would be required to make trade offs in relation to services and the Singapore issues as a quid pro quo for the elimination of the discrimination against their trade. The permanence of the reciprocity rationale, according to which concessions must be paid for, pointed to the fact that the elimination of trade distortions by developed countries would have not been unconditional. However, the extent to which the US and EU were prepared to compromise the overall results of the Doha Development Round, had their market access demands not been met, was not clear in 2001.

The negotiating process from 2001 to 2009 would bring to light the contradiction between the rhetoric of the round and the reality of the negotiations. As argued below, the persistent refusal of the US and EU to eliminate their agricultural support not only defies the objectives of the Doha Declaration, it violates the trade-liberalisation rationale they have consistently purported to embrace since the UR negotiations were launched. In other words, the negotiations followed the GATT practice of employing free-trade principles while pursuing '[sectorally] selective' free trade.[64] In addition, the fact that during the Doha Round the US and EU exerted a level of bilateral pressure on developing countries comparable to that under the UR does not just expose the WTO development myth, it also demonstrates the willingness of the US and EU to actively forego the multilateral trade arena when their agenda is not fulfilled. In what follows, the negotiating practice of the Doha Round is analysed with a view to exposing the WTO rhetoric about free trade, multilateralism and ultimately development.

III FROM CANCUN TO GENEVA: EMERGING OPPOSITIONS

The negotiating process began soon after Doha and was supposed to end in 2005 with a Ministerial Conference to be held in Cancun in 2003 where the negotiating modalities would be set. Contrary to the UR, which had witnessed the breaking down of developing countries' coalition, the Doha negotiating process witnessed a political convergence of developing and

[63] This has been the developed countries' consistent practice under GATT. See RE Hudec, *Developing Countries in the GATT Legal System* (London, Trade Policy Research Centre, 1987) 56.

[64] This expression has been borrowed from F Macmillan, 'Looking Back to Look Forward: Is There a Future for Human Rights in the WTO?' (2005) 11 *International Trade Law and Regulation* 163, 166.

least-developed countries. At Cancun, two groups were established. A group of 20 developing countries (the so-called G20) included Argentina, Bolivia, Brazil, Chile, China, Colombia, Costa Rica, Cuba, Ecuador, El Salvador, Guatemala, India, Mexico, Pakistan, Paraguay, Peru, the Philippines, South Africa, Thailand and Venezuela.[65] Another group, the G90, included the least-developed countries, the African, Caribbean and Pacific countries and the African Union. The organised efforts of both groups played a central role in counteracting the US and EU strategy with respect to agriculture and the Singapore issues.

On agriculture, the US and EU were not prepared to concede an end date for the elimination of export subsidies or precise figures concerning the reduction of domestic support.[66] The EU pointed to the fact that it had already undertaken a comprehensive reform of its Common Agricultural Policy (CAP), reducing distortion in agricultural trade.[67] However, as Stiglitz and Chartlon aptly note in relation to both the 2003 CAP reform and the 2002 US Farm Bill:

> The EU reform shifts support from production-limiting subsidies (the so-called Blue Box subsidies) to other, more acceptable forms of farm support (ie the Green Box subsidies, which are deemed to be less trade-distorting). However, the level of producer support will remain virtually constant—projected to fall only from 57 per cent to 56 per cent (OECD 2004). In addition, the 2002 US Farm Bill had further increased the level of domestic support (under the so-called Blue Box subsidies) for farmers adversely affected by world prices.[68]

Not only did the US and EU refuse to agree on a precise end date for export subsidies and concrete figures for the reduction of domestic support, they also presented a framework agreement which contained a formula for the reduction of tariffs on agricultural products,[69] according to

[65] See F Jawara and A Kwa, Behind the Scenes at the WTO: The Real World of International Trade Negotiations: Lessons of Cancun (London, Zed Books, 2003) xv.

[66] *Ibid* xxv–xxviii.

[67] *Ibid*.

[68] As Stiglitz and Charlton point out, this 'provides counter-cyclical payments (CCPs) to US farmers which respond negatively to world prices. This type of measures has allowed the US to dump its farm surplus on world markets. For example, the US exports corn at prices 20% below the cost of production and wheat at 46% below costs'. Also, 'the US Farm Security and Rural Investment Act (FSRIA) of May 2002 has a value of about US$190 bn over the next 10 years, about US$ 83 bn more than under previous programmes. It sets target prices which are lower than the pre-1996 levels, but the total effective support is larger because average world commodity prices have declined and the range of commodities included in the FSRI is larger than in the 1996 FAIR Act. That Act was intended to phase out farm subsidies, but even before the passage of FSRIA, farmers had achieved support through emergency measures'. Stiglitz and Charlton (n 1) fns 5 and 6.

[69] This formula reflected the compromise between the US and EU and consisted of a proportion of tariffs to be cut by a certain percentage, while the majority of tariffs would be cut according to the so-called Swiss formula (which cut higher tariffs more than lower tariffs), and some tariffs cut to zero or near to zero. See Jawara and Kwa (n 65) xxiv fn 7.

which developing countries would have been required to make further tariff cuts. Given the depressing effects of the EU CAP reform and the US Farm Bill on the economies of developing countries, the US-EU proposal clearly contradicted the principles and objectives of the Doha Declaration. Although the G20 opposed the framework agreement proposed by the US and EU, the Geneva draft text embodied the US and EU position without incorporating developing countries' official opposition. As a consequence, the G20 rejected the draft as failing to reflect their positions.[70]

The other area of controversy between the United States and developing countries concerned the depressing effects on the West and Central African countries' cotton exports of the US export subsidies and domestic support.[71] Benin, Burkina Faso, Chad and Mali proposed an agreement to eliminate all forms of subsidies for cotton over time.[72] They emphasised that this was necessary as cotton was the only export sector of interest to them:

> Any outcome of the negotiations that does not help to ensure respect for the principles of free trade and competition in global trade in cotton will be seen by the WCA countries [West and Central African countries] as unbalanced, unfair and contrary to the objectives approved by all the members countries at Doha.[73]

Despite the unity of the developing countries behind the cotton issue, the US refused to negotiate and, significantly, argued that affected countries should diversify their production away from cotton.[74] The US response was not just at odds with the Doha's commitment to 'assist' least-developed countries. Since West and Central African countries are supposed to be the most competitive cotton producers in the world, its recipe for production diversification violated the free-trade rationale purported by the developed countries themselves. At the insistence of the United States, however, former Director-General Supachai Panitchpakdi suggested the issue be linked to the overall agricultural discussions.[75] Cotton liberalisation was therefore made conditional on an agreement on the contentious US-EU agricultural proposal.

[70] Bridges Daily Update on the Fifth Ministerial Conference, no 4 (Geneva, International Centre for Trade and Sustainable Development, 11 September 2003).

[71] As Jawara and Kwa note, 'over-production as a result of global subsidies estimated at US$6 bn in 2001/2 (mostly from the US, EU and China) has led world cotton prices collapsing over the past decade. While the WCA [West and Central African countries] production—among the most efficient in the world—increased by 14 percent between 1999/2000 and 2001/2002, their export earnings fell by 31 percent'. Jawara and Kwa (n 65) xxix.

[72] WTO Committee on Agriculture, 'WTO Negotiations on Agriculture. Poverty Reduction: Sectoral Initiative in Favor of Cotton' (16 May 2003) WTO Doc TN/AG/GEN/4.

[73] *Ibid.*

[74] Bridges Daily Update on the Fifth Ministerial Conference, No 2 (Geneva, International Centre for Trade and Sustainable Development, 11 September 2003).

[75] Bridges Daily Update on the Fifth Ministerial Conference, no.4 (Geneva, International Centre for Trade and Sustainable Development, 13 September 2003).

On the issue of SDT, contrary to the Doha commitment of making SDT provisions 'more precise, effective and operational', the only 24 included in the Cancun text were 'best endeavour' commitments which had no legal force.[76] Despite the reaction of the Africa Group, which had tabled meaningful SDT commitments, the Cancun text did not change the Geneva draft.[77] This suggested that the Doha mandate on SDT, which seemed to point to a moderation of the WTO reciprocity rationale, reproduced GATT history of developed countries' hortatory statements with regard to development-related trade reforms.

In relation to the negotiations regarding TRIPs, the Doha Declaration required WTO members to find an 'expeditious' solution to the problem affecting countries with insufficient or no manufacturing capacity in the pharmaceutical sector, which, as such, could not avail themselves of compulsory licensing. In August 2003, only a month before Cancun, ministers agreed to an 'interim waiver'[78] which allowed countries to produce patented products under compulsory licence and export them to eligible importing countries, provided that a compulsory licence has also been granted in the importing country.[79] However, as Correa points out, the fact that the waiver was made conditional on certain requirements does not make it a practicable solution.[80] All these conditions impose considerable costs on generic manufacturers. More importantly, according to Correa, the assessment of whether a country has insufficient or no manufacturing capacity is not a matter of self-judgement, but can be subject to challenge by another WTO member. Thus, the onerous conditions of the *interim* decision seemed to impose new obstacles to the achievement of the Doha Declaration's objective of ensuring access to medicines for all.

On the Singapore issues, the Doha Declaration had required members to agree by 'explicit consensus' on both the launch of the negotiations and their negotiating modalities. The Geneva Draft for discussion at Cancun provided two alternatives.[81] The first consisted of launching negotiations

[76] WTO, 'Cancun Ministerial, 2003: Summary of 11 September' www.wto.org/english/thewto_e/minist_e/min03_e/min03_11sept_e.htm.

[77] See C Raghavan, 'Trade: Implementation Issues, S&D Treatment Get Short Shrift' (South–North Development, Third World Network, 26 August 2004).

[78] WTO, 'Implementation of Paragraph 6 of the Doha Declaration on the TRIPs Agreement and Public Health' Decision of the General Council (30 August 2003) WTO Doc WT/L/540.

[79] See C Correa, 'Access to Drugs under TRIPs: A Not So Expeditious Solution' (Geneva, Bridges, International Centre for Trade and Sustainable Development, 2004) 21 www.ictsd.org/monthly/bridges/BRIDGES8–1.pdf.

[80] For instance, the products for export need to be distinguishable from the original patented version (shape, colouring, labelling and packaging); the generic manufacturer needs to prove the 'bio-equivalence' and 'bio-availability' of the generic product and, if data are not disclosed by the patent holder, the generic manufacturer needs to conduct its own 'toxicity and efficacy' studies. *Ibid.*

[81] See Jawara and Kwa (n 65) xxiv.

on all four issues, setting out modalities for each in Annexes, and the second provided for the continuation of the study process. A week before Cancun, more than 40 countries led by Malaysia made a statement in which they argued that the draft gave

> a distorted view that the Annexes have been discussed by Members ... the text on transparency in government procurement was introduced by the proponents in a small group meeting. We are not aware of any text having been put forward by the proponents on trade facilitation. The text on competition policy was discussed only in a small group meeting. Only the proponents' paper was introduced and discussed inconclusively in the HOD [Heads of Delegations] level meeting. Thus, members did not have an opportunity to discuss the modalities identified by the proponents in all the Annexes to the Draft Ministerial text.[82]

These issues were to precipitate the meeting. Although Lamy, the European Commissioner for Trade, was prepared to drop two or three of the Singapore issues, insisting on trade facilitation being negotiated immediately,[83] the opposition of the developing countries and least-developed countries was firm. As the International Development Committee pointed out, 'the timing of the Commission's offer to un-bundle the issues left countries with little time to consider their position, consult their allies and respond constructively'.[84] As a result of the irreconcilable positions on the Singapore issues, the meeting was suspended. The controversy, however, concerned not only the Singapore issues, but the refusal of the US and EU to settle the agricultural and cotton issues in a manner supportive of the Doha mandate.

IV REACTION TO CANCUN: SILENCING DISSENT

The opposition of the G20 and G90 had therefore been essential to the rejection of the Singapore issues and the criticism of the Cancun text on agriculture, cotton and SDT. The reaction to the new developing countries' coalitions was immediate. Dismissing their arguments, which were solidly founded on the Doha Declaration, US Trade Representative Zoellick asserted that 'whether developed or developing countries, there were "can do" and "won't do" countries. The harsh rhetoric of the "won't do"

[82] WTO, 'Paragraphs 13,14,15 &16, Dealing with the Singapore Issues of the Draft Cancun Ministerial Text Contained in Document Job (03)/150/Rev.1. Communication from Bangladesh (on behalf of the LDC Group), Botswana, China, Cuba, Egypt, India, Indonesia, Kenya, Malaysia, Nigeria, the Philippines, Uganda, Venezuela, Zambia and Zimbabwe' WTO Doc WT/MIN(03)/W/4.

[83] International Development Committee, 'Trade and Development at the WTO: Learning the Lessons of Cancun to Revive a Genuine Development Round' in Jawara and Kwa (n 65) xlviii.

[84] *Ibid.*

overwhelmed the concerted efforts of the "can do"'.[85] The US reaction to the newly-formed developing countries' coalitions was to demonstrate clearly that the Doha Round was much more about its market-access opportunities than its commitments to redress the UR imbalances. As Bello points out:

> [I]nstead of understanding why it was isolated in Cancun, the US intensified its efforts to destroy the G21. In a recent visit to Colombia, US Senator Norm Coleman warned President Alvaro Uribe that 'remaining in that Group will not lead to good relations between Colombia and the United States' ... Similarly, the negotiations around the proposed Central American Free Trade Area (CAFTA) have been used by the United States to try to break the Group of 21. In a visit to the region post-Cancun, Mr Zoellick bluntly warned that the negotiations were endangered by Costa Rica and Guatemala's membership in the G21. 'I told them that the emergence of the G20 might pose a big problem to this agreement since our Congress resents the fact that members of CAFTA are also in the G20', he stated. 'If we want to construct a common future with them, resistance and protest do not constitute an effective strategy. In my talks with some of these countries, I sense that they are drawing the right conclusions'.[86]

And the 'right conclusions' were soon drawn. Colombia withdrew from the G20 in September, and in March 2004 the US Trade Representative opened bilateral negotiations for a free-trade area.[87] Costa Rica and Guatemala followed in October and both were included in CAFCA when negotiations were concluded the following January.[88] Peru and Ecuador announced their withdrawal from the group and Zoellick included them in the US-Andean Free Trade Area (FTA).[89] Given the fact that their export-oriented markets could not afford to lose their major importer, Colombia, Costa Rica, Guatemala, Peru and Ecuador abandoned the G20 by January 2004. The United States also used bilateral free-trade agreements in the case of Thailand. In a letter to President Bush on the eve of the APEC (Asia-Pacific Economic Cooperation) meeting where discussions of a US-Thailand FTA were announced, Senator Grassley suggested that before initiating negotiations with the country, 'repudiation by the Government of Thailand of the unbalanced approach displayed in Cancun by the G21 would be a good first step'.[90] Although Thailand did not withdraw from the group, it 'released a statement after Cancun stressing its role as a

[85] USTR, 'US Trade Representative Robert Zoellick Evening Press Conference', Cancun, Mexico. Press Release (14 September 2003).

[86] W Bello, 'Washington Pursues Post-Cancun Vendetta Against Group of 21' (Inside Costa Rica, 2003) insidecostarica.com/specialreports/washington_pursues_vendetta_agaisnt_g21.htm.

[87] See Jawara and Kwa (n 65) lix.

[88] *Ibid* lviii.

[89] *Ibid* lix.

[90] 'Grassley urges President to Consider Ag Concerns Before US-Thailand Trade Agreement', Cancun, Mexico. Press Release, 17 October 2003; quoted in Jawara and Kwa (n 65) lx.

moderate influence within the G20'.[91] In addition, all APEC heads of states accepted the Geneva Draft in October, a month after it was rejected at Cancun.[92]

The US and EU refusal to eliminate export subsidies and reduce domestic support in agriculture and cotton, while requiring developing countries to accept deeper tariff cuts in agriculture and negotiations on the Singapore issues, reveals the extent to which the trade liberalisation rhetoric of the WTO is contradicted by the actual negotiating practice of its developed country members. Both the Cancun meeting and the post-Cancun bilateral pressure on developing countries demonstrate that the US and EU negotiating practice does not substantially differ from that carried out under the GATT. This, as Hudec has put it in relation to development-related GATT reforms, was the developed countries' consistent practice of making impressive statements to give the illusion of greater commitment without undertaking any definable legal obligation.[93]

In contrast to the UR, which failed to deliver substantial market access for developing countries' competitive exports, the Doha Round was supposed to remedy this situation rather than enhancing market-access opportunities for developed countries. Cancun, however, showed this was not the case. As with the UR, market access remains the principal objective of the US and EU negotiating agenda. The qualitative difference with respect to the GATT, however, concerns the fact that WTO competence is not limited to trade in goods, but extends to sensitive areas of domestic regulation concerning investment, services and IP. If the bilateral pressures exerted on developing countries to abandon the G20 and G90 might be beyond the reach of the WTO, the US and EU's aggressive market approach in the new areas, however, is made possible because of the legal provisions of the WTO agreements. The legal examination of the GATS and TRIPs Agreement has suggested that their provisions have the potential to greatly enhance the movement of corporate capital at the expense of the regulatory space of WTO members. The examination of the US and EU negotiating strategy both within and outside the WTO complements the legal analysis carried out so far to corroborate this claim.

V GATS 'FLEXIBILITY': RHETORIC AND NEGOTIATING PRACTICE

As seen in chapter five, the GATS purports to be a flexible agreement in that it allows countries, especially developing countries, to: (a) maintain the right to regulate in order to meet domestic policy objectives; (b)

91 *Ibid* lix.
92 *Ibid.*
93 Hudec (n 63).

exclude from the scope of the agreement 'services provided in the exercise of governmental authority'; and (c) decide about the extent and pace of their liberalisation commitments.[94] The legal examination of the agreement suggested that the first two qualifications needed to be treated very cautiously.[95] First, the legal scope of the 'governmental exception' is not clear. Secondly, the hurdles involved in withdrawing previously made commitments and the operation of the Most Favoured Nation (MFN) make it difficult to reverse the liberalisation process once undertaken. Thirdly, the preamble's reference to the right to regulate cannot be construed as excusing Members' regulations from complying with the GATS provisions. As a result, it was argued that the agreement has the potential to further the interest of corporate capital and adversely impact on the domestic regulatory autonomy of WTO members in ways never realised before under a multilateral treaty on investment. However, it was also pointed out that the materialisation of these implications depends on WTO members' decisions to fully commit under National Treatment (NT) and market access.[96] This section therefore looks at the negotiation process that commenced in 2000 under the GATS and argues that the US and EU practice demonstrates how the potential effects described above have already materialised.

A The Safeguard Mechanism and Liberalisation of GATS Mode 4: An Uncertain Future

The GATS mandated new negotiations in order to achieve progressive liberalisation in the area of services.[97] In order to take account of national policy objectives and the level of development of individual members, negotiations were to be informed by 'appropriate flexibility for individual developing country Members for opening fewer sectors, liberalizing fewer types of transactions, progressively extending market access in line with their development situation'.[98] Furthermore, the participation of developing countries should have been enhanced through 'the liberalization of market access in sectors and modes of supply of export interest to them'.[99] Both the GATS principles were incorporated by trade ministers in the Doha Declaration.[100] In addition, taking into consideration that the specific

[94] See WTO, GATS-Facts and Fiction Booklet, GATS-Facts and Fiction (WTO, Services, 2001) www.abcdoha.org/services/pdfs/WTO_Paper_GATS.pdf. Hereafter WTO Booklet.

[95] See ch 5, II D.

[96] *Ibid.*

[97] GATS Art XIX.1.

[98] GATS Art XIX.2.

[99] GATS Art IV.1(c).

[100] Doha Declaration (n 23) para 15.

commitments undertaken by members can lead to unanticipated consequences requiring regulatory adjustments, the GATS provided for

> multilateral negotiations on the question of emergency safeguard measures based on the principle of non-discrimination. The results of such negotiations shall enter into effect on a date not later than three years from the date of entry into force of the WTO Agreement.[101]

Thus, the GATS posited, as guiding principles for successive negotiations, that members did not expect developing countries to liberalise extensively, that they favoured liberalisation of the movement of natural persons and established a safeguard system that allowed members to temporarily suspend their commitments if these caused unintended and adverse effects on their economy.

Despite the fact that these objectives are clearly stated, their achievement has not yet occurred. The US and EU have delayed commitments on the liberalisation of GATS mode of supply 4, namely movement of natural persons, because of their immigration policy concerns.[102] Thus, contrary to the free-trade rationale of the WTO and the objectives of the Doha Declaration, the liberalisation of developing countries' most competitive service sector has not taken place. In addition, since negotiations began in 2000, the US and EU have consistently refused to negotiate on the safeguard measures. The US in particular has argued that the flexibility provided by the GATS with respect to specific commitments does not require a safeguard mechanism.[103] However, the importance of such a mechanism, which is provided in relation to trade in goods,[104] cannot be overstated with respect to services. As Trebilcock and Howse aptly note:

> *[E]x ante* limitations on commitments do not perform the same function as safeguards: safeguards necessarily adjust obligations *ex post* and temporarily, given some anticipated social and economic consequences from the implementation of GATS commitments. If anything, the case for a mechanism to perform this function in GATS is even stronger than in GATT … specific commitments and other GATS disciplines have the effect of locking in particular approaches to regulatory reform and privatisation.[105]

[101] GATS Art X.1.

[102] See S Chaudhuri, A Mattoo and R Self, 'Moving People to Deliver Services: How Can the WTO Help?' (2004) 38 *Journal of World Trade* 363.

[103] See Trebilcock and Howse (n 34) 374.

[104] GATT Art XIX provides that in case of unforeseeable circumstances causing a surge of imports that seriously threatens domestic industries, countries are allowed to temporarily suspend their concessions under GATT.

[105] Trebilcock and Howse (n 34) 374.

Even though developing countries have repeatedly expressed their frustration in relation to negotiations on the safeguard mechanism and the liberalisation of GATS mode 4, there has been no substantial progress since Cancun.[106]

B Targeting Non-Discriminatory Domestic Regulation: GATS Article VI

Whereas negotiations on the movement of natural persons and the safeguard mechanism have been hampered by the US and EU, the intrusion in the domestic regulatory space of members is further evidenced in the negotiations on domestic regulation required by the GATS to ensure that 'measures relating to qualifications requirements and procedures, technical standards and licensing procedures do not constitute unnecessary barriers to trade in services ... and are not more burdensome than necessary'.[107] In order to appreciate the level of intrusion into the domestic regulatory space of WTO members, the negotiations required under GATS Article VI need to be viewed together with the provisions on NT, MFN and Market Access. Whereas NT and MFN aim to eliminate discriminatory measures,[108] and market access targets quantitative non-discriminatory measures,[109] negotiations on 'domestic regulation' under Article VI aim to eliminate qualitative non-discriminatory government measures. As Sinclair and Grieshaber-Otto point out, qualifications requirements may include professional and educational certification. Licensing requirements concern not only professional licensing, but broadcast licences, university accreditation and facilities licensing for clinics, hospitals and laboratories.[110] Moreover,

> [t]echnical standards refer not only to regulations affecting the technical characteristic of the service itself but also the rules according to which services must be performed. Water quality standards, pipeline safety, and toxic waste disposal and storage standards are just a few important examples.[111]

[106] C Manduna, 'The GATS Negotiations: Development Considerations Towards Hong Kong' Trade Briefs (Trade Law Centre for Southern Africa, 2005) www.tralac.org/scripts/content.php?id=4022.

[107] GATS Art VI.4.

[108] Under NT, members are prevented from discriminating against foreign services and service providers in favour of domestic services and service providers. Under MFN, members are required not to discriminate between similar services and service providers of different WTO members.

[109] If members fully commit under market access, Art XVI lists a number of measures they are prevented from adopting, even if the measure at issue does not discriminate between domestic and foreign services and between domestic service providers and foreign service providers. See ch 5, II D iii.

[110] S Sinclair and JG Grieshaber-Otto, *Facing the Facts: A Guide to the GATS Debate* (Ottawa, Canadian Centre for Policy Alternatives, 2002) 65.

[111] *Ibid* 65.

Thus, the qualitative non-discriminatory regulations that the current GATS negotiations aim at disciplining concern important policy choices until now outside the scope of WTO regulation. Furthermore, whereas countries can list exceptions under NT and Market Access,[112] no exception can be invoked by members under Article VI. In 2001, the WTO Secretariat pointed out that what states need to argue before a panel in order to defend a certain measure is that this 'is actually necessary to achieve the specified legitimate objective'.[113] The current draft of the disciplines does not include the necessity test. However, it requires states to ensure their regulations are 'objective' and 'relevant' to the supply of the services to which they apply. Therefore, regardless of whether the final draft incorporates the necessity test or the objectivity and relevance criteria, the point is that unlike the GATT, where additional requirements have been imposed in order to save discriminatory measures intended to fulfil a legitimate objective, GATS Article VI.4 extends its reach by targeting non-discriminatory regulation. In effect, this is a large intrusion into the regulatory space of members. The Doha Declaration states that 'Members shall aim to complete negotiations under art. VI.4 ... prior to the conclusion of negotiations on specific commitments'.[114] Thus, the conclusion of negotiations on 'domestic regulation', and more importantly without a safeguard mechanism yet in place, clearly points to the aggressive market approach of the US and EU. The WTO Secretariat has emphasised that the GATS recognises the right to regulate 'and to introduce new regulations on the supply of services within their territories in order to meet national policy objectives'.[115] The efficacy of this preambular reference has already been questioned.[116] However, if current negotiations on Article VI were to be successful, the so-called right to regulate would be further compromised.

C Enter Specific Commitments: The Request-Offer Approach

Thus, the negotiating process under the GATS has been characterised by the US and EU refusal to agree on a safeguard mechanism and to liberalise the movement of natural persons. Conversely, the US and EU have focused on negotiations in the area of domestic regulation that will further reduce WTO members' autonomy to adopt non-discriminatory regulations. This contradicts not only the language of the GATS, but the spirit of the Doha

[112] GATS Arts XVI and XVII.
[113] WTO Secretariat, 'Application of the Necessity Test: Issues for Consideration' 2 May, 2000; quoted in Sinclair and Grieshaber-Otto (n 110) 65–66.
[114] Doha Declaration (n 23) para 7.
[115] WTO Booklet (n 94).
[116] See ch 5, II D iv.

Development Round. To substantiate this claim, it is necessary to turn to the last pillar of the so-called GATS flexibility, namely the claim that countries can autonomously decide about the degree and pace of liberalisation by freely choosing their specific commitments under NT and Market Access.

To reinforce this flexibility, the Doha Declaration has reiterated that developing countries are expected to liberalise fewer service sectors in accordance with their development needs. Moreover, GATS Article XIX:3 provides that prior to negotiating guidelines and modalities for future negotiations, the Council for Trade in Services is to carry out a comprehensive assessment in order to evaluate the impact of the liberalisation commitments already undertaken by members. In other words, negotiations should not begin unless a comprehensive study on the effects of liberalisation has been made.

Crucially, this assessment has not taken place, whereas negotiating modalities were nonetheless adopted in 2001.[117] This means that developing countries have been denied the right under the GATS to assess the impact of service liberalisation already undertaken prior to negotiating new commitments. Further, there is a more problematic aspect linked to the negotiating guidelines adopted in 2001. These stipulate that negotiations on specific commitments will be carried out on a request-offer basis with no sector 'excluded a priori'.[118] Thus, a country submits initial requests to another country from which it requires certain specific commitments to be made. The recipient country then tables its initial offers and negotiations start between the two countries. Due to the nature of the modalities, only offers made by recipient countries are accessible on the WTO website.

This has made it difficult to assess the negotiating practice of the requesting parties, especially in light of public statements such as those released by developed countries' officials after Doha. For instance, Patricia Hewitt, former UK Secretary of State for Trade and Industry, declared that the EU would not require least-developed countries to liberalise more than three to five sectors, and that, in the case of developing countries, requests were made in line with their levels of development.[119] However, thanks to a EU document leaked to the Polaris Institute in Canada, the reality of the GATS negotiations has been disclosed.[120] The document shows that the EU has targeted 109 countries, 94 of which are developing countries, economies in

[117] WTO, 'Guidelines and Procedures for the Negotiations on Trade in Services' (29 March 2001) WTO Doc S/L/93.

[118] *Ibid.*

[119] *Hansard*, 'Rt Hon Patricia Hewitt MP Response to UK Parliamentary Question from Julia Drown MP' (26 June 2002); quoted in World Development Report, 'Whose Development Agenda? An Analysis of the European Union's GATS Requests of Developing Countries' (WDM: 2003) 9. Hereafter, World Development Report.

[120] World Development Report (n 119) 6.

transition and least-developed countries, requesting the liberalisation of service sectors well beyond the level stated by Hewitt.[121]

In order to show how negotiations are carried out and the extent to which they impact on the domestic regulatory autonomy of targeted countries, it is necessary to analyse the relationship between the GATS initial commitments,[122] the 2001 negotiating modalities and the content of the requests countries have made, for which the leaked EU document is important. In accordance with the bottom-up approach to liberalisation adopted under the UR, countries have selected the sectors they were prepared to liberalise and listed specific limitations under NT and market access. For instance, Kenya has committed its telecommunication sector. At the same time it has listed an exception that limits foreign investments to 30 per cent.[123] India has liberalised its banking sector but placed a ceiling of 15 per cent on assets of foreign banks in the total assets of the banking system.[124] Colombia has also committed its financial services sector. However, it has listed as an exception the right to offer special conditions to Colombian nationals.[125] The specific commitments made by countries during the UR represent the baseline for the negotiations commenced in 2000 to be conducted under the request offer approach. This means that WTO members need to make further specific commitments in order to achieve progressive liberalisation.

In relation to the content of the EU requests, the leaked document shows that the EU is requesting developing countries and least-developed countries to liberalise more than a few service sectors, contrary to Hewitt's statement and the Doha Declaration's language. It also shows that the EU is precisely targeting those exceptions developing countries have listed to their schedules of commitments, contrary to the so-called flexibility of Articles XIX and IV. Thus, the above-mentioned exceptions listed by Kenya, India and Colombia have been targeted by the EU, with the aim of eliminating existing market-access restrictions to its foreign investors. The EU's aggressive market approach is apparent in the concentration of requests made in areas such as telecommunication, with all 94 countries targeted, followed by the business sector with 93 countries, the transport sector with 86 countries and the financial sector with 68 countries.[126] The

[121] *Ibid* 9. Ecuador, Guatemala, Peru, El Salvador, Trinidad and Tobago have received 11 sector requests. China, India, Kuwait Pakistan, Tanzania, Thailand, Malaysia, South Africa, Paraguay, Colombia, Costa Rica, Mexico, the Philippines, Qatar, Egypt, Tunisia and Venezuela have received 12 requests. Sri Lanka has received 10; Kenya, 9; Zimbabwe, 8; Tanzania, 7; and Mozambique has received 6 sector requests.

[122] Namely, the specific commitments made during the UR.

[123] See World Development Report (n 119) 17.

[124] *Ibid.*

[125] *Ibid.*

[126] See Summary Table of EU Requests in World Development Report (n 119) 37–42.

EU negotiating practice under the GATS points to the fact that although it has renounced negotiations on investments under the Singapore issues,[127] it is nonetheless aggressively pursuing market access for its foreign investors in the service area. At a more fundamental level, the EU leaked document shows that, contrary to the argument that negotiations under the WTO occur on a multilateral basis, the request offer approach means that negotiations are conducted on de facto bilateral terms.

Hence, if the so-called flexibility that GATS offers and the negotiating practice of the EU are duly taken into consideration, the assault on the domestic regulatory autonomy of WTO members should give cause for great concern. However, since negotiations on services are an integral part of market access under the SUA, as the 2005 Report of the Chairman to the Trade Negotiations Committed has remarked,[128] liberalisation on agriculture is made conditional on liberalisation of services. Thus, since Cancun, about 71 initial offers have been made and 31 revised offers have been submitted.

VI TRIPS: TRANSFER OF TECHNOLOGY V INVESTORS' RIGHTS

Despite the enormous costs developing countries are incurring in complying with the TRIPs Agreement provisions,[129] the central argument advanced by developed countries during the UR was that developing economies will, in the long run, benefit from the transfer of technology and increasing investment flows that IP holders' security entails.[130] To support this objective, TRIPs requires that the enhanced protection of IP rights be balanced with the 'transfer and dissemination of technology'[131] and the right of states to adopt measures to prevent IP holders from 'adversely affect[ing] the international transfer of technology'.[132] Furthermore, it has been stressed that the TRIPs Agreement provisions do not posit the

[127] This was made official in 2004, with the adoption of the so-called July Framework for resuming negotiations under the Doha Round. See WTO, Doha Work Programme: Decision of the General Council (2 August 2004) WTO Doc WT/L/579.

[128] See Mancuna (n 106).

[129] The implementation costs to reform their legal systems have been analysed by Finger and Schuler (n 20) 525. In a survey concerning the US, the UK, Germany, Japan, France and Switzerland, Finger also notes that patent rents from TRIPs amount to US$40 bn per year while total IP payment outflows deriving from full implementation of TRIPs amount to US$60 bn per year. See JM Finger, 'The Doha Agenda and Development: A View from the Uruguay Round' ERD (Asian Development Bank: Working Paper No 21, 2002) 13–25.

[130] For an early critique of these arguments within GATT, see FM Abbott, 'Protecting First World Assets in the third World: Intellectual Property Negotiations in the GATT Multilateral Framework' (1989) 22 *Vanderbilt Journal of Transnational Law* 689, 698.

[131] TRIPs Art 7.

[132] TRIPs Art 8.

exclusive[133] rights of investors as absolute; they provide for several exceptions that limit investors' rights.[134] One particular instance of this is the right of states to issue compulsory licences,[135] namely the government authorisation to third parties to use a patent without the consent of the IP holder, provided the conditions stipulated in TRIPs Article 31 are met.[136] In addition, it has been suggested that if developing countries had accepted multilateral negotiations on IP, the US would have refrained from negotiating on a bilateral basis.[137] The TRIPs Agreement was thus supposed to put an end to the unilateral and bilateral pressure that left developing countries isolated against US economic and political influence.

More than a decade into the operation of the TRIPs Agreement, it is possible to assess the validity of each claim. With regard to the 'transfer of technology' argument, the legal examination of TRIPs Articles 7, 8, 66 and 67 has suggested that their legal enforceability, and therefore their usefulness as means on which developing countries can rely to ensure that technology transfer takes place, is doubted.[138] This is evidenced both by the fact that no country has yet relied on these provisions and by the fact that empirical evidence that transfer of technology has occurred is at best 'sketchy and anecdotal'.[139] Furthermore, empirical evidence that correlates the increased protection of IP with higher flows of foreign direct investments is not conclusive.[140]

As to the argument that the TRIPs Agreement provides for the right to issue compulsory licences, the post-UR phase has highlighted the difficulty developing countries encounter in availing themselves of such a right. The so-called access to medicine debate brought to the fore the controversy over the legal interpretation of the TRIPs Agreement provisions on compulsory licences, in particular with regard to states with insufficient or

[133] These are the IP holder's rights to exclude third parties from using, producing or commercialising the IP subject matter without authorisation.

[134] See TRIPs Arts 13, 17 and 30, 31.

[135] TRIPs Art 31.

[136] For the conditions attached to the issuance of compulsory licences, see ch 4 (fn 61).

[137] As Emory Simon, Director for Intellectual Property at the Office of the United States Trade Representative (USTR) remarked in relation to the failure to negotiate TRIPs, 'What happens if we fail [to obtain TRIPS]? I think there are a number of consequences to failure. First, will be an increase in bilateralism. For those of you who think bilateralism is a bad thing, a bad thing will come about' in P Drahos, 'BITs and BIPs: Bilateralism in Intellectual Property' (2001) 4 *The Journal of World Intellectual Property* 791, 791.

[138] For instance, the question arises as to whether both provisions allow states to deny TRIPs protection to IP holders who have not complied with measures aimed at facilitating the transfer of technology or preventing anti-competitive abuses. See ch 5 II E ii.

[139] Trebilcock and Howse (n 34) 400.

[140] See CA Primo Braga and C Fink, 'The Relationship Between Intellectual Property Rights and Foreign Direct Investments' (1998) 9 *Duke Journal of Comparative and International Law* 163, 181.

no manufacturing capacity.[141] As a result of this controversy, ministers at Doha clarified that the TRIPs Agreement should not prevent the availability of essential medicines. In addition, the Doha Declaration required members to find a solution to address the concerns of states with insufficient production capabilities. Members arrived at this solution in August 2003.[142] The effectiveness of this decision, however, needs to be assessed in light of the limits posed by post-UR bilateral activity promoted by the US and EU in particular.

This relates to the third claim concerning the beneficial impact of the TRIPs Agreement on developing countries, namely the suggestion that multilateral negotiations on IP would put an end to the bilateral and unilateral pressure developed countries, in particular the United States, have exerted on developing countries since the beginning of the 1980s. Rather than witnessing the decline of unilateral and bilateral pressure, the post-UR phase has been characterised by an increase in bilateral activity between developed and developing countries deriving from the interaction between the TRIPs Agreement provisions and a number of Bilateral Investment Treaties (BITs), Free Trade Areas (FTAs) and Regional Trading Areas (RTAs).[143] As most investment agreements define IP as a protected 'investment', the aim of this activity has been to give more extensive protection to IP than what is provided in the TRIPs Agreement.

However, the basis for doing so is to be found in the TRIPs Agreement itself. The agreement sets only minimum standards that countries are supposed to abide by, which means that agreements negotiated after TRIPs can provide for more extensive protection. This has to be seen within the context of the operation of the MFN clause, according to which if a WTO member provides for higher standards of IP protection, the new protection will be extended to all WTO members. The reasons for signing investment agreements are several. First, despite the elusive evidence on the correlation between the conclusion of such agreements and the increased flows of investments, countries in need of foreign capital may hope that the enhanced protection of foreign investors will encourage inflows of foreign investment. Secondly, the enhanced protection of IP standards through the conclusion of such agreements may be posed as a condition for obtaining

[141] The issue arose with regard to several pharmaceutical companies challenging a South African legislation allowing for the import of patented medicines that had been sold in another market without the consent of the patent holder before the High court of Pretoria. The complaint, supported by the European and American governments, was that the South African Act violated TRIPs in that it allowed for 'parallel imports'. This notwithstanding the fact that TRIPs Art 6 recognises the possibility of parallel imports as it allows states to decide about the 'exhaustion of rights'. The complaint was withdrawn by the pharmaceutical companies in April 2001 due to public pressure. See Trebilcock and Howse (n 34) 429–32; Abbott, 'WTO TRIPs Agreement' (n 46).

[142] For the conditions attached, see above, n 80.

[143] Hereafter referred to as Investment Agreements.

preferential trading arrangements[144] or deemed necessary in order to escape the pressure mechanism of the US Section 301.[145]

A Substantive TRIPs-plus Standards in Investment Agreements

Although many investment agreements do not set specific standards of IP protection, they protect the IP rights of investors by including IP in the definition of investments.[146] As Drahos puts it, an agreement that requires '—a Member to implement a more extensive standard or—which eliminates an option for a Member under a TRIPs standard' can be said to incorporate TRIPs-plus measures.[147] Since the coming into force of the TRIPs Agreement, both kinds of agreements, those requiring a state to grant more extensive protection than that required by TRIPs and those eliminating an option available under TRIPs, have been concluded between developed and developing countries. Examples of the first category include investment agreements that contain requirements to:

1. extend the term of patent protection in order to compensate patent owners for regulatory delays in being able to exploit the patent;[148]
2. grant patents for 'new uses' of known compounds;[149]

[144] For instance, Drahos points out that both the US-Caribbean Basin Initiative of 1983 and the US African Growth and Opportunity Act (2000), which provide for preferential access to the US market in favour of Caribbean and sub-Saharan states, pose as a condition for eligibility that states give 'effective protection' to US IP rights. Drahos (n 137) 801.

[145] In the case of the BIT signed by the US with Nicaragua in 1995, its entry into force was made conditional on Nicaragua signing a Bilateral Intellectual Property agreement (BIP) providing adequate and effective protection of US IPRs. Two years later, the USTR added Nicaragua to its Special 301 'Other observation' list as negotiations on BIP were still proceeding. In 1998, the BIP between Nicaragua and the US was signed and was to be implemented in 1999, ahead of the transitional period under TRIPS. *Ibid* 796.

[146] See C Correa, 'Bilateral Investment Agreements: Agents of New Global Standards for the Protection of Intellectual Property Rights' (GRAIN, 2002) 6 www.grain.org/briefings_files/correa-bits-august-2004.pdf.

[147] Drahos (n 137) 793.

[148] See US-Jordan FTA, in Drahos (n 137) 797. See also, CAFCA, Art 15.9(6), US-Chile FTA, Art 17.9(6), US-Morocco FTA, Art 15.9(7), US-Singapore FTA, Art 16.7(7)–(8) in FM Abbott 'Toward a New Era of Objective Assessment in the Field of TRIPS and Variable Geometry for the Preservation of Multilateralism' (2005) 8 *Journal of International Economic Law* 77, 89, fn 45. This is not required by the TRIPS Agreement as made clear by the WTO, *Canada: Patent Protection of Pharmaceutical Products, Report of the Panel* (adopted 17 March 2000) WT/DS114/R.

[149] See eg, US-Morocco FTA, Art 15:9(2). As Abbott notes, 'In a typical case, a pharmaceutical compound known to be effective for treating one form of disease may be found to treat another disease, and a person seeks a patent on the "new use"… the TRIPs Agreement is silent regarding whether such patents should be granted, leaving countries with flexibilities to decide the question'. Abbott, *ibid*, 89, fn 44.

3. ensure protection of IP rights in conformity with the highest international standards;[150]
4. apply NT at the pre-establishment phase;[151] and
5. give effect to the Union for the Protection of Plant Varieties.[152]

These are examples of investment agreements increasing the standards of protection beyond TRIPs. Agreements that eliminate options states can adopt under TRIPs are those that:

1. impose limits on the exclusion from patentability;[153]
2. prevent parallel importation[154] and limit the right to issue compulsory licences;[155] and
3. require countries to implement TRIPs before the transitional period has expired.[156]

B Investor-to-State Dispute Resolution

In addition to incorporating higher standards of IP protection than those set under the TRIPs Agreement, investment agreements provide for both state-to-state and investor-to-state dispute resolution. This means that, contrary to the inter-states dispute resolution system envisaged under the WTO, investment agreements confer on investors the right to sue the host state through ad hoc proceedings often involving arbitration. Since 1997, the majority of the disputes concerning such agreements have involved

[150] Correa argues this is the case with bilateral agreements concluded between the EC and South Africa (1999), Tunisia (1998) and the Palestinian Authority (1997). See Correa, 'Bilateral Investment Agreements' (n 146) 20.

[151] See US model BIT (2004) Art.3.2 and US-Singapore FTA Art15.1.17. The latter is the first agreement which seems to extend NT in relation to the 'acquisition' of rights to the pre-establishment phase, departing from TRIPs Part IV; in Correa, 'Bilateral Investment Agreements' (n 146) 3 fn 4.

[152] See US-Jordan FTA, US-Nicaragua BIP and EC Mexico FTA; in Drahos (n 137). TRIPs Art 27 provides for the obligation of states to protect plant varieties. However, states can decide whether to grant patents or devise a *sui generis* system of plant variety protection.

[153] TRIPs Art 27.3 allows states to exclude from patent protection plants and animals. However, as Abbott points out, the US-Chile FTA Art 17.9(2), (best efforts), CAFTA Art 15.9(2), (best efforts) and the US-Morocco FTA Art 15.9(2), preclude the exclusion from patentability of plants and animals. See Abbott, 'Toward a New Era' (n 148) 89, fn 43.

[154] Despite the fact that the Doha Declaration and the subsequent Decision of 2003 have clarified that parallel imports are consistent with the TRIPs Agreement, some FTAs prohibit them. See US-Morocco, Art 15.9(4); in Abbott, 'Toward a New Era' (n 148) 90 fn 46.

[155] Whereas the TRIPs Agreement lays down the conditions under which compulsory licences can be granted, investment agreements limit the granting of compulsory licences to specific circumstances, such as cases of national emergencies or extreme urgency. See US-Jordan FTA; in Drahos (n 137) 797. Also, see US-Singapore FTA Art 16.7(6); in Abbott, 'Toward a New Era' (n 148) 90, fn 47.

[156] US-Nicaragua; in Drahos (n 137) 796.

investors and host states rather than the states party to the agreement.[157] As Hallward-Driemeir points out, investor-state proceedings

> are not bound by precedents, are not necessarily obliged to be open to the public, or to publish final decisions. The decisions have only limited appeal and cannot be amended by the domestic legal system or a supreme court. The nature of the dispute resolution can provide a great deal of leeway in how cases will be decided ... [T]hey could encourage investors to pursues their case even if the merits are not all that strong.[158]

Thus, the inclusion of investor-to-state dispute resolution signals a departure from the WTO interstate system, giving private investors strong rights in relation to the protection of their investments. The significance of this departure has to be viewed in the context of the protection against expropriation these agreements confer on investors.

C Expropriation

Investment agreements usually contain provisions aimed at protecting foreign investments against expropriation by the host state. Expropriation, however, does not refer only to the direct taking of foreign property. Investment agreements increasingly refer to 'de facto', 'indirect' and 'creeping' expropriation or acts 'tantamount' to expropriation.[159] Although these terms are differently construed, they refer to government acts that cause a loss for the foreign investor or diminish the value of its investment.[160] The issue of expropriation touches on several of the TRIPs Agreement flexibilities, such as compulsory licences and parallel imports, as well as the rights host states enjoy under the CBD.[161]

With regard to compulsory licences and parallel imports, they may be construed under investment agreements as government actions limiting the economic gains 'a patent owner may obtain from his "investment"'.[162] As Correa observes:

> [T]he mere fact that [a compulsory licence] may have an adverse economic effect on an investment, standing alone, does not establish that a *de facto* or *indirect* expropriation has occurred ... [however] cases may arise in which claims of this

[157] See Correa, 'Bilateral Investment Agreements' (n 146) 27.
[158] Hallward-Driemeier, 2003; quoted in Correa, *ibid.*
[159] See Correa, 'Bilateral Investment Agreements' (n 146) 15; M Sornarajah, *The International Law on Foreign Investments* (Cambridge, Cambridge University Press, 2004) 350–54.
[160] See Sornarajah, *ibid.*
[161] UN Convention on Biological Diversity (n 43).
[162] Correa, 'Bilateral Investment Agreements' (n 146) 15.

type could be made—for instance, when a patent owner is dissatisfied with the determination of the level or mode of remuneration.[163]

Similarly, if parallel imports are enacted according to the conditions posed by the Decision on Public Health and the 2003 waiver, they should be considered legitimate under the TRIPs Agreement and therefore should not give rise to expropriation claims. However, Correa notes that the decisions taken under the North American Free Trade Agreement (NAFTA) Chapter 11 to consider market shares as investments pose the question of possible expropriation claims in cases where it is successfully argued that parallel imports diminish the IP owner's market share.[164] Thus, while the August 2003 waiver has made clear that parallel imports are consistent with TRIPs, investment agreements may well allow foreign investors to bring expropriation claims against the host state thanks to the investor-to-state dispute resolution. The intention, as Abbott puts it, is clear: 'the new bilateral and regional arrangements are providing the legal basis for the reduction of critical policy space within developing countries'.[165]

i TRIPs, CBD and Investment Agreements

Abbott's argument is corroborated by the examination of the intricate relationship between the TRIPs Agreement, the CBD and investment agreements. The CBD requires access to genetic resources to occur on the basis of 'prior informed consent of the Contracting Party providing such resources'[166] and 'mutually agreed terms'[167] between the provider and the user of such resources. Thus, the Convention requires states to enact legislation or regulation ensuring that the use of biological resources and 'Traditional Knowledge' is made dependent on the requirement to inform the country of origin of their source.[168]

This requirement represented an important achievement for developing countries seeking to prevent unauthorised exploitation of their resources and knowledge. The TRIPs Agreement, on the other hand, does not provide for a 'disclosure of source of origin' obligation as a condition for granting a patent. The controversy between developed and developing

[163] *Ibid* 15–16. Under the TRIPs Agreement, one of the conditions for the granting of compulsory licences to third parties is that adequate remuneration is provided to the patent owner.

[164] Correa, 'Bilateral Investment Agreements' (n 146) 19.

[165] Abbott, Toward a New Era' (n 148) 91.

[166] UN Convention on Biological Diversity (n 43) Art 15.5.

[167] *Ibid* Art 15.4.

[168] Countries such as Brazil, Costa Rica, India and the Andean Community have already enacted legislation concerning the 'disclosure of source of origin' obligation, providing for the revocation of a patent granted in absence of such requisite. See Correa, 'Bilateral Investment Agreements' (n 146) 18.

countries[169] over a possible conflict between the two international treaties led trade ministers at Doha to instruct the Council to study the relationship between the TRIPs Agreement and the CBD. However, the US[170] and EU in particular have since refused to amend the TRIPs Agreement, arguing that no conflict between the two agreements exists since countries are free to enact domestic legislation to fulfil the convention's objectives.[171] However, several questions arise in relation to expropriation claims under investment agreements and their relationship with TRIPs and the CBD.

The first issue concerns the revocation of a patent for failing to disclose the source of origin of the biological resources or the 'Traditional Knowledge' incorporated in the patent. As Correa writes, it may be argued that such a legislative provision corresponds to 'a new requirement for patentability not provided in TRIPs art. 27.1'.[172] This interpretation would not only give states the possibility of bringing an action before the WTO, but in the context of an investment agreement that considers patents as a protected 'investment', investors may well bring before arbitration tribunals' closed-doors expropriation claims against host states. Similar problems arise in relation to another area disciplined by the Convention. Article 15 requires Contracting Parties to take legislative, administrative or policy measures 'with the aim of sharing in a fair and equitable way the results of research and development and the benefits arising from the commercial and other utilization of genetic resources with the Contracting Party providing such resources'.[173]

Thus, one important objective of the CBD is to ensure that Contracting Parties providing the biological resources share, in an equitable and fair manner, the benefits arising from commercial and other uses[174] of the resources, such as in the case of patents. However, in addition to the fact that the TRIPs Agreement does not pose 'benefit sharing' as a condition for the granting of patents, some investment agreements explicitly prohibit

[169] For an exposition of developing countries' positions in relation to the conflict between the two agreements, see the arguments submitted by Bolivia, Brazil, Cuba, Dominican Republic, Ecuador, India, Peru, Thailand and Venezuela in 'The Relationship between the TRIPs Agreement and the Convention on Biological Diversity and the Protection of Traditional Knowledge' (24 June 2003) WTO Doc IP/C/W/403.

[170] The US signed the Convention in 1993 but has not ratified it yet. For the complete list of countries, see www.biodiv.org/world/parties.asp.

[171] For an overview of the differing positions between developed and developing countries, see 'The Relationship between the TRIPs Agreement and the Convention on Biological Diversity: Summary of Issues Raised and Points Made' (09 March 2006) WTO DocIP/C/W/368/Rev.1.

[172] Correa, 'Bilateral Investment Agreements' (n 146) 18.

[173] UN Convention on Biological Diversity (n 43) Art 15.7.

[174] For instance, the transfer of technology and 'know-how' associated with the utilisation of resources.

performance requirements such as transfer of technology.[175] From this standpoint, the chances for foreign investors to bring expropriation claims and succeed seem to increase. Moreover, as Correa writes, these agreements accomplish another objective: they are intended to 'limit the ability of parties to apply "performance requirements" in a manner that goes well beyond the standards set forth by the WTO Agreement on Trade Related Investments Measures'.[176]

The legal analysis of the GATS, TRIMs Agreement and TRIPs Agreement carried out in chapter five suggested that the regulatory autonomy of WTO members may have been substantially eroded in favour of the extension of investors' rights. However, it is the examination of the negotiating practice both within and outside the WTO that poignantly reveals the US and EU agenda. As a result of the power the G20 and G90 have increasingly acquired in the context of the WTO multilateral negotiations, developed countries are shifting between multilateral and bilateral negotiating forums. Thus, negotiations on services are still carried out under the WTO since the request offer approach amounts to de facto bilateral negotiations between developed and developing countries. Since negotiations on investment have been dropped from the negotiating agenda and those on IP are not progressing, developed countries have turned to bilateral deals to advance the protection of their corporate interests.

VII FROM HONG KONG TO GENEVA: THE LAST BREATH OF THE DOHA ROUND?

By 2004, the negotiations that effectively remained within the WTO multilateral arena were those concerning agricultural liberalisation, NAMA and SDT.[177] The process that led to the suspension of the Doha Round in July 2006 and again in July 2008 focused on the disagreement between developed and developing countries over these issues. The subject matter of the impasse reinforces the argument that the Doha Round, contrary to the development rhetoric, is about achieving substantial access in developing countries' markets without undertaking meaningful liberalisation in the areas of interest to them. This contradicts not only the spirit of the Doha Round, which is supposed to take development seriously, but the free-trade principles that underpin the liberalisation rationale of the WTO.

[175] See US-Singapore FTA, Art 15.8.1(f); in Correa, 'Bilateral Investment Agreements' (n 146) 25.
[176] *Ibid.*
[177] This is not to say that services and IP are excluded from WTO negotiations. It is to emphasise that both the IP bilateral activity and de facto bilateral negotiations under the GATS challenge claims about the multilateral nature of WTO negotiations.

A The July Framework

In July 2004, members agreed on the modalities for final negotiations to be concluded in December 2005. The so-called 'July Package'[178] seemed to contain three achievements the developing countries had sought since Cancun. First, a commitment was made by developed countries to eliminate agricultural export subsidies and tighten disciplines on other forms of export subsidisation.[179] Secondly, the decision stated that developing countries would have had the flexibility to designate an appropriate number of so-called Special Products, based on criteria of food security, livelihood security and rural development needs, and that these products were eligible for 'more flexible treatment' in the context of tariff cuts.[180] The decision also stated that a special safeguard mechanism would be established for use by developing countries.[181] Finally, the decision officially dismissed three of the four Singapore issues, namely investment, competition policy and government procurement.[182]

However, the extent to which these commitments were to produce tangible results was conditioned by the undefined language of the decision. First, no end date for the elimination of export subsidies was agreed and the reduction of domestic support was left for future negotiations.[183] Similarly, with regard to the Special Products and safeguard mechanism concerning developing countries' food and livelihood security, the concrete criteria were to be specified during the negotiations. Secondly, the proposals advanced by the Western and Central African countries which focused on the immediate elimination of cotton subsidies independently of the agricultural negotiations were not included in the decision, which limited itself to 'recognising the importance of cotton for a certain number of countries' and addressing the issue 'ambitiously, expeditiously and specifically'.[184] Thirdly, on SDT and issues relating to implementation of the WTO agreements, the decision only set new deadlines for the issues to be considered and for reports to be submitted by July 2005.[185] Finally, although negotiations on investments were abandoned, the US and EU

[178] WTO, Doha Work Programme (n 127).

[179] *Ibid* Annex A, paras 13–17.

[180] *Ibid* Annex A, para 41.

[181] *Ibid* Annex A, para 42.

[182] Negotiations on trade facilitation would instead proceed. However developing countries' obligations are made conditional on their receipt of adequate assistance in order to overcome the costs of implementation. *Ibid* Annex D.

[183] In particular, para 13 of the decision provided that Art 6.5 concerning subsidies under the so-called 'blue box', namely those used under the US Farm Bill and the reformed EU CAP, would be reviewed in future negotiations.

[184] *Ibid* Annex A, para 4.

[185] *Ibid* para 1(d).

were pursuing their market-access agenda under the GATS request-and-offer approach and through the bilateral activity on investments and IP.

In exchange for the modest commitments made in these areas, developing countries were asked to make trade offs in the areas of interest to the developed countries. Thus, in exchange for the limited concessions made in agriculture, cotton and the Singapore issues, developing countries accepted a new framework on NAMA,[186] which replicated the Cancun text. Khor identified two aspects of the framework contained in Annex B whose implications for developing countries' industrial policy were enormous. First, the decision adopted a 'non-linear' formula that requires sharp tariff reduction, especially for higher tariffs.[187] As Khor points out 'in the history of GATT and WTO, the developing countries have never had to come under a "formula approach", let alone an aggressive non-linear formula, not even during the Uruguay Round'.[188] Secondly, the decision required countries to bind at least 95 per cent of their tariff lines, therefore eliminating the WTO flexibility to decide what industrial products' tariffs to bind and at what rate. Khor concluded that 'as many developing countries have low applied rates for many products (as a result of structural adjustment loan conditionalities), the result of the NAMA exercise may be to depress the industrial tariffs (both bound and applied) of developing countries to unbearably low levels'.[189] Moreover, the NAMA framework violated the Doha Declaration requirement that developing countries be allowed 'less than full reciprocity' when negotiating their commitments.

B The Hong Kong Ministerial Declaration

The Hong Kong Ministerial Meeting in December 2005 was supposed to conclude the Doha Round. However, as disagreement between developing and developed countries over agriculture and NAMA persisted, ministers adopted a declaration setting out the negotiating objectives to be achieved by 2006.[190] The major achievement of the Hong Kong Ministerial Meeting was the commitment to end export subsidies by 2013.[191] Thus, ten years after the entry into force of the UR Agreement on Agriculture, an end date

[186] *Ibid* Annex B.

[187] For instance, under this formula, a 40 per cent tariff on a product would be reduced to 7 per cent. See M Khor, 'Preliminary Comments on the WTO's Geneva July Decision' (Third World Network, SUNS Working Paper, 2004) 3.

[188] *Ibid.*

[189] *Ibid* 5.

[190] WTO, Hong Kong Ministerial Declaration (adopted 18 December 2005) WTO Doc WT/MIN(05)/DEC.

[191] *Ibid* para 6.

for export subsidies was finally agreed on, although developing countries would have to wait eight years for their complete phase out. Moreover, the Declaration contained no meaningful commitments on the reduction of domestic support, the area in which most US and EU subsidies are concentrated,[192] and no agreement on the reduction of import tariffs was reached. Developed countries also committed to eliminate all forms of export subsidies on cotton in 2006 and to give duty-free and quota-free access for cotton exports from the least-developed countries.[193] However, the United States refused to set an end date for reducing domestic subsidies. The other achievement was in the area of TRIPs and Public Health, where members welcomed the Decision of the General Council of 6 December 2005 on an Amendment of the TRIPs Agreement.[194] This decision transformed the 2003 'interim waiver' into an amendment to the TRIPs Agreement.[195]

On the other issues, however, the Ministerial Declaration largely reiterated the language of the Doha Declaration and the commitments of the July Framework.[196] Similarly, in relation to NAMA, the Hong Kong Declaration incorporated the ambitious cut formula of the July Framework, pointing to the need to establish modalities as soon as possible in order to conclude the negotiations no later than 31 July 2006.[197] Thus,

[192] *Ibid* para 5.

[193] *Ibid* para 11.

[194] *Ibid* para 40.

[195] WTO, Amendment of the TRIPs Agreement, Decision of the General Council (adopted 6 December 2005) WTO Doc WT/L/641.

[196] Thus, with regard to the Special Products and the Special Safeguard mechanism referred to by the July Decision, members recognised that 'Developing Country Members will have the flexibility to self-designate an appropriate number of tariff lines as Special Products guided by indicators based on the criteria of food security, livelihood security and rural development. Developing country Members will also have the right to have recourse to a Special Safeguard Mechanism based on import quantity and price triggers, with precise arrangements to be further defined'. WTO, Hong Kong Ministerial Declaration (n 190) para 7. No progress was made in the area of Special and Differential Treatment, with members recognising that 'substantial work still remains to be done' and instructing 'the Committee on Trade and Development in Special Session to expeditiously complete the review of all the outstanding Agreement-specific proposals and report to the General Council, with clear recommendations for a decision, by December 2006'. *Ibid* para 36. As to negotiations on services, the declaration urged 'all Members to participate … towards achieving a progressively higher level of liberalization of trade in services'. *Ibid*. Also, and possibly in response to the mounting criticism with regard to bilateral negotiations, Annex C provided the option that the request-offer negotiations be pursued on a plurilateral basis. Two rounds of plurilateral negotiations were conducted in 2006 with about 21 collective requests made by 'clusters'. This did not mean however that negotiations were conducted on an open, multilateral basis. Furthermore, Lamy reported in 2007 that as a result of the 'prevailing sentiment among WTO members that 'plurilaterals' had served their purpose', negotiations had reverted to the request/offer approach. WTO, Key Stages in the Negotiations www.wto.org/english/tratop_e/serv_e/key_stages_e.htm

[197] *Ibid* paras 12–23.

between January and July 2006, intensive negotiations focused on the two crucial issues, namely agricultural liberalisation, in particular with regard to domestic support, and NAMA.

C Suspension, Crisis, Resumption

On 24 July 2006, Pascal Lamy, the newly-elected Director-General of the WTO, announced the suspension of the Doha Round. During an informal meeting at the level of Head of Delegations, he stated:

> [I]t is clear that the main blockage is on the Agriculture legs of the triangle of issues . . .the gap in level of ambition between market access and domestic support remained too wide to bridge. This blockage was such that the discussion did not even move on to the third leg of the triangle—market access in NAMA ... Faced with this persistent impasse, I believe that the only course of action I can recommend is to suspend the negotiations across the Round as a whole to enable the serious reflection by participants which is clearly necessary.[198]

Once again, the impasse concerned agriculture. The US and EU refused to substantially reduce their domestic support, which had been increasing since the end of the UR. As Bello pointed out:

> [E]ven if the United States had conceded to the terms of WTO Director General's compromise on cutting its domestic support, this would still have left it with a massive $20 billion worth of allowable subsidies. Even with the European Union agreeing to phase out its export subsidies, this would still have left it with 55 billion euros in other forms of export support. In return for such minimal concessions, the US, EU, and other developed countries wanted radically reduced tariffs for their agricultural exports in developing country markets.[199]

US Trade Representative Susan Schwab also attacked the provisions for 'Special Products' and 'special safeguard mechanisms', in particular with regard to the 'self-designation' flexibility provided by the December 2005 Hong Kong Ministerial Declaration.[200] With no progress on the agricultural issue, developing countries refused to negotiate on NAMA, which according to the formula adopted under the July Framework and reiterated in the Hong Kong Declaration, would have resulted in developing countries' industrial tariff cuts in the range of 60 to 70 per cent.[201]

[198] P Lamy, 'Time out needed to review options and positions' (WTO, Trade Negotiations Committee, 24 July 2006) www.wto.org/english/news_e/news06_e/tnc_dg_stat_24july06_e.htm

[199] W Bello, 'Why Monday's Collapse of the Doha Round Negotiations is the Best Outcome for Developing Countries' (Focus on the Global South, 25 July 2006) www.focusweb.org/content/view/984/36/.

[200] *Ibid.*

[201] *Ibid.*

The tone with which negotiators and commentators presented the suspension of the talks made their resumption look very unlikely. Indian trade minister Nath, for instance, referred to the Round as being somewhere 'between intensive care and the crematorium' while for Bello its collapse represented 'the best outcome for developing countries'.[202] However, following a plot rehearsed so many times since 2001, talks 'resumed fully across the board'[203] in 2007 only to break down, once again, in July 2008 when trade ministers met in Geneva. The formal reason concerned the special safeguard measure in agriculture. The US had demanded a high trigger level of 140 per cent (which corresponds to 40 per cent surge in imports). Although Brazil supported the US position, India and China together with the group of 33 developing countries rejected it arguing that farmers would be seriously damaged should states be required to demonstrate a 40 per cent surge before they could act.[204]

Just as the long Doha saga seemed to have finally reached an end, the Group of Twenty (G-20) finance ministers and Central Bank governors intervened and bestowed new meaning on the Round. The financial crisis which had hit the United States in 2007, and whose impact was being felt in different parts of the world, was seen as imposing a new sense of responsibility. Thus, in 2008, WTO members were called on to avoid protectionist impulses and work towards 'a successful conclusion to the WTO's Doha Development Agenda with an ambitious and balanced outcome'.[205] Doha is thus no longer only a 'political must for development'. As Lamy has put it, it also promises to 'play the role of a global stimulus package ... [and] act as a structural reform package'.[206] The conclusion of the negotiations is now scheduled for 2010.

CONCLUSIONS

The agenda of developing countries within the Doha negotiations did not substantially challenge the neo-liberal assumptions on which the WTO rests. Their request for agricultural liberalisation, in particular the elimination of domestic support that harmed their competitiveness, is entirely

[202] ICTSD, 'WTO Doha Round put on hold indefinitely' (ICTSD: Bridges Trade BioRes, 6:14, 2006) ictsd.org/i/news/biores/9500/. W Bello (n 199).

[203] On 07/02/07 Pascal Lamy announced that Members have resumed negotiations 'fully across the board'. See P Lamy www.wto.org/audio/2007_02_07_GC_Lamy.mp3.

[204] See M Khor, 'Reflections begin on the WTO Failure and the Future Work' (Third World Network: SUNS Working Paper, 2008).

[205] G-20, 'Washington Declaration: G-20 Summit on Financial Markets and the World Economy' (Washington, G-20, 2008).

[206] P Lamy, 'Doha Success can yield double dividend of Global Stimulus and Structural Reform' (WTO News-Speeches, 13 October 2009) www.wto.org/english/news_e/sppl_e/sppl137_e.htm.

consistent with the logic behind international specialisation based on comparative advantage. The suspension of the Doha talks in 2006 and 2008 owes much to the refusal by the US and EU in particular to live up to the trade principles whose universal beneficial validity they have promoted since the end of the 1970s.

The history of the Doha Round negotiations is thus indicative of three major flaws in the assumptions regarding the nature and purpose of the WTO. First, despite the fact that the WTO Preamble cites 'mutually advantageous arrangements directed to the substantial reduction of tariffs and other barriers to trade and to the elimination of discriminatory treatment in international trade relations' as the means to expand 'the production of and trade in goods and services, while allowing for the optimal use of the world's resources',[207] the Doha Round has confirmed that the WTO does not pursue trade liberalisation on the basis of comparative advantage. Although the Uruguay Round (UR) agreements do not mention free trade as an ultimate goal and the Agreement Establishing the World Trade Organisation does not refer to free trade as one of its institutional objectives, the raison d' etre of the WTO system rests on the assumption that trade liberalisation based on comparative advantage is universally beneficial in that it leads to the most efficient allocation of worldwide resources. However, as Macmillan aptly notes, 'the institution of the WTO serves the cause of the (sectorally selective) free traders, rather than free trade serving the cause of greater institutionalism in multilateral trading relations'.[208]

Secondly, the WTO does not provide a multilateral system of negotiations where countries reach 'mutually advantageous arrangements' within a rules-based system. As the Doha Round has shown, the nature of the Single Undertaking Approach (SUA), the de facto bilateral negotiations under the GATS and the minimum standards of protection under the TRIPS Agreement, combined with the increasing bilateral activity in the area of investment, confirm the permanence of the threats the multilateral system was supposed to eradicate. In particular, the US and EU tendency to revert to bilateral negotiations when their agenda is not satisfied within the WTO defies not only the neo-liberal assumptions about the so-called level playing field, but the possibility of multilateralism itself.

Finally, the Doha Development Round has confirmed the development rhetoric of the international trading regime, which, as Hudec pointed out with regard to the GATT, consists of the developed countries' practice of making impressive statements in relation to development-related trade reforms without undertaking substantial obligations.[209] More importantly,

[207] See WTO Preamble (n 3).
[208] Macmillan (n 64).
[209] See Hudec (n 63).

it has confirmed the continuity of the modality through which development has operated within the international trading system since the immediate postwar period. Its scientific authority continues to operate within the WTO in order to advance the interests of the major capitalist powers.

Although it can only be expected that, absent a successful conclusion of the Round, the bilateral activity of the developed countries will intensify in the foreseeable future, the analysis of the negotiations has suggested that the belief in WTO multilateralism needs to be seriously questioned. In other words, rather than concentrating efforts to conclude negotiations on the WTO's current terms, time should be taken for rethinking not only the neo-liberal rationale that posits the universal beneficial role of trade liberalisation and deeper integration but, at a more fundamental level, the persistence of the development framework originated in the immediate postwar period.

Conclusions

The Development Mission of the WTO

I RETURN IN conclusion to this book's originating question: what is to be made of the six-decades' long development enterprise of the multilateral trade regime? In the Introduction, I argued that there are two different and interrelated angles from which to assess the development dimension of both the GATT and the WTO. One is to look from within the development framework set up in the immediate postwar period, that is, engaging with its terms without challenging its underlying assumptions. From this perspective, I have shown that the WTO follows the GATT history of active discrimination against developing countries' trade. In over 30 years of development-related policies, the GATT produced numerous initiatives, declarations, reports and amendments that made its legal disciplines more flexible with respect to the concerns of its developing country members. However, hardly any measure contained legally binding commitments by developed countries. In other words, GATT practice towards developing countries violated the very development principle it purported to promote, namely economic growth and industrialisation by means of trade. With the WTO, this practice has continued. Despite the neo-liberal emphasis on market openness and reciprocity as the means to achieve successful integration in the global economy, the US and EU have pursued market access for their corporate capital while impeding the full liberalisation of the sectors in which developing countries are most competitive. Hence both the GATT's and the WTO's history point to a discrepancy between their stated development objectives and their actual negotiating practices. From this perspective, it would follow that the elimination of the asymmetry in trade rules could finally deliver the promise of development. In other words, the concerted efforts of the international community should be directed at the elimination of the double standards of trade liberalisation.

The second angle, however, complicates this view. The central claim of this book is that an appreciation of the modality through which the 'science of development' has operated since decolonisation is necessary to understanding the rationale behind the six-decades' long 'failure' and 'promise' of development within the postwar international trading regime. The argument in this respect has been twofold. First, as the premise of development, namely the need for the so-called developing countries to rely on a universal economic rationality in order to replicate the experience of the so-called developed countries, is established as unquestionable, its means can be constantly transformed to both reconceptualise the 'failure' of development and posit anew the 'promise' of its overcoming. Thus, notwithstanding the transformation from the GATT to the WTO as to the means through which to achieve development, both regimes have participated in the creation and transformation of a development apparatus that links forms of knowledge about Third World societal organisations with forms of power and intervention that continuously require the restructuring of the economic, social and political arrangements of so-called developing countries.

Secondly, the development mission so construed has been central to the re-articulation of the imperial project that followed the demise of colonialism. Despite the fact that the development enterprise of the multilateral trading regime cannot be explained in terms of the influence of theories, states, international institutions and economic processes alone, I have argued that the processes that have led to the establishment of the GATT and the WTO represent two clear instances of the efforts of the imperial powers to shape and reshape the contours of the 'science of development' in order to organise the international division of labour to their advantage.

Thus, the GATT participated in the consolidation of the postwar development norm by institutionalising the so-called failure of developing countries to trade as efficiently as the industrialised nations. By positing the need to overcome this failure by means of tariff reductions and elimination of quantitative restrictions on a Most Favoured Nation (MFN) basis, it provided the ex-colonial powers with access to the markets of the newly independent countries, from which they could extract raw materials and in which they could place surplus produce. At the same time, by exempting from trade liberalisation the sectors in which newly independent countries were supposed to have a comparative advantage, it provided the ex-colonial powers with the means to constrain the 'development' of their competitors.

With the WTO, the so-called failure of developing countries is made to rest on the adoption of their erroneous economic policies and legal claims during the 1960s and 1970s, which are deemed to have led to the inefficient allocation of domestic and worldwide resources. By establishing the undisputed need to abandon these strategies in order to become 'effective players' in the multilateral trading system, the WTO requires developing countries to extend market access beyond trade in goods to include services and investments while providing extensive protection to the intellectual property rights of corporate capital. However, the discrimination against the developing countries' competitive exports has not been eradicated.

This concluding chapter aims to provide an alternative account of the development debate within the WTO. By integrating the two perspectives described so far, it makes the case for a challenge to be brought not only to the neo-liberal rationale underlying the WTO agreements, but to the assumptions on which the development framework established in the postwar period rests.

I THE FIRST PERSPECTIVE: THE REFORM OF THE INTERNATIONAL TRADING SYSTEM

The first perspective on development suggests that a number of reforms can be attempted to ameliorate the impact of the WTO agreements on the economies of developing countries. The first set of proposals has focused on the role of uniform liberalisation implied in the adoption of the WTO's Single Undertaking Approach (SUA). In 2004, for instance, Hoekman suggested that WTO disciplines be divided into core and non-core rules in order to make the WTO 'more supportive of development'.[1] The former would entail unconditional acceptance by all developing countries of a set of rules including transparency, MFN treatment, the non-use of quotas, the binding of all tariffs and the willingness to reduce tariffs in the course of negotiations.[2] In a less defined way, he suggested that non-core principles be identified through consultative mechanisms within the WTO, such as the Trade Policy Review Mechanism (TPRM), that evaluate the feasibility of developing countries' departure from WTO non-core rules on the basis of the adverse effects this is likely to have on other WTO members.

According to Hoekman, this system implies a departure from the SUA that imposes the same set of obligations on all countries regardless of their development needs, while ensuring at the same time predictability in the multilateral trading system. Although this proposal aims to create a system of less than uniform obligations between developed and developing countries as far as non-core rules are concerned,[3] it retains all the core WTO substantive reciprocal obligations so that no departure from the market-access mindset is contemplated. Indeed, any departure from those rules is

[1] B Hoekman, Making the WTO More Supportive of Development (Mimeo, World Bank, 2004) 15.

[2] *Ibid* 16.

[3] In addition to the fact that non-core rules are not specified by Hoekman, a possible departure is made conditional upon consultation between the country at issue, the specialised international organisations and the likely adversely affected countries in order to find a solution that accommodates all parties. *Ibid.*

presented as a threat to the stability and predictability of the multilateral trading system. As Hoekman maintains:

> Allowing for 'policy space'—or leeway for countries to pursue policies that would otherwise be subject to multilateral discipline [sic.]—will increase uncertainty and could reduce the willingness of major trading countries to make commitments in the first place.[4]

In a different proposal, Charlton and Stiglitz suggest that

> all WTO members commit themselves to providing free market access in all goods to all developing countries poorer and smaller than themselves. Thus, all developing countries could expect free access to all markets with (1) a larger GDP and (2) a larger GDP per capita.[5]

This proposal is different from Hoekman's in that it contemplates a departure from the WTO's neo-liberal assumption about uniform liberalisation by positing a system that distinguishes between countries with different levels of development and embracing the principle that 'all countries should participate in an enforceable system of preferential market access in which rights and obligations are distributed progressively according to the objective criteria'.[6]

However, although this proposal makes the case for a progressively qualified trade liberalisation, it retains the WTO's underlying rationale according to which trade liberalisation and market access are conducive to development. Hence, so-called objective criteria such as GDP are relied on to provide the threshold for determining the degree of market access each country is expected to grant to other WTO members. The underlying assumption, however, is that when a country has achieved a certain level of economic growth, it will then be required to abide by WTO obligations. In other words, the desirability of the liberalisation mindset of the WTO is not called into question. The insistence on market access for developing countries' competitive exports is another manifestation of the acceptance of the WTO's liberalisation mindset. Thus, proposals for the elimination of support from the US and EU on agriculture and cotton and the liberalisation of GATS mode of supply 4, have characterised much of the development debate prior to and during the Doha Round.[7]

[4] *Ibid.*

[5] JE Stiglitz and A Charlton, *Fair Trade For All: How Trade Can Promote Development* (Oxford, Oxford University Press, 2005) 94.

[6] *Ibid.*

[7] See eg Oxfam International, 'Africa and the Doha Round: Fighting to Keep Development Alive', Briefing Paper No 80 (London, Oxfam, November 2005); see also S Chaudhuri, A Mattoo and R Self, 'Moving People to Deliver Services: How Can the WTO Help?' (2004) 38 *Journal of World Trade* 363; W Martin and K Anderson, 'Agricultural Trade Reform under the Doha Agenda: Some Key Issues' (2008) 52 *The Australian Journal of Agricultural and Resource Economics* 1.

A number of concrete suggestions have also been made in relation to the GATS and the TRIPs Agreements. For instance, in order to address the relationship between the TRIPs Agreement minimum standards of protection and the bilateral activity in investment agreements, it has been proposed that the TRIPs Council be converted 'from a body that secures a platform to one that polices a ceiling'.[8] In relation to the GATS, it has been suggested that the request offer approach be replaced by open multilateral negotiations to ensure transparency and accountability in the liberalisation requests made by governments.[9] It has also been argued that a proper emergency safeguard mechanism be put in place to allow countries to find temporary relief from liberalisation commitments when they have adverse social and economic consequences.[10] Furthermore, it has been stressed that further negotiations should not take place until a complete assessment of the impact of service liberalisation, as provided in GATS, is made.[11]

Before assessing these various proposals from the two interrelated perspectives, one speculation can be made with regard to their feasibility. As argued in chapters three and four, the greatest achievement of the US and EU in the course of the UR was the conclusion of the GATS, the TRIPS Agreement and to a lesser extent, the TRIMs Agreement. As a result of the alliance forged between corporate capital and northern states, these agreements have provided the necessary legal framework for extending the model of trade-service-investment driven market integration from the three industrial poles to the rest of the world.[12] The US and EU will therefore be unlikely to reverse the unprecedented gains they have obtained through the legal provisions of these agreements. This becomes apparent if one looks at the way in which the liberalisation of financial services has been pursued under the GATS framework despite growing concerns about international financial instability. As argued below, the requests made with regard to the liberalisation of financial services, including certain financial innovations, point to the protection and advancement of corporate capital regardless of the economic, political and social costs this might entail. More importantly, the reticence with which the WTO has acknowledged the potential adverse impact of GATS negotiations on financial stability is symptomatic of its unwillingness to call into question the universal beneficial role of liberalisation.

[8] P Drahos and J Braithwaite, *Information Feudalism: Who Owns the Knowledge Economy* (London, Earthscan, 2002) 208.

[9] See ICTSD, 'Trade in Services' (ICTSD, Doha Round Briefing Series, 1:3, 2003).

[10] See MJ Trebilcock and R Howse, The Regulation of International Trade (London; New York, Routledge, 2005) 374.

[11] See M Msayekhi and M Juisant, 'Assessment of Trade in Services in the Context of the GATS 2000 Negotiations', Working Paper No 13 (London, South Centre, 2002).

[12] See chs 3 and 4.

A The GATS and the Financial Crisis

As mentioned in chapter six, it is in the context of the financial crisis which originated in the United States in 2007 that the Doha Round has gained a renewed sense of urgency. WTO members are called on to behave responsibly and conclude the current round of negotiations as this will, in the words of Lamy, 'provide the world economy with a much needed global stimulus package'.[13] Neither the Group of Twenty (G-20) finance ministers and Central Bank governors nor the WTO, however, has acknowledged the possible linkages between the liberalisation of financial services on the one hand and the financial instability of the kind that has led to the current crisis on the other.

Despite the different interpretations of the crisis' underlying factors,[14] it is accepted that the unregulated proliferation of innovative financial instruments has been one of its most important triggers. Thanks to a process called 'securitisation', US subprime mortgages were bundled into different financial products sold internationally together with a number of innovative instruments supposed to calculate and reduce their risks, including the risk of people defaulting on them, for instance through so-called Credit Default Swaps (CDSs). The fact that financial institutions could generate mortgages and related securities they could quickly sell to international investors meant not only that they were able to move them off their balance sheets quickly, thereby circumventing capital reserve requirements and engaging in ever riskier activities.[15] It also meant that the traceability of the origins as well as the assessment of the quality of these instruments became virtually impossible. Thus, when the 'miscalculation' of their risks fully emerged, these previously acclaimed innovations became, almost overnight, 'toxic assets' able to send shock waves through the international financial system. Indeed, one of the objectives of the reforms first discussed by the G20 was the regulation of CDSs and

[13] P Lamy, 'Doha Success can yield double dividend of Global Stimulus and Structural Reform' (WTO News-Speeches, 13 October 2009) www.wto.org/english/news_e/sppl_e/sppl137_e.htm.

[14] See eg D McNally, 'From Financial Crisis to World-Slump: Accumulation, Financialisation and the Global Slowdown' (2009) 17 *Historical Materialism* 49; P Gowan, 'Crisis in the Heartland: Consequences of the New Wall Street System' (2009) 55 *New Left Review* 1; J Bellamy Foster and F Magdoff, *The Great Financial Crisis: Causes and Consequences* (New York, Monthly Review Press, 2009).

[15] As Gould notes, 40 per cent of sub-prime backed bonds were outside the US in 2007. E Gould, *Financial Instability and the GATS negotiations*, Trade and Investment Series, 9:4 (Ottawa, Canadian Centre for Policy Alternatives, 2008) 5.

so-called over the counter (OTC) derivatives, namely those financial instruments companies have been negotiating directly rather than through an official exchange.[16]

What is worthy of note is the fact that while at the G20 level countries have been pondering how best to regulate financial services in general and financial innovations in particular, their liberalisation is being simultaneously pursued under the GATS. This has happened despite the fact that the links between services liberalisation and financial instability had been established as early as 2003. Since then, policy analysts have been pointing to the fact that many requests made with regard to financial services, most of which target developing countries, have the potential of adversely impacting on the financial stability of states.[17] In analysing the 2002 EU requests, for instance, Stichele looked at the potential risks deriving from the opening up of markets to derivative products and investment fund management services, including pension fund management services, without appropriate prudential regulation in place.[18] She also focused on the requests concerning the removal of restrictions on full ownership of banks, including the obligation to invest in a joint venture, and argued that taken together these have the potential to lead to market consolidation and concentration. She therefore warned already in 2003 against the risk of creating financial institutions which could become 'too difficult to monitor and "too big to fail"'.[19] Other requests directly pertaining to prudential regulation, and therefore having potentially destabilising effects, included those asking states to remove measures that (1) require the authorisation of their central banks in order to pay dividends abroad and/or (2) impose a time limitation before foreign invested capital can be repatriated.[20]

The revised requests the EU made in 2005 largely reiterated the content of the 2002 requests. They contained, however, one additional element worth emphasising. Some developing countries, including India and Thailand, have been asked to liberalise according to the so-called Understanding.[21] Unlike the GATS which formally adopts a bottom-up approach to

[16] G20, 'Progress Report on the Immediate Actions of the Washington Actions Plan' (London, G20, 2009) www.g20.org/Documents/g20_washington_actionplan_progress_140309.pdf.

[17] MV Stichele, *Potential Risks of Liberalisation of Financial Services in GATS* (Amsterdam, SOMO, 2003) 1–3.

[18] *Ibid* 4.

[19] *Ibid* 5–6. In 2008, the United States would intervene to bail out AIG, the world's largest insurance company which held around US$1 trillion in Credit Default Swaps (CDSs) after the company defaulted on US$14 bn of these instruments. See McNally (n 14).

[20] MV Stichele, *GATS Negotiations in Financial Services: The EU Requests and their Implications for Developing Countries* (Amsterdam, SOMO, 2005) 3

[21] *Ibid* 1–2. She also points to the fact that out of the 94 targeted countries, 20 were least developed and 30 low income countries.

liberalisation, the Understanding promotes a top-down model of liberalisation by applying National Treatment and Market Access automatically, that is unless states have listed exceptions. This means that countries will need to know at the moment of signing in the Understanding exactly what exceptions they want to list. This is important since the Understanding requires each Member to refrain from introducing new measures (the so-called standstill provision) and to allow 'financial service suppliers of any other Member established in its territory to offer any new financial service'.[22] Further, as scholars have observed in relation to the interpretation of the GATS provisions by the Appellate Body (AB), once states have made a commitment for a classification of services under Market Access, they can no longer exclude any service within that classification.[23]

The far reaching effects of the Understanding can be readily appreciated by looking at a real case. As a result of the speculation on food prices, India has recently introduced a ban on derivatives trading, in particular on futures trading in sensitive food products. The EU has asked India to remove this measure as well as to sign in the Understanding. Were India to accept these requests, it would find it extremely difficult to reintroduce a similar measure in the future as a result of both the standstill provision of the Understanding and the 'ban on bans' deriving from the AB interpretation in the US Gambling case.[24] These provisions therefore have an enormous significance for the domestic regulatory space of Member States, especially in light of the aggressive market approach to liberalisation the EU requests have revealed.

These concerns, however, have not affected the WTO negotiations on services: not only has finance become, after tourism, the most committed sector under the GATS, but the liberalisation of financial services also continues to be presented as a driver of progress and modernisation. In 2006, the US Coalition of Service Industries published a study which argued for the expansion of commitments under the GATS, claiming that the adoption of 'sophisticated' Western financial innovations would benefit both consumers, who could avail themselves of new products meeting their

[22] The Understanding on Commitments in Financial Services, Part B, Art 2.7. The standstill provision refers to part A of the Understanding which provides that 'Any conditions, limitations and qualifications to the commitments noted below shall be limited to existing non-conforming measures'. Part B also states that 'Each Member shall list in its schedule pertaining to financial services existing monopoly rights and shall endeavour to eliminate them or reduce their scope'.

[23] WTO, United States: Measures Affecting the Cross Border Supply of Gambling and Betting Services, Report of the Appellate Body (adopted 7 April 2005) WT/D285/AB/R. Hereafter, the US Gambling case.

[24] Gould (n 15) 10.

diverse needs, and financial institutions which could use efficient mechanisms of risks calculation and management.[25]

The financial industry has been a driving force behind the negotiations of the GATS since the early days of the UR so to ensure that financial services received a special treatment.[26] It is therefore not surprising that it continues to employ powerful rhetorical tools to promote, and create the market for, its products abroad. What is interesting is that only one year after this study was published the same financial innovations so highly valued by Western governments and institutions have turned into 'financial weapons of mass destruction'.[27] They have contributed to a crisis which, contrary to predictions, has happened not in countries where regulation is supposed to be endemically weak but at the heart of the 'advanced' financial system, a system which countries are expected to learn from and replicate.

This should have, if not called into question the principles and rationale of the Western financial system, at least warned against making further requests to liberalise financial innovations before a careful assessment of the potential impact of commitments already undertaken could be carried out. However, both the G20 and the WTO have, until recently, remained silent. Indeed in 2008, Lamy satisfactorily reported that 71 new offers and 31 revised offers had been made, most of which were in the area of financial services.[28]

B Addressing the Challenge, Strengthening the Mindset

It is only in March 2009 that the potential links between GATS liberalisation and financial instability were first discussed in the context of a workshop organised by the WTO to mark the tenth anniversary of the fifth protocol to the GATS. Most contributions acknowledged the problems that lack of appropriate regulation might pose to the financial stability of the international system.[29] However, they found no connection between

[25] US Coalition of Service Industries Research and Education Foundation, Making the most of the Doha opportunity: Benefits from Services Liberalization'; in Gould (n 15) 5.

[26] Gould (n 15) 1–7.

[27] Warren Buffet was the first to use this term in 2002 when he sent a letter to his Berkshire Hathaway's shareholders. Since 2007, however, the term has repeatedly been used by the media. See eg N Pratley, 'Wall Street Crisis: is this the death knell for derivatives?' *Guardian* (15 September 2008).

[28] WTO, Services Negotiations, www.wto.org/english/tratop_e/serv_e/s_negs_e.htm; see also WTO, Lamy Circulates Report on Market Access Commitments in Services (WTO News-DDA, 30 July 2008) www.wto.org/english/news_e/news08_e/serv_signalling_july08_e.htm.

[29] See WTO, 'Workshop to Mark the Tenth Anniversary of the Fifth Protocol to the GATS' (WTO, Services, 13 March 2009) www.wto.org/english/tratop_e/serv_e/finance_e/workshop_march09_e/workshop_march09_e.htm.

the latter and the liberalisation of financial services. Two arguments were presented. The first is that financial liberalisation neither coincides with, nor does it encourage, deregulation.[30] The second argument is that, provided appropriate regulation is put in place by states, liberalisation augments global welfare and developing countries stand to gain the most from the liberalisation of financial services.[31]

It is important to scrutinise these two claims to better appreciate the extent to which the WTO's liberalisation mindset is open to challenge and the kind of reform attempts that are likely to succeed. The reason adduced in support of the first argument is that the Annex to the GATS provides states with the right to enforce prudential regulation.[32] The so-called prudential carve out provides that

> notwithstanding any other provisions of the Agreement, a Member shall not be prevented from taking measures for prudential reasons, including for the protection of investors, depositors, policy holders or persons to whom a fiduciary duty is owed by a financial service supplier, or to ensure the integrity and stability of the financial system.[33]

However, three points need to be made in this respect. First, the carve out is qualified by the following proviso: 'where such measures do not conform with the provisions of the agreement, they shall not be used as a means of avoiding the Members' commitments or obligations under the Agreement'. As Gould observes, this means that the more commitments countries make, the more likely they will be challenged for using prudential measures in order to circumvent their obligations. There is, however, another difficulty with the prudential carve out and this is the fact that what is deemed prudential as opposed to protectionist is the object of intense controversy. Divergences of opinion on the matter have already been articulated within the WTO Committee on Trade in Financial services.[34] Ultimately it will be up to panellists and AB members to decide on the meaning of prudential and protectionist. This relates to the second point about the 'freedom to regulate'. As seen in chapter six, all domestic regulations, including those on financial services, will be subject to the rules emerging as a result of the current negotiations under Article VI. This means they might be challenged if they do not meet the objectivity and relevance test of Article VI, which leads to the third point: if panellists and

[30] *Ibid.*

[31] Both arguments are made by Sergio Marchi, former Canadian trade minister and current Chairman of the General Council of the WTO, during a video debate organised by the WTO with, interestingly enough, Myriam Vander Stichele. See WTO, 'What is the Role of WTO Services Rules in the Context of the Current Financial Crisis?' (WTO Public Forum, 2009) www.wto.org/english/forums_e/debates_e/debate17_e.htm.

[32] WTO, 'Workshop to Mark the Tenth Anniversary' (n 29).

[33] GATS, Annex on Financial Services, Art 2.

[34] See Gould (n 15) 8.

AB members have to make a determination as to whether a domestic, non-discriminatory, measure is prudential or protectionist, absent a clear cut definition of what is prudential and taking into account the proviso attached to the carve out, they will very likely resort to the test of ArticleVI. Thus, the decision as to whether a measure will be GATS-compatible or not will be made by WTO bodies.

The second argument that has emerged from the WTO exercise is that developing countries are the main beneficiaries, as well as supporters, of services liberalisation and this is because liberalisation promotes competition and efficiency.[35] This argument is made even though studies carried out in the last two years have shown how the liberalisation of financial services in developing countries has had a series of adverse effects. For instance, the 2009 report by the World Development Movement has focused on the impact that the entry and presence of foreign banks in Mexico and India have had on the access by small business and households to financial credit. The report found, among other things, that

> the entry and presence of foreign banks is associated with the 'cherry-picking' of richer customers (both individuals and large businesses) and a decline in services and credit for poorer customers and smaller businesses. Rural Communities are especially affected; foreign banks rarely have a meaningful presence outside large urban areas.[36]

This has produced 'a discernible and negative shift of credit away from productive activities (investment in agriculture, industrial production or local services) which can boost local development, and towards personal consumption, via credit cards and credit for items such as cars and mortgages'.[37] UNCTAD had also reported similar findings in its 2007 paper, pointing to the cherry-picking phenomenon as well as to the lack of investment in rural areas and the macroeconomic problems deriving from the relaxation of performance requirements on foreign providers, which has been a consequence of National Treatment and Market Access commitments.[38]

Thus, it might well be that some customers have benefited from the liberalisation of financial services. However, as the findings of these reports suggest, competition and efficiency are abstract concepts that say very little about who accesses credit, how and for what purposes. They are therefore unable to account for a whole set of important economic, social and political effects that access to credit generates. What is revealing, however,

[35] See WTO Forum (n 31).

[36] World Development Movement, '*Taking the Credit: How Financial Services Liberalisation Fails the Poor*' (London, World Development Movement, 2009) 6

[37] *Ibid*.

[38] UNCTAD, 'Trade and Development Implications of Financial Services' (3 August 2007) TD/B//COM1/EM, in Gould (n 15) 14.

is the fact that the superiority of the Western financial system continues to be upheld, not only despite the various analyses which since 2003 have challenged claims about competition and efficiency, but despite the fact that this crisis has shown how financial innovations supposed to calculate and reduce risks have turned out to amplify, if not generate, them.

What do these arguments, persisting at a time when the call for urgent and responsible action is made all over the world, say about the possibility of reforming the WTO? Starting with a more immediate and practical observation, the fact that the resumption of the talks and their successful conclusion have been posited as necessary in order to deal responsibly with the challenges of the crisis when such challenges are not, however, allowed to affect the WTO mindset, warns exactly against accepting such a necessity. The claim that trade liberalisation, albeit with appropriate regulation in place, is universally beneficial, and particularly so for developing countries, is symptomatic of the unwillingness of the WTO and certainly of its major trading players to call into question the way in which the international trading regime has worked since decolonisation. The advancement of the power of transnational capital and the employment of the development rhetoric to facilitate this process continue to operate as strongly as ever. This is not to say that reforms should not be attempted. Indeed the call for bringing to a standstill further negotiations under the GATS, particularly in relation to financial services, and introducing a ceiling on the standards of protection mandated by the TRIPs Agreement, should be answered if the advancement of the power of corporate capital vis-à-vis the regulatory autonomy of WTO members is to be halted.

However, and taking into account that the Doha Round negotiations have fully resumed across the board, it is also imperative to reflect on the normative assumptions on which the WTO's development enterprise rests. Recognising the permanence of the civilising mission within the WTO is the first step in articulating a critique of the way in which the 'science of development' has operated since its inception. As I argue below, the significance of the three pillars on which the science of development was built, namely the unquestionable dichotomy between developed and developing countries, the necessary reliance on economic rationality and the desirability of the guidance and expertise of developed countries, has increased with the shift from the GATT's approach to development to the WTO's. Assessing the WTO development framework on its own terms is crucial not only in order to argue against the successful conclusion of the current Development Round, but because it offers the opportunity to evaluate the suggested reforms, in particular those that rely on the market-access argument, from a different perspective.

II THE SECOND PERSPECTIVE: THE WTO AND ITS CIVILISING MISSION

The WTO embodies the neo-liberal rejection of the postwar economic rationality that considered the state the prime agent for achieving development, which was identified with both rapid economic growth and industrialisation. With the so-called counter-revolution in development thinking, reliance on neo-classical assumptions about rational economic behaviour and the price mechanism provided the premise for the replacement of development economics with the universality of neo-liberal economic laws.[39] The WTO agreements embody the neo-liberal development rationale by positing as unquestionable the universal beneficial role of trade liberalisation to be pursued through reciprocal binding commitments. Thus, although the content of postwar economic rationality is transformed to embrace the neo-liberal revolution of the development norm, the undisputed reliance on its universality remains unaffected. A similar observation can be made with respect to the neo-liberal transformation of the other two pillars of the development norm, namely the early assumptions about the backwardness of non-Western societies and the consequent need for guidance and assistance by the so-called developed members of the international community.

Within the WTO, not only are developing countries characterised by their failure to develop their trade as efficiently as that of the industrialised nations, as they were in the case of the GATT, but the dichotomy between developed and developing countries is reconceptualised to extend to the latter's failing institutional and social arrangements, which are posited as the obstacles to development. North's suggestion in 1993 that 'transferring the formal political and economic rules of successful western market economies to Third World and Eastern European economies is not a sufficient condition for good economic governance … [as] it is essential to change both the institutions and the belief systems for successful reform since it is the mental models of the actors that will shape choices'[40] has been incorporated in the post-Washington consensus. As Rodrik points out:

> [T]he resulting 'augmented Washington Consensus' goes beyond liberalization and privatization to emphasize the need to create the institutional underpinnings of market economies. The reforms on the list include financial regulation and prudential supervision, governance and anti-corruption, legal and administrative reform, labor-market 'flexibility', and social safety nets. Operationally, these institutional reforms have two noteworthy features. First, they are heavily influenced by an Anglo-American conception of what constitutes desirable institutions … Second, they are driven largely by the requirements of integration

[39] See ch 3.

[40] DC North, 'The New Institutional Economics and Development' (Smithian Forum, Working Paper, 1993) 6 www.nju.edu.cn/cps/site/NJU/njuc/dep/shangyuan/2.doc.

> into the world economy. The latter explains the emphasis on the international harmonization of regulatory practices, as in the case of financial codes and standards and of the WTO agreements.[41]

Thus, although the post-Washington consensus seems to point to a softening of the neo-liberal development norm in that the role of the state is reintroduced to run parallel to that of the market, it is in fact the former that is supposed to facilitate the natural and rational working of the latter, whose status therefore remains uncontested.[42] As far as developing countries are concerned, however, the post-Washington consensus reinforces the assumption that the ineffective working of the market is due to their inappropriate institutional and social arrangements. In other words, its emphasis on institution building and good governance reinforces the neo-liberal assumptions about the impropriety of developing countries' political, social and institutional arrangements. As a consequence, their integration into the global economy, posited as necessary to achieve development, is to be pursued through harmonisation of regulatory practices in addition to trade liberalisation. As former WTO Director-General Moore puts it:

> Trade is one component of a policy framework for growth, poverty reduction and development. Trade must be part of the equation, but it is only a part of that framework. Sound macroeconomic policies, debt reduction, capacity building and good governance are critical to any programme of development and poverty reduction.[43]

In this respect, the WTO agreements on Sanitary and Phytosanitary Measures, Technical Barriers to Trade and Customs Evaluation require developing countries to reform their administrative practices in accordance with the 'proper' standards that have long been adopted by developed countries.[44] Similarly, the reforms of developing countries' legal and administrative systems to comply with the TRIPs, TRIMs and GATS requirements of transparency, undue delay and due process are all regulatory steps the WTO considers necessary to ensure 'good governance'.[45]

[41] See D Rodrik, 'The Global Governance of Trade as if Development Really Mattered' (UNDP, 2001) www.servicesforall.org/html/Governance/Rodrik-Trade%20&%20Development.pdf

[42] Indeed, one common misunderstanding that the post-Washington consensus has brought to light is that neo-liberalism was founded on the rejection of the state, when in actual fact the state has always been central to the establishment and the functioning of the market.

[43] WTO, 'Integrated Framework (IF) Joint Core Agency Seminar on the Policy-Relevance of Mainstreaming Trade into Country Development Strategies: Perspectives of LDCs'. Statement by M Moore (WTO, Development, 17 January 2001) www.wto.org/english/tratop_e/devel_e/sem02_e/ifseminar_moorestat_jan01_e.htm.

[44] See ch 5, I D.

[45] Indeed, good governance and institution building are not an integral part of the WTO mandate. However, they are referred to in several provisions of the WTO agreements. See eg

The point is not to vilify good governance and institution building; rather, the aim is to consider the way in which they operate to order hierarchically different societal organisations and become instrumental in requiring countries at the lower end of the development spectrum to abide by the rules, models and standards as defined by those at the top of the hierarchy. In other words, it is crucial to appreciate that despite the transformation the civilised/uncivilised, advanced/backward, developed/developing dichotomy has undergone, the civilising mission continues to operate through these regulatory mechanisms. Developing countries are therefore constantly required to recognise the desirability of the prevailing economic, political and legal rationality and reform their regimes accordingly guided by the help and expertise of the developed countries.

Technical and financial assistance is therefore deployed in a manner reminiscent of the *modus operandi* of the Mandate System under the League of Nations that aimed to assist those peoples 'not yet able to stand by themselves under the strenuous conditions of the modern world'.[46] Thus, the Integrated Framework (IF) inaugurated in 1997 by the WTO, the United Nations Conference on Trade and Development, the World Bank, the International Monetary Fund, the United Nations Development Programme and the International Trade Centre aims to encourage 'LDCs [least developed countries] to be full and active players and beneficiaries of the multilateral trading system'.[47] By coordinating the activities of donors and recipient governments and providing them with the 'specific field of competence'[48] of the six organisations involved, the IF recalls the economic neutrality invoked by the Mandate System in order to achieve 'the well-being and development of such peoples'.[49] Assistance under the IF is therefore made conditional on the acceptance by the recipient country of the economic rationality of the international economic institutions. Hence, the recipient country needs to 'prove that [it] has created an environment which helps the integration of trade in its plans for economic growth and development. This should include providing an institutional arrangement, implementing domestic reforms that favour trade, and engaging donors'.[50]

WTO 'General Transparency and Other "Good Governance" Obligations' (WTO, GATS Training Module, Basic Purpose and Concept) www.wto.org/english/tratop_e/serv_e/cbt_course_e/c1s5p1_e.htm.

[46] League of Nations, *Covenant of the League of Nations*, Art 22, para 1; quoted in A Anghie, 'Time Present and Time Past: Globalisation, International Financial Institutions, and the Third World' (2000) 32 *New York University Journal of International Law & Politics* 243, 276.

[47] WTO, 'The Integrated Framework for Least Developed Countries (IF)' (WTO, Development, Integrated Framework) www.wto.org/english/tratop_e/devel_e/teccop_e/if_e.htm.

[48] *Ibid.*

[49] League of Nations, Covenant of the League of Nations, Art 22, para 1 (n 46).

[50] WTO, 'The Integrated Framework' (n 47).

Similarly, the 'technical and financial' instruments provided in the WTO agreements, including the legal provisions for longer transition periods, are intended to assist developing and least-developed countries in complying with WTO rules, whose rationale, however, is not open to challenge. Furthermore, the instruments at WTO disposal for surveillance and compliance with its legal provisions have been enhanced. Through the Trade Policy Review Mechanism,[51] WTO members are subject to a detailed analysis of conformity with the WTO agreements followed by the Secretariat 'perspective on the Member's trade policies'.[52] Finally, the establishment of the Dispute Settlement System, which Weiler describes as 'a world economic court in all but name',[53] provides the WTO with an effective enforcement mechanism to ensure compliance with its provisions.

III THE WTO'S MARKET-ACCESS MINDSET

The development mechanisms of the WTO show that the space for development is confined to assistance and guidance that enable developing and least-developed countries to comply with its legal provisions, while the implicit normative assumptions these embody are not open to challenge. Reforms can be attempted and might be successful as long as they do not question the universal desirability of the prevailing economic rationality. They can certainly point to trade imbalances and suggest that, in virtue of their specific development needs, countries are entitled to temporarily depart from WTO rules until they become able 'to stand by themselves'. However, the spirit of these reforms is gauged in terms of exceptions to the universal validity of the WTO economic rationality.

From this perspective, it is evident that redressing the 'asymmetry' in trade rules does not question the normative assumptions on which the WTO and its development mission rests. Any attempt at challenging this framework should take into consideration all three elements, namely the way in which the dichotomy operates to order hierarchically different societal organisations, the linear and consequent reading of history that posits the desirability for countries at the lower end of the development spectrum to abide by the economic rationality of those at the top and the necessary guidance and assistance of the developed members of the

[51] See Preamble of Agreement Establishing the World Trade Organization (15 April 1994) LT/UR/A/1, Annex 3. For the WTO explanation of the role played by the TPRM, see 'Overseeing National Trade Policies: the TPRM' (WTO, Trade Policy Reviews, 2001) www.wto.org/english/tratop_e/tpr_e/tp_int_e.htm.

[52] *Ibid.*

[53] JHH Weiler, 'The Rule of Lawyers and the Ethos of Diplomats: Reflections on the Internal and External Legitimacy of WTO Dispute Settlement' (Harvard Law School, Jean Monnet Working Paper 2000) 21.

international community to achieve development. It is beyond the scope of this book to provide such an agenda. However, I suggest that one way to start articulating a critique of the trade-development relationship within the WTO is to question the universality and desirability of the current economic rationality, or what Rodrik defines as 'the Enlightened Standards View that posits the universal beneficial nature of trade liberalisation, market access and global integration in all trade-related matters'.[54] Neoliberal economic rationality demanded of all WTO members requires acceptance of free trade and market openness. Developing countries have themselves, since the UR, adopted the language of market openness in relation to the areas in which they possess a comparative advantage.[55] Thus, after the UR, emphasis has been placed on the need to address specific asymmetries in market access, such as tariff peaks against developing country exports, industrialised countries' protection in agriculture and textiles, and the request for special and differential treatment.[56]

I do not suggest that double standards do not seriously impede the trade of developing countries. However, as development is viewed in terms of market access and special and differential exceptions, the result is the gradual elimination of policy autonomy for any WTO member, let alone developing country members. As Rodrik observes, 'the only way they [WTO Developing Country Members] can gain enhanced market access is by restricting their own policy autonomy in exchange'.[57] The examination of the GATS, TRIPs and TRIMs Agreements has indeed shown this is already the case with the unprecedented rise of the power of transnational capital at the expense of the regulatory domestic policy of WTO developing members.

It seems necessary therefore to interrogate once more the relationship between the free-trade rhetoric of the WTO and the selective liberalisation process it promotes. Since the desirability of 'free markets' is at the core of the WTO's market-access mindset, the issue concerning the universal validity of free trade, and ultimately its possibility, needs to be examined further if the economic rationality of the WTO is to be called into question. In this respect, the work of Bhagwati is important as he recognises that some countries, and the United States in particular, have discontinuously used the free-trade discourse in order to promote their 'vested interests'. He nonetheless asserts that if the substance of each argument is duly rectified, no authority, however powerful, can reasonably

[54] Rodrik (n 41) 1.
[55] See ch 4 VI A.
[56] Rodrik (n 41) 2.
[57] *Ibid* 4. See also HJ Chang, *The Myth of Free Trade and the Secret History of Capitalism* (New York, Bloomsbury Press, 2007) 78–80.

justify any departure from free trade.[58] In terms of the current development debate within the WTO, this means that if the asymmetry in market access is eliminated, free trade can deliver growth and prosperity for all. However, it is exactly this possibility that is questioned here from two interrelated standpoints.

The first concerns the theoretical incongruity on which the supremacy of free-trade theory is built, namely the claim that an open economy is superior to any other system because markets are more efficient than governments in allocating resources. Market efficiency rests on the assumption that when market prices mirror real prices, the 'invisible hand' can be trusted to lead to the best allocation of worldwide resources and, consequently, to the creation of the greatest material wealth.[59] Since the classical formulation of free-trade theory by Smith and Ricardo, international specialisation and comparative advantage have constituted its central pillars. To put it simply, each country should specialise in the production of the good it produces at the lowest cost along its production possibilities frontier: as every country has a comparative advantage in producing something, the international community will benefit equally from free trade.[60]

In the past two centuries, however, free-trade theory has been assailed by doubts that have prompted economists to advocate a departure from free trade in particular circumstances.[61] Bhagwati notes that in all these instances, the basic reason for departing from free-trade theory has been the presence of so-called markets failures: if market prices diverge from real prices, resources may be wrongly allocated and free trade cannot be considered the best policy. However, Bhagwati's argument is that the fact that markets do not work well, or are imperfect, only implies that free trade cannot be asserted to be the first best policy; it does not mean that its

[58] See JN Bhagwati, *Free Trade Today* (Princeton, Princeton University Press, 2002).

[59] *Ibid* 28.

[60] The theory of international specialisation as formulated by Adam Smith posits that nations can mutually benefit from trade by specialising in the production of certain goods when they differ in their cost ability to produce them. See A Smith, *An Enquiry into the Nature and Causes of the Wealth of Nations* [1776] (Oxford, Clarendon Press, 1979) Book IV ii,12. Whereas, according to Smith, the basis for trading is absolute advantage, Ricardo introduces the concept of comparative advantage by showing how two countries can still gain from specialisation even if one of them has an absolute advantage in producing both goods. So long as the two countries have a difference in the costs of production between the two goods, it is still convenient for them to specialise in the production of the one whose cost is the lowest. See D Ricardo, *Principles of Political Economy and Taxation* [1817] (London, Everyman's Library, 1978) 82. International specialisation and comparative advantage constitute the pillars of classic free trade theory.

[61] For an extensive account of the economic objections to free-trade theory, see DA Irwin, *Against the Tide: An Intellectual History of Free Trade* (Princeton, Princeton University Press, 1996). See also G Dunkley, *The Free Trade Adventure: The WTO, the Uruguay Round and Globalism: A Critique* (London, Zed Books, 2000) 118.

conditions cannot be restored. In particular, his proposition is that in the presence of domestic failures that prevent market prices from mirroring real prices, governments can intervene in order to offset the distortion so that free trade can be restored.[62]

However, the assumption that governments are able to identify the distortion and apply the appropriate measure in order to tackle it seems to contrast with the very reason according to which governments should abstain from intervention in their trade regimes. The main argument against protection, since Smith, is that the political process cannot be trusted to produce the right kind of intervention.[63] Therefore, the point to be emphasised here is that if in order to be corrected markets need government intervention, then the free-trade axiom of market superiority cannot be upheld.[64] This theoretical incongruity can only be overcome if the debate goes beyond the binary opposition between free trade and protectionism and it is recognised that 'free' markets, as well as regulated markets, are outcomes of political processes.

Therefore, the second interrelated point is that, if markets are recognised to be the result of political processes, free-trade theory and liberalisation practice cannot be assessed separately from the historical, political and economic contexts in which they are deployed. Thus, it is important to ask what kind of political process neo-liberal theories, states, international institutions, and the WTO in particular, promote through the deployment of 'free-trade' discourse. As observed in chapters three and four, the renewed emphasis on free trade in the 1980s coincided with the attempt to restructure the international economy along the lines of the service-investment-technology driven market integration pursued by the Americans and the Europeans in particular. This has resulted in the legal framework of the GATS, TRIMs and TRIPs Agreements which, as seen in chapter five, aim at conferring unprecedented rights on foreign investors while restricting the policy autonomy of recipient states. At the same time, the negotiating activity of the WTO shows that the US and EU continue to actively hinder the trade interests of their competitors.

Thus, if the analysis of the historic, political and economic contexts in which the WTO has come into force is taken into account, then it becomes important to recognise that the current emphasis on free trade to deliver development is misplaced. This is possibly the more immediate and practical answer to the question with which I have started this concluding chapter. Without an appreciation of the imperial framework under which

[62] Bhagwati (n 58) 28–31.

[63] See Bhagwati (n 58) 31. See also Irwin (n 61) 229.

[64] See D Alessandrini, 'Transnational Corporations and the Doctrine of Comparative Advantage: A Critique of Free Trade Normative Assumptions' (2005) 1 *International Trade Law and Regulation Journal* 14.

the 'science of development' has operated since its outset, and which the WTO has embodied, even the most ardent advocates of free trade, such as Bhagwati, who have been critical of the US trade policy, end up overlooking the fact that the WTO is not a free-trade organisation. It did not come into force to promote universal trade liberalisation but, as Macmillan puts it, to serve the cause of the sectorally selective free traders.[65] Equally important, upholding the case for free trade as conducive to development without such an appreciation reinforces the belief in a universal economic rationality and a linear, consequential reading of history that does nothing to challenge the 'political rationality' of development.

IV THE 'POLITICAL RATIONALITY' OF DEVELOPMENT

As argued in chapter one, the institutional separation between the economic and political realms of international law and institutions was based on the assumption that technocratic institutions could best serve the interests of the international community by specialising in their respective areas of expertise and away from political interference.[66] However, as Anghie has noted with regard to the International Financial Institutions (IFIs) and the development knowledge they produce, this separation seems to have undergone a qualitative transformation, with the World Bank, for instance, expanding its prior focus on economic matters to incorporate 'human rights' and 'good governance' in its development strategies.[67] The increased competence of the international financial institutions is noticeable also with respect to the international trading regime. It is not just the case that the WTO legal regime implies a 'degree of intrusiveness into domestic sovereignty [that] bears little resemblance to the shallow integration of the GATT model of negative regulation'.[68] Unlike the GATT, the WTO is also endowed with effective surveillance and disciplinary mechanisms that ensure compliance with its rules. Moreover, the WTO's focus on free trade and the market as the means to alleviate poverty, eliminate

[65] F Macmillan, 'Looking Back to Look Forward: Is there a Future for Human Rights in the WTO?' (2005) 11 International Trade Law and Regulation 166.

[66] For the discussion on the functionalist approach to international organisations, see ch 1.

[67] Anghie argues that 'With regard to the interference in political affairs, the Bank, for example, prescribes policies relating to a huge range of matters which traditionally related to the "political affairs" of a state. For example, the Bank's concern for "good governance" raises a number of troubling issues. The Bank's argument that it can bring within its purview any activity that affects "development" suggests that there are few limits to the activities which the Bank seeks to influence. Thus, the Bank is working to "strengthen the role and effectiveness of the press", as well as dealing with a wide-ranging set of issues including environmental policy, judicial reform, public service reform, and governmental auditing functions'. Anghie (n 46) 266–67.

[68] S Ostry, 'The Changing Scenario in International Governance' (Ottawa, Royal Society of Canada, 20 November 1999).

marginalisation, avoid corruption and promote good governance is indicative of the shift Anghie identifies with regard to the IFIs:

> The dual mandate, Civilization and Commerce, was embodied in the policies of the Mandate System which, although principally concerned with bringing about political development, ultimately sought to achieve this through economic development. By contrast, the Bank, beginning with a concern for economic development, has now assumed increased authority over political matters. The circle has been completed but in the reverse direction, as the Bank also undertakes its own version of the dual mandate.[69]

Thus, the neo-liberal transformation of the science of development has entailed a qualitative shift in the understanding of social and political life, and its effects are certainly not confined to the development field. The powerful hold of neo-liberalism over political and social life exceeds the traditional economic realm by positing the market mechanism and rational choice as the universal interpreters of human behaviour. Wendy Brown has crucially argued that neo-liberalism entails a political rationality that

> is not equivalent to an ideology stemming from or masking an economic reality, nor is it merely a spillover effect of the economic on the political or the social. Rather, as Foucault inflected the term, a political rationality is a specific form of normative political reason organizing the political sphere, governance practices, and citizenship. A political rationality governs the sayable, the intelligible, and the truth criteria of these domains. Thus, while neoliberal political rationality is based on a certain conception of the market, its organization of governance and the social is not merely the result of leakage from the economic to other spheres but rather of the explicit imposition of a particular form of market rationality on these spheres.[70]

Similarly, the neo-liberal shift in development thinking has involved the reconceptualisation of Third World societal organisations in terms of the market logic so that exchange, utility maximisation and individual responsibility increasingly become the parameters for evaluating all institutional and social arrangements. The WTO and the international economic institutions with which it cooperates have embodied precisely this political rationality, extending unprecedented market discipline to areas previously exempted from regulation.[71] In the context of the discussion this book has engaged with, namely that concerning the modality through which the 'science of development' has operated within the multilateral trade regime,

[69] Anghie (n 46) 285.

[70] W Brown, 'American Nightmare: Neoliberalism, Neoconservatism, and De-Democratization' (2006) 34 *Political Theory* 690, 693.

[71] For instance, the idea that WTO negotiations involve a bargaining process according to which players are positioned on an equal footing with one another and engage in 'trade-offs' in order to maximise their welfare conforms to the neo-liberal political rationality that explains every arrangement in terms of market efficiency and profitability.

this raises the question of what exactly is involved in the shift from the GATT's to the WTO's approach to development.

I have argued that, since its inception, the functionalist separation between the economic and political realms of international law served to conceal the deeply political nature of the supposedly neutral economic rules and institutions put in place to promote development.[72] In the immediate postwar period, one crucial preoccupation of the imperial powers was to gain access to the natural resources of the ex-colonies and incorporate them within the expanding world capitalist system. Development thinking supported this enterprise by positing the need for newly-independent countries to replicate the 'successful' experience of Western societies. Thus, the wholesale transformation of Third World societies which the postwar development thinking engendered, and in which GATT participated, was no less 'political' than the current degree of 'intrusiveness' imposed by the neo-liberal approach to development that the WTO promotes.

This is not to downplay the qualitative difference involved in this shift and, as Anghie puts it, in the completion of the circle encompassing the economic and political dimensions of development.[73] It is rather to say that the conditions for the possibility of this shift are to be found in the premise on which the science of development rests, in particular the three normative assumptions that have allowed its scientific authority to persist. These assumptions have provided the science of development with its 'political rationality', that is, the rationality that governs the 'sayable, the intelligible, and the truth criteria' of this domain.[74]

At the same time, although the pervasive effects of development cannot be reduced to any single determining agenda, the imperial mission of the major capitalist powers has certainly played a central role in reshaping the contours of the 'sayable and the intelligible' in the development domain. The insistence of this work on the interaction between the forms of knowledge and the forms of power and intervention that the 'science of development' articulates does not aim at presenting any alternative as contained within this mutual reinforcing relationship. As Brown puts it, if 'Neoliberalism as a form of political reasoning that articulates the nature and meaning of the political, the social, and the subject must be underscored because it is through this form and articulation that its usurpation of other more democratic rationalities occurs',[75] then the political rationality of the 'science of development' must be exposed to

[72] See ch 1.
[73] See above, text to n 69.
[74] See above, text to n 70.
[75] Brown (n 70) 694–95.

denounce the modality through which it usurps other practices by rendering them unintelligible and unsayable.

The aim of this work has been to expose the development assumptions of the WTO and its consequent development-related trade disciplines as deeply political rather than the result of a linear, rational and ultimately desirable progression of history. The questioning of the universal beneficial impact of the WTO agreements is, however, only one of the challenges that needs to be brought to the imperial development framework that has allowed, since its inception, for the hierarchical ordering of different societal organisations. I have focused on particular forms of intervention that representations of Third World societies have given rise to within the international trading regime since the early 1940s. On the basis of this analysis, I have suggested that if development is viewed through the lenses of the imperial framework within which it has operated, then the focus might not be on how to make the WTO 'more supportive of development' but rather on what experiments and practices can be thought of that depart from the 'failure' and 'promise' that perpetuate its 'political rationality'.

Bibliography

ABBOTT, FM, 'Protecting First World Assets in the Third World: Intellectual Property Negotiations in the GATT Multilateral Framework' (1989) 22 *Vanderbilt Journal of Transnational Law* 689.

——, 'WTO TRIPs Agreement and its Implications for Access to Medicines in Developing Countries' (UK Commission on Intellectual Property Rights: Study Paper 2a, 2002).

——, 'Toward a New era of Objective Assessment in the Field of TRIPS and Variable Geometry for the Preservation of Multilateralism' (2005) 8 *Journal of International Economic Law* 77.

ALESSANDRINI, D, 'Transnational Corporations and the Doctrine of Comparative Advantage: A Critique of Free Trade Normative Assumptions' (2005) 1 *International Trade Law and Regulation Journal* 14.

ALMANSI, A, Jaastad, A and Hurtado, C, 'The Debt Crisis in Latin America' in D Lal and M Wolf (eds), *Stagflation, Savings and the State: Perspectives on the Global Economy* (Oxford; New York, Oxford University Press, 1986).

ALSTON, P, 'Resisting the Merger and Acquisition of Human Rights by Trade Law: a Reply to Petersmann' (2002) 13 *European Journal of International Law* 815.

AMERICAN ENTERPRISE INSTITUTE, *International Trade in Services: An Overview and Blueprint for Negotiations* (Washington DC, AEI, 1988).

AMIN, S, *Imperialism and Unequal Development* (Hassocks, Harvester Press,1977).

——, *Obsolescent Capitalism: Contemporary Politics and Global Disorder* (London; New York, Zed Books, 2003).

ANGHIE, A, 'Francisco de Vitoria and the Colonial Origins of International Law' (1996) 5 *Social and Legal Studies* 321.

——,'Finding the Peripheries: Sovereignty and Colonialism in the Nineteenth Century International Law' (1999) 40 *Harvard International Law Journal* 1.

——, 'Time Present and Time Past: Globalisation, International Financial Institutions, and the Third World' (2000) 32 *New York University Journal of International Law & Politics* 243.

——, *Imperialism, Sovereignty and the Making of International Law* (Cambridge, Cambridge University Press, 2005).

Anghie, A, Chimni, BS, Mickelson, K and Okafor, O (eds), The *Third World and International Legal Order: Law, Politics and Globalisation* (Leiden, Brill Academic Publishers, 2003).

ARMSTRONG, P, Glynn, A and Harrison, J, *Capitalism since World War II: The Making and Break up of the Long Boom* (London, Fontana, 1984).

ARRIGHI, G, *The Long Twentieth Century: Money, Power and the Origins of our Time* (London, Verso, 2000).

ATLANTIC CHARTER, DEPARTMENT OF STATE BULLETIN, SEPTEMBER 27, 1941 (Washington DC, Government Printing Office, 1941).

BALASSA, B, *Development Strategies in Semi-Industrialised Countries* (Baltimore, Johns Hopkins University Press, 1982)

——, 'Interest of Developing Countries in the Uruguay Round' (1988) 11 *The World Economy* 39.

——, *New Directions in the World Economy* (Basingstoke, The Macmillan Press, 1989).

BAUER, PT, *Equality, the Third World and Economic Delusion* (London, Methuen, 1981).

——, Reality and Rhetoric: Studies in the Economics of Development (London, Weidenfeld & Nicolson, 1984).

BELLAMY FOSTER, J and MAGDOFF, F, *The Great Financial Crisis: Causes and Consequences* (New York, Monthly Review Press, 2009).

BELLO, W, *The Future in the Balance: Essays on Globalisation and Resistance* (Oakland, Food first Books, 2001).

——, *Deglobalisation: Ideas for a New World Economy* (London; New York, Zed Books, 2002).

——, 'Washington Pursues Post-Cancun Vendetta Against Group of 21' (Inside Costa Rica, 2003).

——, 'Why Monday's Collapse of the Doha Round Negotiations is the Best Outcome for Developing Countries' (Focus on the Global South, 2006).

BERGSTEN, CF, 'APEC and World Trade' (1994) 73(3) *Foreign Affairs* 1

BERNE CONVENTION FOR THE PROTECTION OF LITERARY and ARTISTIC WORKS (9 September 1886) 1161 UNTS 3.

BHAGWATI, JN, *Anatomies and Consequences of Exchange Control Regimes* (NewYork, National Bureau of Economic Research, 1978).

——, 'Splintering and Disembodiment of Service and Developing Nations' (1984) 7 *The World Economy* 133.

——, *Free Trade, 'Fairness' and Protectionism: Reflections on the Agenda for the WTO* (London, Institute Of Economic Affairs for the Wincott Foundation, 1995).

——, *Free Trade Today* (Princeton, Princeton University Press, 2002).

——, 'Don't Cry for Cancun' (2004) 83 *Foreign Affairs* 52.

BRAITHWAITE, J and DRAHOS, P, *Global Business Regulation* (Cambridge, Cambridge University Press, 2000).

BRIDGES DAILY UPDATE ON THE FIFTH MINISTERIAL CONFERENCE, NO 2 (Geneva, International Centre for Trade and Sustainable Development, 11 September 2003).

BRIDGES DAILY UPDATE ON THE FIFTH MINISTERIAL CONFERENCE, NO4 (Geneva, International Centre for Trade and Sustainable Development, 11 September 2003).

BRIDGES DAILY UPDATE ON THE FIFTH MINISTERIAL CONFERENCE, NO 4 (Geneva, International Centre for Trade and Sustainable Development, 13 September 2003).

BROWN, W, *Edgework: Critical Essays on Knowledge and Politics* (Princeton, Princeton University Press, 2005).

——, 'American Nightmare: Neoliberalism, Neoconservatism, and De-Democratization' (2006) 34 *Political Theory* 690.

BROWN, WA, *The United States and The Restoration of World Trade* (Washington DC, Brookings Institution Press, 1950).

BULAJIC, M, 'A Changing World Calls for International Development Law' in P Sarcevic and HV Houtte (eds), *Legal Issues in International Trade* (London; Boston, Graham and Trotman, 1990).

——, *Principles of International Development Law: Progressive Development of the Principles of International Law relating to the New International Economic Order* (Dordrecht; London, Martinus Nijhoff, 1993).

BURCHELL, G, et al (eds), *The Foucault Effect: Studies in Governmentality: With two lectures by and an interview with Michael Foucault* (London, Harvester Wheatsheaf, 1991).

BURT, EM, 'Developing Countries and the Framework for Negotiations on Foreign Direct Investments in the World Trade Organisation' (1997) 12 *American University International Law Review* 1015.

CHANG, HJ, *Globalisation, Economic Development and the Role of the State* (London; New York, Zed Books, 2003).

——, *The Myth of Free Trade and the Secret History of Capitalism* (New York, Bloomsbury Press, 2007).

CHATTERJEE, P, *Nationalist Thought and the Colonial World: A Derivative Discourse* (Minnesota, University of Minnesota Press, 1993).

CHATTERJEE, SK, 'The Stabilization Clause Myth in Investment Agreements' (1988) 5 *Journal of International Arbitration* 97.

CHAUDHURI, S, Mattoo, A and Self, R, 'Moving People to Deliver Services: How Can the WTO Help?' (2004) 38 *Journal of World Trade* 363.

CHIMNI, BS, 'The World Trade Organisation, Democracy and Development: A View from the South' (2006) 40 *Journal of World Trade* 5.

CLAUDE L, *Swords into Plowshares: The Problems and Process of International Organisation* (New York, Random House, 1971).

CORREA, C, 'Bilateral Investment Agreements: Agents of New GlobalStandards for the Protection of Intellectual Property Rights' (GRAIN, 2002).

——, 'Access to Drugs under TRIPs: A Not So Expeditious Solution' (Geneva, Bridges, International Centre for Trade and Sustainable Development, 2004).

COWEN, MP and SHENTON, RW, *Doctrines of Development* (London, Routledge, 1996).

CROOME, J, *Reshaping the World Trading System: A History of the Uruguay Round* (The Hague; London, Kluwer Law International, 1999).

DAM, KW, *The GATT Law and International Economic Organisation* (Chicago, University of Chicago Press, 1970).

DARCH, C, Halbert, D and Story, A, *The Copy/South Dossier: Issues in the Economics, Politics and Ideology of Copyrights in the Global South* (Canterbury, The Copy/Couth Research Group, 2006).

DATTU, R, 'A Journal from Havana to Paris: the Fifty-years Quest for the Elusive Multilateral Agreement on Investments' (2000–01) 24 *FORDHAM International Law Journal* 275.

DOMMEN, C, 'Raising Human Rights concerns in the World Trade Organisation: Actors, Processes and Possible Strategies' (2002) 24 *Human Rights Quarterly* 1.

DRAHOS, P, 'BITs and BIPs: Bilateralism in Intellectual Property' (2001) 4 *The Journal of World Intellectual Property* 791.
DRAHOS, P and BRAITHWAITE, J, *Information Feudalism: Who Owns the Knowledge Economy* (London, Earthscan, 2002).
DUMENIL, G and LEVY, D, *Capital Resurgent: Roots of the Neoliberal Revolution* (Cambridge MA; London, Harvard University Press, 2004).
DUNKLEY, G, *The Free Trade Adventure: The WTO, The Uruguay Round and Globalism: A Critique* (London, Zed Books, 2000).
EDWARDS, S, 'Comments' in SHaggard (ed), *Developing Nations and the Politics of Global Integration* (Washington DC, Brookings Institution Press, 1995).
ESCOBAR, A, *Encountering Development: The Making and Unmaking of the Third World* (Princeton, Princeton University Press, 1995).
FEDERAL RESEARCH DIVISION, 'Appendix B – Dominican Republic and Haiti:Caribbean Basin Initiative' (The Library of Congress, Federal Research Division, 1983).
FERGUSON, J, *The Anti-Politics Machine: 'Development', Depoliticization, and Bureaucratic Power in Lesotho* (Cambridge, Cambridge University Press, 1990).
JM FINGER, 'The Grand Bargain: Will the WTO get over it?' in DLM. Kennedy and JD Southwick (eds), *The Political Economy of International Trade Law: Essays in Honour of Robert Hudec* (Cambridge, Cambridge University Press, 2002).
—, 'The Doha Agenda and Development: A View from the Uruguay Round' ERD (Asian Development Bank, Working Paper No. 21, 2002).
——, 'Comment: The Uruguay Round North-South Bargain: Will the WTO Get Over It?' in DLM Kennedy and JD Southwick (eds), *The Political Economy of International Trade Law: Essays in Honour of Robert Hudec* (Cambridge, Cambridge University Press, 2002).
FINGER, JM, NG, F and WANGCHUK, S, *Antidumping as Safeguard Policy* (Washington DC, World Bank, 2001).
FINGER, JM and SCHULER, P, 'Implementation of the Uruguay Round Commitments: the Development Challenge' (2000) 23 *The World Economy* 511.
FOUCAULT, M, *Power/Knowledge: Selected Interviews and Other Writings 1972–1977* ed C Gordon (Brighton, Harvester Press, 1980).
FRANK, AG, *Capitalism and Underdevelopment in Latin America: Historical Studies of Chile and Brazil* (New York, Monthly Review Press, 1967).
FRIEDMAN, M, *Why Government is the Problem* (Stanford, California, Hoover Institution on War, Revolution and Peace, 1993).
——, *Foreign Economic Aid, Means and Objectives* (Stanford, California, Hoover Institution on War, Revolution and Peace, 1995).
FURTADO, C, *Development and Underdevelopment* (Berkeley, University of California Press, 1964).
——, *Teorie dello Sviluppo Economico* (Bari, Laterza, 1970).
——, 'Underdevelopment: To Conform or Reform' in GM Meier *et al* (eds), *Pioneers in Development* (New York, Oxford University Press, 1984).
GARCIA-AMADOR, FV, 'The Proposed New International Economic Order: A New Approach to the Law of Governing Nationalization and Compensation' (1980) 12 *Lawyer of the Americas* 1.
——, 'State Responsibility in Case of "Stabilization Clauses"' (1993) 2 *Journal of Transnational Law and Policy* 23.

——, *The Emerging International Law of Development: A NewDimension of International Economic Law* (New York; London, Oceana Publications, 1990).

GARDNER, RN, *Sterling-Dollar Diplomacy: Anglo-American Collaboration in the Reconstruction of Multilateral Trade* (Oxford, Clarendon Press, 1956).

GATHII, JT, 'International Law and Eurocentricity' (1998) 9 *European Journal of International Law* 184.

——, 'The Legal Status of the Doha declaration on Trips and Public Health under the Vienna Convention on the Law of Treaties' (2002) 15 *Harvard Journal of Law and Technology* 291.

GATT, GENERAL AGREEMENT ON TARIFFS and TRADE, 55 UNTS 194.

——, *International Trade 88–89* (Geneva, GATT, 1990).

——, Punta del Este Ministerial Declaration (20 September 1986) BISD 33S/19.

——, 'Services Sectoral Classification List' (10 July 1991) Uruguay Round Document MTN.GNS/W/120.

——, Thirty-Eighth Session at Ministerial Level: Ministerial Declaration (1982) BISD 29th Supp 29S/11.

——, 'Trends in International Trade: A Report by a Panel of Experts' (Geneva, GATT Publications, 1958).

——, Twelfth Session of the Contracting Parties (1957) BISD 6th Supp (1958).

——, Twenty-first Session of the Contracting Parties (1963) BISD 12th Supp (1964).

GELINAS, J, *Freedom from Debt* (London; New York, Zed Books, 1998).

GIBBS, M, 'Special and Differential Treatment in the Context of Globalisation' Note Presented to the G15 Symposium on Special and Differential Treatment in the WTO Agreements (New Delhi, 10 December 1998).

GIBSON, J, *Community Resources: Intellectual Property, International Trade and Protection of Traditional Knowledge* (Aldershot, Ashgate, 2005).

GOULD, E, *Financial Instability and the GATS Negotiations*, Trade and Investment Series, 9:4 (Ottawa, Canadian Centre for Policy Alternatives, 2008).

GOWAN, P, *The Global Gamble: Washington's Faustian Bid for World Dominance* (London, Verso, 1999).

——, 'Crisis in the Heartland: Consequences of the New Wall Street System' (2009) 55 *New Left Review* 1.

GRAMSCI, A, *Selections from the Prison Notebooks* (London, Lawrence and Wishart, 1971).

GRAY, J, *False Dawn: The Delusions of Global Capitalism* (London, Granta, 1998).

G-20, 'Washington Declaration: G-20 Summit on Financial Markets and the World Economy' (Washington, G20, 2008).

——, 'Progress Report on the Immediate Actions of the Washington Actions Plan' (London, G20, 2009).

HAQUE, MS, *Restructuring Development Theories and Policies: A Critical Study* (Albany, State University of New York Press, 1999).

HARDT, M and NEGRI, A, *Empire* (Cambridge MA; London, Harvard University Press, 2000).

HARVEY, D, *Spaces of Capital: Towards a Critical Geography* (Edinburgh, Edinburgh University Press, 2001).

——, *A Brief History of Neo-liberalism* (Oxford, Oxford University Press, 2005).

——, *The New Imperialism* (Oxford, Oxford University Press, 2003).

HELLEINER, E, *States and the Re-emergence of Global Finance: From Bretton Woods to the 1990s* (Ithaca; London, Cornell University Press, 1994).

HERTEL, TW and MARTIN, W, 'Liberalising Agriculture and Manufactures in a Millennium Round: Implications for Developing Countries' (2000) 23 *The World Economy* 455.

HIRSCHMAN, AO, *The Passions and the Interests: Political Arguments for Capitalism* before its Triumph (Princeton, Princeton University Press, 1977).

HOEKMAN, B, 'Strengthening the Global Trade Architecture for Development: The Post Doha Agenda' (2002) 1 *World Trade Review* 23.

——, *Making the WTO More Supportive of Development* (Mimeo, World Bank, 2004).

HOEKMAN, BM and KOSTECKI, MM, *The Political Economy of the World Trading System: From GATT to WTO* (Oxford, Oxford University Press, 1995).

HOWSE, R and MUTUA, M, 'Protecting Human Rights in a Global Economy: Challenges for the World Trade Organisation' (Rights and Democracy, Working Paper, 2000).

HUDEC, RE, *Developing Countries in the GATT Legal System* (London, Trade Policy Research Centre, 1987).

HYDE, JN, 'Economic Development agreements' (1962) 105 *Hague Recueil* 271.

ICTSD, 'Trade in Services' (ICTSD, Doha Round Briefing Series, 1:3, 2003).

——, 'WTO Doha Round put on hold indefinitely' (ICTSD, Bridges Trade BioRes, 6:14, 2006).

ILO, 'Employment, Growth and Basic Needs: A One World Problem'. Report of the Director General of the International Labour Office to the Tripartite World Conference on Employment, Income Distribution and Social Progress, and the International Division of Labour (Geneva, ILO, 1976).

IRWIN, DA, *Against the Tide: An Intellectual History of Free Trade* (Princeton, Princeton University Press, 1996).

A Jaastad, A Almansi and C Hurtado, 'The Debt Crisis in Latin America' in D Lal and M Wolf (eds), *Stagflation, Savings and the State: Perspectives on the Global Economy* (Oxford and New York, Oxford University Press, 1986).

JACKSON, JH, *World Trade and the Law of GATT* (New York, Bobbs-Merrill, 1969).

——, *The World Trading System: Law and Policy of International Economic Relations* (Cambridge MA, The MIT Press, 1997).

——, *The Jurisprudence of GATT and the WTO: Insights on Treaty Law and Economic Relations* (Cambridge, Cambridge University Press, 2000).

JACKSON, JH, DAVEY, WJ and SYKES, AO, *Legal Problems of International Economic Relations: Cases, Materials and Text on the National and International Regulation of Transnational Economic Relations* (St Paul, Minn.; Great Britain, West Group, 2002).

JAWARA, F and KWA, A, *Behind the Scenes at the WTO: The Real World of International Trade Negotiations: Lessons of Cancun* (London, Zed Books, 2003).

JESSOP, B, *The Future of the Capitalist State* (Oxford, Polity, 2002).

JEWISH VIRTUAL LIBRARY, 'Reagan on Signing the Free Trade Area Implementation Act' (Jewish Virtual Library, A Division of the American-Israeli Cooperative Enterprise, 1985).

KAHLER, M, *International Institutions and the Political Economy of Integration* (Washington DC, Brookings Institution Press, 1995).

KHOR, M, 'Globalisation and the South: Some Critical Issues' (UNCTAD, Working Paper No 147, 2000).

——, 'Preliminary Comments on the WTO's Geneva July Decision' (Third World Network, SUNS Working Paper, 2004).

——, 'Reflections begin on the WTO Failure and the Future Work' (Third World Network, SUNS Working Paper, 2008).

KOSHY, S, 'From Cold War to Trade War: Neo-Colonialism and Human Rights' (1999) 58 *Social Text* 1.

KRUEGER, AO, 'The Political Economy of Rent-Seeking Society' (1974) 64 *American Economic Review* 291.

——, 'Agricultural Incentives in Developing Countries: Measuring the Effects of Sectoral and Economic-wide Policies' (1988) 2 *World Bank Economic Review* 255.

——, *Political Economy of Policy Reform in Developing Countries* (Cambridge MA, The MIT Press, 1993).

——, 'Developing Countries and the Next Round of Multilateral Trade Negotiations' (World Bank Policy Research, Working Paper No 2118, 1999).

KUFUOR, KO, *World Trade Governance and Developing Countries: The GATT/WTO Code Committee System* (London, Blackwell Publishing, 2004).

LAL, D, *The Poverty of 'Development Economics'* (London, Institute of Economic Affairs, 1983).

LAMY, P, 'Talks Suspended. Today there are only Losers' (WTO News-DDA, 24 July 2006).

——, 'Time out needed to review options and positions' (WTO, Trade Negotiations Committee, 24 July 2006).

LAMY, P, 'WTO Doha Development Agenda: Building on the Uruguay Round towards a freer, fairer world trading system' (WTO News-Speeches, 22 November 2006).

LAMY, P, 'Doha Success can yield double dividend of Global Stimulus and Structural Reform' (WTO News-Speeches, 13 October 2009).

LEAGUE OF NATIONS, *Covenant of the League of Nations* (28 April 1919).

LEWIS, D, Rodgers, D and Woolcock, M, 'The Fiction of Development: Knowledge, Authority and Representation' (London, London School of Economics and Political Science, 2005).

LEWIS, WA, *The Theory of Economic Growth* (London, Allen & Unwin, 1955).

LOW, P and SUBRAMANIAN, A, 'Beyond TRIMs: A case for Multilateral Action on Investment Rules and Competition Policy?' in W Martin and LA Winters (eds), *The Uruguay Round and the Developing Countries* (Cambridge, Cambridge University Press, 1996).

MACIEL, GA, *The international Framework for World Trade: Brazilian Proposals for GATT Reform* (London, Trade Policy Research Centre, 1977).

MACMILLAN, F, *The WTO and the Environment* (London, Sweet and Maxwell, 2001).

——, 'International Economic Law and Public International Law: Strangers in the Night' (2004) 6 *International Trade Law and Regulation* 115.
——, 'Looking Back to Look Forward: Is There a future for Human Rights in the WTO?' (2005) 11 *International Trade Law and Regulation* 163.
MANDUNA, C, 'The GATS Negotiations: Development Considerations Towards Hong Kong' (Trade Law Centre for Southern Africa, Trade Brief, 2005).
MANIRUZZAMAN, AFM, 'International Development Law as Applicable Law to Economic Development Agreements: A Prognostic View' (2001) 20 *Wisconsin International Law Journal* 1.
MARLEY, LORD 'The Empire as an Economic Unit' (1938) 9 *The Political Quarterly* 529.
MARTIN, W, and Anderson, K, Agricultural Trade Reform under the Doha Agenda: Some Key Issues' (2008) 52 *The Australian Journal of Agricultural and Resource Economics* 1.
MASKUS, KE, *Intellectual Property Rights in the Global Economy* (Washington DC, Institute for International Economics, 2000).
MATSUSHITA, M, Schoenbaum, TJ and Mavrodis, PC, *The World Trade Organisation: Law, Practice, and Policy* (Oxford, Oxford University Press, 2003).
MCCULLOCH, N, Winters, LA and Cirera, X, *Trade Liberalisation and Poverty: A Handbook* (London, Centre for Economic Policy Research, 2001).
MCNALLY, D, 'From Financial Crisis to World-Slump: Accumulation, Financialisation and the Global Slowdown' (2009) 17 *Historical Materialism* 49.
MEIKSINS WOOD, E, *Empire of Capital* (London, Verso, 2005).
MEWETT, AW, 'The Theory of Government Contracts' (1959) 5 *McGill Law Journal* 222.
MICHALOPOULOS, C, 'The Role of Special and Differential Treatment for Developing Countries in GATT and the World Trade Organisation' (World Bank, Working Paper, 2000).
——, *Developing Countries in the WTO* (Basingstoke, Palgrave, 2001).
MITRANY, D, *A Working Peace System: An Argument for the Functionalist Development of International Organisation* (London, National Peace Council, 1946).
MOORE, M, 'Address by the Director-General, Mr M. Moore at the Inaugural Session' (9 November 2001) WTO Doc WT/MIN(01)/12.
MORRISSEY, O, 'Investments and Competition Policy in the WTO: Issues for Developing Countries' (2002) 20 *Development Policy Review* 63.
MSAYEKHI, M and JUISANT, M, 'Assessment of Trade in Services in the Context of the GATS 2000 Negotiations' (South Centre, Working Paper No13, 2002).
NAU, HR, *Trade and Security: US Policies at Cross-Purposes* (Washington, DC, American Enterprise Institute, 1995).
NICHOLAS, HG, *The United Nations as a Political Institution* 5th edn (Oxford, Oxford University Press, 1975).
NORTH, DC, 'The New Institutional Economics and Development' (Smithian Forum, Working Paper, 1993).
ODELL, JS, 'The Seattle Impasse and its Implications' in DLM Kennedy and JD Southwick (eds), *The Political Economy of International Trade Law: Essays in Honour of Robert Hudec* (Cambridge, Cambridge University Press, 2002).

OECD, Report by the High Level Group on Trade and Related Problems (Paris, OECD, 1982).
OECD, The MAI Negotiating Text (Paris, OECD, 22 April 1998) DAFFE/MAI(98)7REV1.
Ostry, S, *Governments and Corporations in a Shrinking World: Trade and Innovations Policies in the United States, Europe and Japan* (New York; London, Council of Foreign Relations, 1990).
——, *The Post-Cold War Trading System: Who's on First?* (Chicago; London, University of Chicago Press, 1997).
——, The Changing Scenario in International Governance (Ottawa, Royal Society of Canada, 20 November 1999).
——, 'The Uruguay Round North-South Grand Bargain: Implications for Future Negotiations' in DLM Kennedy and JD Southwick (eds), *The Political Economy of International Trade Law: Essays in Honour of Robert Hudec* (Cambridge, Cambridge University Press, 2002).
Oxfam International, 'Africa and the Doha Round: Fighting to Keep Development Alive' (Oxfam, Briefing Paper No 80, 2005).
Oxley, A, *The Challenge of Free Trade* (London, Harvester Wheatsheaf, 1990).
Palmer, BD, *Descent into Discourse: The Reification of Language and the Writing of Social History* (Philadelphia, Temple University Press, 1990).
Paris Convention for the Protection of Industrial Property (20 March 1883) 828 UNTS 305.
Peet, R, *Unholy Trinity: The IMF, World Bank and WTO* (London, Zed Books, 2003).
Petersmann, E, 'Taking Human Dignity, Poverty and Empowerment of Individuals More Seriously: Rejoinder to Alston' (2002) 13 *European Journal of International Law* 845.
Picciotto, S, 'Linkages in International Investment Regulation: The Antinomies of the Draft Multilateral Agreement on Investments' (1998) 19 *University of Pennsylvania Journal of International Economic Law* 731.
——, 'What Rules for the World Economy' in S Picciotto and R Mayne (eds), *Regulating International Business: Beyond Liberalisation* (Basingstoke, Macmillan, 1999).
Pratley, N, 'Wall Street Crisis: is this the death knell for derivatives?' *Guardian* (15 September 2008).
Prebisch, R, *Economic Development of Latin America and its Principal Problems* (New York, United Nations, 1950).
——, 'Commercial Policy in the Underdeveloped Countries' (1959) 49 *American Economic Review* 251.
——, *Towards a Dynamic of Development Policy for Latin America* (New York, United Nations, 1963).
Preeg, EH, *Traders in a Brave New World: The Uruguay Round and the Future of the International Trading System* (Chicago, The University of Chicago Press, 1995).
Primo Braga, CA and Fink, C, 'The Relationship between Intellectual Property Rights and Foreign Direct Investments' (1998) 9 *Duke Journal of Comparative and International Law* 163.

RAGHAVAN, C, 'Trade: Implementation Issues, S&D Treatment Get Short Shrift' (Third World Network, South-North Development, 26 August 2004).

RAJAGOPAL, B, *International Law from Below: Development, Social Movements and Third World Resistance* (Cambridge, Cambridge University Press, 2003).

RICARDO, D, *Principles of Political Economy and Taxation* [1817] (London, Everyman's Library, 1978).

RICUPERO, R, 'Ministerial Round Table on Trade and Poverty in Least Developed Countries' (UNCTAD, 19 March 2001).

RODRIK, D, 'Globalization, Social Conflict and Economic Growth', Prebisch Lecture (Geneva, UNCTAD, 24 October 1997).

——, 'The Global Governance of Trade as If Development Really Mattered' (UNDP, Working Paper, 2001).

ROSTOW, WW, *The Process of Economic Growth* (New York, W.W. Norton & Co., 1962).

ROY, G, 'Is the Law of State Responsibility Part of Customary International Law?' (1959) 55 *American Journal of International Law* 552.

RUGGIERO, R, 'Towards GATS 2000—A European Strategy' (WTO News-Speeches, 2 June 1998).

RYAN, MP, *Knowledge Diplomacy: Global Competition and the Politics of Intellectual Property* (Washington, DC, Brookings Institution Press, 1998).

SACHS, W, (ed) *The Development Dictionary: A Guide to Knowledge as Power* (London, Zed, 1992).

SALACUSE, JW, 'BIT by BIT: the Growth of Bilateral Investment Treaties and their Impact on Foreign Investments in Developing Countries' (1990) 24 *International Lawyer* 654.

SALDANA-PORTILLO, MJ, THE REVOLUTIONARY IMAGINATION IN THE AMERICAS and THE AGE OF DEVELOPMENT (Durham; London, Duke University Press, 2003).

SARKAR R, Development Law and International Finance 2nd edn (The Hague; London, Kluwer Law International, 2002).

SCOTT, CV, GENDER and DEVELOPMENT: RETHINKING MODERNIZATION and DEPENDENCY THEORY (Boulder, Colo.; London, L. Rienner, 1995).

SCHUH, GE, 'Developing Countries Interests in WTO Agricultural Policy' in DLM Kennedy and JD Southwick (eds), *The Political Economy of International Trade Law: Essays in Honour of Robert Hudec* (Cambridge, Cambridge University Press, 2002).

SELL, SK, *Private Power, Public Law: The Globalisation of Intellectual Property Rights* (Cambridge, Cambridge University Press, 2003).

——, 'Multilateral Corporations as Agents of Change: The Globalisation of Intellectual Property Rights' in AC Cutler, V Haufler and T Porters (eds), *Private Authority and International Affairs* (Albany, SUNY Press, 1999).

SEN, AK, *Development as Freedom* (Oxford, Oxford University Press, 2001).

SINCLAIR, S and GRIESHABER-OTTO, JG, *Facing the Facts: A Guide to the GATS Debate* (Ottawa, Canadian Centre for Policy Alternatives, 2002).

SINGH, JP, 'Wiggle Rooms: New Issues and North-South Negotiations during the Uruguay Round'. Paper prepared at the Conference on Developing Countries and the Trade Negotiation Process (Geneva, UNCTAD, 6–7 November 2003).

SMITH, A, An Enquiry into the Nature and Causes of the Wealth of Nations [1776] (Oxford, Clarendon Press, 1979).
SORNARAJAH, M, *The International Law on Foreign Investments* (Cambridge, Cambridge University Press, 1994).
——, *The International Law on Foreign Investments* 2nd edn (Cambridge, Cambridge University Press, 2004).
SOUTH CENTRE, 'Intellectual property in Investment Agreements: the TRIPs-plus implications for Developing Countries' (GRAIN, Analytical note, 2005).
SRINIVASAN, TN, *Developing Countries and the Multilateral Trading System: From the GATT to the Uruguay Round and the Future* (Oxford, Westview Press, 1997).
——, 'Trade and Development: Developing Countries in the World Trading System, 1947–1999' (Yale University, Department of Economics, 1999).
——, 'Developing Countries and the Multilateral Trading System after Doha' (Economic Growth Centre, Discussion Paper No 842, 2002).
STICHELE, MV, *Potential Risks of Liberalisation of Financial Services in GATS* (Amsterdam, SOMO, 2003).
——, *GATS Negotiations in Financial Services: The EU Requests and their Implications for Developing Countries* (Amsterdam, SOMO, 2005).
STIGLITZ, JE, *Globalisation and its Discontents* (London, Penguin, 2002).
JE STIGLITZ and A CHARLTON, *Fair Trade For All: How Trade Can Promote Development* (Oxford, Oxford University Press, 2005).
A Story, C Darch and D Halbert, *The Copy/South Dossier: Issues in the Economics, Politics and Ideology of Copyrights in the Global South* (Canterbury, The Copy/Couth Research Group, 2006) 49.
SUNKEL, O, 'National Development Policy and External Dependence in Latin America' (1969) 6 *Journal of Development Studies* 23.
SUTHERLAND, P, 'Global Trade: The Next Challenge' in GATT, News of the Uruguay Round (NUR082) Geneva, 28 January 1994.
TOYE, JFJ, *Dilemmas of Development: Reflections on the Counter-Revolution in Development Economics* 2nd edn (Oxford, Blackwell, 1993).
TREBILCOCK, MJ and HOWSE, R, *The Regulation of International Trade* (London; New York, Routledge, 2005).
TRUMAN, H, *Public papers of the President of the United States: Harry S. Truman, 1949* (Washington DC, U. Government Printing Office, 1964).
TUSSIE, D, *The Less Developed Countries and the World Trading System: A Challenge to the GATT* (London, Pinter, 1987).
TYSON, LD *Who's Bashing Whom: Trade Conflicts in High-Technology Industry* (Washington DC, Institute for International Economics, 1992).
UN, CHARTER OF ECONOMIC RIGHTS and DUTIES OF STATES (adopted 12 December 1974) UNGA Res 3281 (XXIX).
——, Convention on Biological Diversity (adopted 5 June 1992) 31 ILM 818.
——, Resolution on Permanent Sovereignty over Natural Resources (adopted 14 December 1962) UNGA Res 1803 (XVII).
——, Resolution on the New International Economic Order (adopted 14 December 1974) UNGA 3306 (XXIX).

United Nations Conference on Trade and Employment, Havana Charter for an International Trade Organization, Final Act and Related Documents (New York, Lake Success, April 1948).

UNCTAD, *Beyond Conventional Wisdom in Development Policy: An Intellectual History of UNCTAD 1964–2004* (New York and Geneva, United Nations, 2004).

——, Resolution 159 (VI) Belgrade (adopted 2 July 1983).

——, *Technology Transfer*, UNCTAD Series on Issues in International Investment Agreements (New York and Geneva, United Nations, 2001).

UNDP, *Making Global Rules Work for People* (New York, Earthscan Publications Ltd, 2003).

US International Trade Commission, *Foreign Protection of Intellectual Property Rights and the Effect on US Industry and Trade*, Publication 2065 (Washington DC, ITC, February 1988).

USTR, 'US Trade Representative Robert Zoellick Evening Press Conference, Cancun, Mexico' Press Release (14 September 2003).

VerLoren van Themaat, P, *The Changing Structure of International Economic Law: A Contribution of Legal History, of Comparative Law and of General Legal Theory to the Debate on a New International Economic Order* (The Hague, London, Nijhoff, 1981).

Virno, P, *A Grammar of the Multitude* (New York, Semiotext(e), 2004).

Wade, R, 'What Strategies are Viable for Developing Countries Today? The World Trade Organization and the Shrinking of "Development Space"' (2003) 10 *Review of International Political Economy* 621.

Wallerstein, I, *The Capitalist World Economy: Essays* (Cambridge, Cambridge University Press, 1979).

Watal, J, *Intellectual Property Rights in the WTO and Developing Countries* (The Hague; London, Kluwer Law International, 2001).

Weiler, JHH, 'The Rule of Lawyers and the Ethos of Diplomats: Reflections on the Internal and External Legitimacy of WTO Dispute Settlement' (Harvard Law School, Jean Monnet Working Paper, 2000).

Weiss, F, Denters, E and de Waar P (eds), *International Economic Law with a Human Face* (The Hague; London, Kluwer Law International, 1998).

Wilcox, C, *A Charter of World Trade* (New York, The MacMillan Company, 1949).

Williamson, J, 'What Washington means by Policy Reform' in J Williamson (ed), *Latin American Adjustment: How Much Has Happened?* (Washington DC, Institute for International Economics, 1990).

World Bank, 'Trade, Development and Poverty Reduction'. Paper prepared jointly by the staff of the World Bank and the IMF for the consideration of the Development Committee (31 March 2000).

——, 'World Development Report 1985' (Oxford and New York, Oxford University Press, 1985).

World Development Movement, 'Taking the Credit: How Financial Services Liberalisation Fails the Poor' (London, World Development Movement, 2009).

——, 'Whose Development Agenda? An Analysis of the European Union's GATS requests of developing countries' (London, World Development Movement, 2003).

WTO, 'Accession of Viet Nam: Report of the Working Party' (27 October 2006) WTO Doc. WT/ACC/VNM/48.
——, Agreement on Agriculture (15 April 1994) LT/UR/A-1A/2.
——, Agreement on Implementation of Article VI of the General Agreement on Tariffs and Trade 1994 (15 April 1994) LT/UR/A-1A/3.
——, Agreement on Implementation of Article VII of the General Agreement on Tariffs and Trade 1994 (15 April 1994) LT/UR/A-1A/4.
——, Agreement on Safeguards (15 April 1994) LT/UR/A-1A/8.
——, Agreement on Subsidies and Countervailing Measures (15 April 1994) LT/UR/A-1A/9.
——, Agreement on Technical Barriers to Trade (15 April 1994) LT/UR/A-1A/10.
——, Agreement on Textiles and Clothing (15 April 1994) LT/UR/A-1A/11.
——, Agreement on the Application of Sanitary and Phytosanitary Measures (15 April 1994) LT/UR/A-1A/12.
——, Agreement on Trade-Related Aspects of Intellectual Property Rights(15 April 1994) LT/UR/A-1C/IP/1.
——, Agreement on Trade-Related Investment Measures (15 April 1994) LT/UR/A-1A/13.
——, Amendment of the TRIPs Agreement, Decision of the General Council (adopted 6 December 2005) WTO Doc WT/L/641.
——, 'Day 9: Talks collapse despite progress on a list of issues' (WTO News-DDA, 29 July 2008).
——, Decision on Negotiations on Basic Telecommunications (15 April 1994) LT/UR/D-5/4.
——, Declaration on the TRIPs Agreement and Public Health (20 November 2001) WTO Doc. WT/MIN(01)/DEC/2.
——, Doha Declaration (14 November 2001) WTO Doc WT/MIN(01)/DEC/1
——, Doha Work Programme: Decision of the General Council (2 August 2004) WTO Doc WT/L/579.
——, Final Act Embodying the Results of the Uruguay Round of MultilateralTrade Negotiations (15 April 1994) LT/UR/A/1.
——, 'GATS-Facts and Fiction Booklet' (WTO, Services, 2001).
——, 'GATS: Rules for Growth and Investments' (WTO, Understanding the WTO, The Agreements).
——, General Agreement on Tariffs and Trade 1994 (15 April 1994) LT/UR/A-1A/1/GATT/1.
——, General Agreement on Trade in Services (15 April 1994) LT/UR/A-1B/S/1.
——,'General Transparency and Other "Good Governance" Obligations' (WTO, GATS Training Module, Basic Purpose and Concept).
——, 'Golden Jubilee of the Multilateral Trading System' Press Release (5 February 1998).
——, 'Guidelines and Procedures for the Negotiations on Trade in Services' (29 March 2001) WTO Doc S/L/93.
——, Hong Kong Ministerial Declaration (adopted 18 December 2005) WTO Doc WT/MIN(05)/DEC.
——, 'Implementation of Paragraph 6 of the Doha Declaration on the TRIPs Agreement and Public Health', Decision of the General Council (30 August 2003) WTO Doc. WT/L/540.

——, 'Implementation of Special and Differential Provisions in WTO Agreements and Decisions' WTO Doc WT/COMTD/W/77.
——, 'Integrated Framework (IF) Joint Core Agency Seminar on the Policy-Relevance of Mainstreaming Trade into Country Development Strategies: Perspectives of LDCs'. Statement by M. Moore (WTO, Development, 17 January 2001).
——, 'Lamy Circulates Report on Market Access Commitments in Services' (WTO News-DDA, 30 July 2008).
——, Marrakesh Agreement Establishing the World Trade Organization (15 April 1994) LT/UR/A/2.
——, 'Overseeing National Trade Policies: The TPRM' (WTO, Trade Policy Reviews, 2001).
——, 'Paragraphs 13,14,15 &16, Dealing with the Singapore Issues of the Draft Cancun Ministerial Text Contained in Document Job (03)/150/Rev.1: Communication from Bangladesh (on behalf of the LDC Group), Botswana, China, Cuba, Egypt, India, Indonesia, Kenya, Malaysia, Nigeria, Philippines, Uganda, Venezuela, Zambia and Zimbabwe' WTO Doc. WT/MIN(03)/W/4.
——, 'Preparations for the Fourth Session of the Ministerial Conference:Proposal for a Framework Agreement on Special and Differential Treatment'. Presented by Cuba, Dominican Republic, Honduras, India, Indonesia, Kenya, Malaysia, Pakistan, Sri Lanka, Tanzania, Uganda and Zimbabwe' (2001) WTO Doc WT/GC/W/442.
——, 'The Integrated Framework for Least Developed Countries (IF)' (WTO, Development, Integrated Framework).
——, 'The Relationship between the TRIPs Agreement and the Convention on Biological Diversity: Summary of Issues Raised and Points Made' (9 March 2006) WTO Doc IP/C/W/368/Rev.1.
——, Understanding on Commitments in Financial Services (15 April 1994) LT/UR/U/1.
——,'What is the Role of WTO Services Rules in the Context of the Current Financial Crisis?' (WTO Public Forum, 2009).
——, 'Workshop to Mark the Tenth Anniversary of the Fifth Protocol to the GATS' (WTO, Services, 13 March 2009).
——, 'WTO Negotiations on Agriculture. Poverty Reduction: Sectoral Initiative in Favour of Cotton', WTO Committee on Agriculture (16 May 2003) WTO Doc TN/AG/GEN/4.

Index

Where a subject is covered on a large number of pages some minor references have not been indexed and major references are indicated by the page numbers being in bold. Where a topic is covered on the page and elaborated on in a note on the same page the note number is not given. Where a subject is only covered by a note the page number is given followed by the note, eg 73(n22).